# The
# Game
### of
# Hearts

**Felicity Day** qualified as a solicitor before deciding to pursue a writing career. She has since written about British history and heritage – including her favourite period, the Regency – for a wide range of publications, from *The Telegraph*, *The Mail on Sunday*'s *YOU Magazine* and *Country Life*, to specialist history titles such as the BBC's *Who Do You Think You Are?* and *History Revealed*. *The Game of Hearts* is her first book.

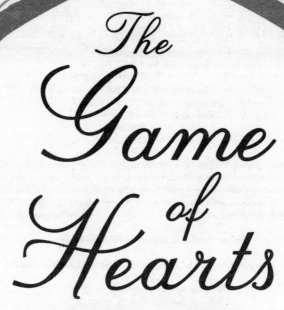

# The Game of Hearts

## TRUE STORIES OF
## REGENCY ROMANCE

# FELICITY DAY

BLINK
bringing you closer

First published in the UK by Blink Publishing
An imprint of The Zaffre Publishing Group
A Bonnier Books UK company
4th Floor, Victoria House
Bloomsbury Square,
London, WC1B 4DA
England

Owned by Bonnier Books
Sveavägen 56, Stockholm, Sweden

Hardback: 978-1-78870-639-1
Trade paperback: 978-1-78870-732-9
Paperback: 978-1-78512-088-6
Ebook: 978-1-78870-640-7
Audio: 978-1-78870-761-9

British Library Cataloguing-in-Publication Data.

A catalogue record for this book is available from the British Library.

Design by www.envydesign.co.uk
Internal illustrations © Shutterstock

Printed and bound in Great Britain by Clays Ltd, Elcograf S.p.A

1 3 5 7 9 10 8 6 4 2

Blink Publishing is an imprint of Bonnier Books UK
www.bonnierbooks.co.uk

*For Mum and Dad*

# Contents

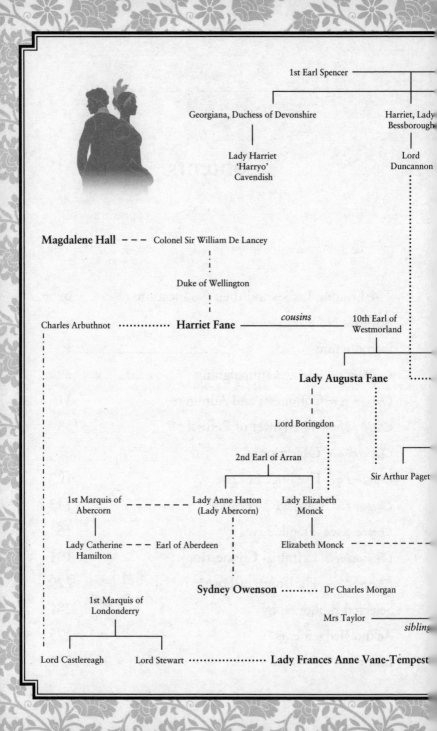

1st Earl Spencer

Georgiana, Duchess of Devonshire

Harriet, Lady Bessborough

Lady Harriet 'Harryo' Cavendish

Lord Duncannon

**Magdalene Hall** – – – Colonel Sir William De Lancey

Duke of Wellington

Charles Arbuthnot ·············· **Harriet Fane** ——— *cousins* ——— 10th Earl of Westmorland

**Lady Augusta Fane**

Lord Boringdon

2nd Earl of Arran

Sir Arthur Paget

1st Marquis of Abercorn – – – – – – Lady Anne Hatton (Lady Abercorn) ··········· Lady Elizabeth Monck

Lady Catherine – – – Earl of Aberdeen
Hamilton

Elizabeth Monck – – – – – – –

**Sydney Owenson** ·········· Dr Charles Morgan

Mrs Taylor ——— *sibling*

1st Marquis of Londonderry

Lord Castlereagh          Lord Stewart ····················· **Lady Frances Anne Vane-Tempest**

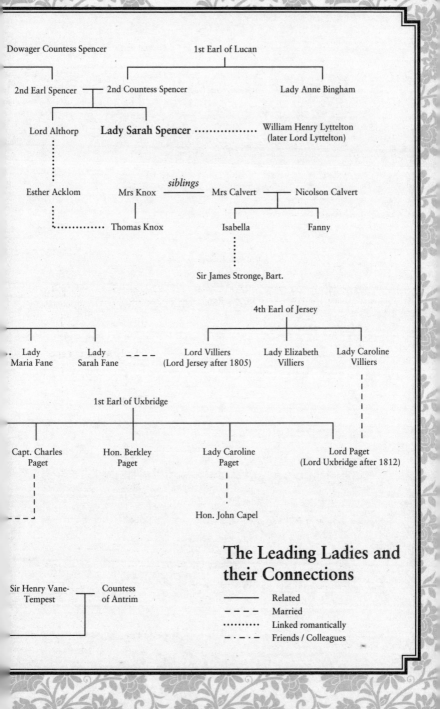

Dowager Countess Spencer ——— 1st Earl of Lucan

2nd Earl Spencer ——— 2nd Countess Spencer

Lady Anne Bingham

Lord Althorp

**Lady Sarah Spencer** ················ William Henry Lyttelton (later Lord Lyttelton)

Esther Acklom

Mrs Knox ——— *siblings* ——— Mrs Calvert ——— Nicolson Calvert

Thomas Knox

Isabella

Fanny

Sir James Stronge, Bart.

4th Earl of Jersey

. Lady Maria Fane

Lady Sarah Fane — — — Lord Villiers (Lord Jersey after 1805)

Lady Elizabeth Villiers

Lady Caroline Villiers

1st Earl of Uxbridge

Capt. Charles Paget

Hon. Berkley Paget

Lady Caroline Paget

Lord Paget (Lord Uxbridge after 1812)

Hon. John Capel

# The Leading Ladies and their Connections

Sir Henry Vane-Tempest ——— Countess of Antrim

——————— Related

– – – – – – Married

················ Linked romantically

– · – · – · Friends / Colleagues

# Author's Note

## On the Regency

The term 'Regency' is often applied to the period of history stretching from roughly 1788 to 1830, but strictly speaking, the Regency lasted only nine years – beginning in February 1811 when the Prince of Wales was named Prince Regent on account of the mental illness of his father, King George III, and ending in January 1820, when he officially ascended to the throne as King George IV. The availability of material, and the desire to ensure depth and variety, means that not all the stories of romance in *The Game of Hearts* date from this 'true' or 'official' Regency era, but, mindful of how much can change within the space of even ten years, every effort has been made to focus on a twenty-year period between 1800 and 1820.

For consistency, George IV has been referred to as the Prince Regent throughout, even if, at the particular time, he was actually Prince of Wales.

## On contemporary material

Original spelling, punctuation and capitalisation have been retained in quotations, though occasionally abbreviations have been rendered in full in square brackets for ease of reading.

# Introduction

'LONDON, I NEVER knew so dull,' one disgruntled resident of Grosvenor Square wrote to her son at the end of March 1810. The streets and squares of the West End might have been woken from their wintertime slumber, echoing once more with the rumble of carriage wheels and coal-wagons, the steady beating of brass door knockers and shouts of servants that signalled their wealthy residents were back in town. The main shopping thoroughfares might have been bustling again as tailors, milliners and dressmakers showed off new-season fashions. Invitation cards to the first 'at-homes' and fashionable assemblies might have been propped on chimney-pieces already. But something was missing. 'I hear of no matches,' she complained, 'the flirtations have not yet begun.'

For Mrs Spencer-Stanhope, romance was the beating heart of the social whirl that was the Regency season, and today it has almost become the beating heart of that entire period of history. From compulsively readable novels to glossy costume dramas, romance and the Regency have become a natural pair, the perfect match. Think of that short stretch between the turn of the nineteenth century and the death of King George IV in 1830, when Jane Austen's books were entertaining their earliest readers, empire-line gowns were in, and post-chaises rather than trains rattled across the countryside, and your first thought is probably not of the wars being waged in Europe and America, or the increasingly angry clamour for political reform, but romance.

Undeniably, there is something endlessly compelling – even covetable – about the era's courtships: when the rules of engagement were clear; when flirting meant lingering looks, locked eyes across the dance floor and the fleeting touch of hands; when singletons went in search of not just a brief encounter but their companion for life. At the very least, the glittering ballrooms in which they mingled, bathed in candlelight, make for an idyllic backdrop to a romantic storyline.

Yet the Regency romance, whether it's on the page or screen, a contemporary or classic, can sometimes feel like utter fantasy. The heroines are all bold and beautiful, independent and opinionated. They hold out for a love match and get it, no matter whether they're blessed with a decent dowry or not. The strict social conventions rarely bother them. Their suitors usually turn out to be enlightened rather than entitled, and they don't often have to worry about what happens when the wedding bells stop ringing.

But what was it really like to go looking for love in the Regency? What did it really mean to be a Regency wife? And are our favourite fictional tales, with their likeable, liberal-minded heroes and spirited heroines, really so far from the truth?

*The Game of Hearts* is the result of a quest to find out, taking us behind drawing room doors, into the ballrooms and boudoirs of their real-life counterparts, to tell true stories of life and love as it was for women of the Regency.

Captured between the pages of this book are, by and large, only the experiences of those whose families rotated between inherited stately homes in the country and imposing houses in town; whose names and titles opened the doors to royal palaces and assured them vouchers for the exclusive Almack's; whose healthy incomes covered everything from opera boxes to smart barouches, extravagant balls to fashions of the first stare. With a rhythm and set of rules all of its own, theirs was a world and a way of life that fascinated even in their own time – a favourite subject for satirical pamphleteers and printmakers, and endlessly chronicled in the popular press, which devoted column upon column to their crowded parties and promising flirtations, scandalous elopements and matrimonial splits.

It's the wealth of material that makes them the obvious focus for a book of this kind. Not just the newspaper reports, but the long letters they had sufficient funds to send back and forth, remarkably well preserved in family archives, and the journals and memoirs that their leisured lives gave them time to write, published enthusiastically by their descendants in the pre-war period. So while Regency courtship customs, and the expectations of wives and mothers, were much the same among the gentry families and members of the so-called squirearchy, who poured into assembly rooms in provincial towns and cities, these are the stories of the women of hedonistic high society – the ladies of the *haut ton,* the beau monde, the fashionable world.

Who exactly was in and who was out of that exclusive contingent was never an exact science. Generally, the *ton* comprised a significant proportion of the nation's peers and their families, along with a generous scattering of landed gentlemen and theirs; but certainly not all aristocratic families had the means or inclination to take their place in its ranks, and not absolutely everyone who squeezed into lavishly gilded saloons for the frenetic round of socialising during the season had aristocratic birth. Knowing the right people, dressing the right way and possessing a remarkable degree of wit or beauty could sometimes provide a coveted passport into high-society circles. What is absolutely certain is that the beau monde was a small and incredibly privileged group, not representative in the least of Regency Britain as a whole.

London was then, as now, a diverse city, home to people of great riches and great poverty, of different races and religions; but the clubs and ballrooms of Mayfair were an entirely different matter, open only to the tiny minority who possessed wealth and power. Those who lived in splendid surroundings, waited on by armies of servants, and whose world was very nearly global, at a time when most British citizens would be lucky to stray much beyond their home town. No more than about 0.1 per cent of the population of roughly 12 million enjoyed the kind of income that made possible an annual migration to town to participate in the season. For all the novels it has inspired, the fashionable world was, in reality, a small one, with prominent families often interconnected by marriage or united by political allegiance.

Rumours of romance and talk of matrimonial prospects preoccupied members like Mrs Spencer-Stanhope with good reason. Watching flirtations unfold and sparks of attraction fly, predicting potential matches and helping to make a few more, were not just pleasurable ways to pass the time. They mattered, because without marriage, there could be no legitimate heirs to inherit noble titles, ancient family names and ancestral acres. The very survival of the elite depended on suitable matches and the spawning of a new generation, into whose hands property and peerages could one day pass. The very survival of a family, too, could hinge on its matrimonial alliances: the brilliant match of one member had the power to make the whole family richer, their circle of influence wider, and their position in fashionable society more secure. A son's new wife might bring money and land. A daughter who married into a powerful political family might be able to send a parliamentary seat or well-paid government post her brother's way, or do a little matchmaking between her sisters and her husband's supremely eligible friends.

How much true love needed to be part of the romantic equation was sometimes still a matter for debate. Yet the parents of the generation of aristocrats who came of age in the Regency – plenty of whom had made marriages of affection themselves – were rarely willing to compel, or even coax, their offspring to marry against their inclination. The whole point of the round of social events that comprised the season – coinciding with the parliamentary session and running roughly from late January to early July – was to send sons and daughters out into ballrooms that were full of suitable partners, to make a match for themselves that combined sense with sensibility, passion with practicality.

It was courtesan Harriette Wilson, the most famous of the 'fashionable impure' of the era, who poetically described the occupational hazard of falling in love as 'the game of hearts' – yet it is a phrase that perfectly encompasses the manoeuvring involved for her high-born female contemporaries in their own romantic lives. The need to balance love with financial security and family duty; the strategies necessitated by strict social conventions, double standards and severe legal handicaps; and the pitfalls of making a wrong move.

This is the story of how six women, along with their siblings, cousins, close friends and acquaintances, fared. From the richest heiresses to those whose talent alone gave them a place in the *ton*; from ladies who found navigating the marriage market a chore to those who had a surfeit of suitors to choose from; those who ran away from a marriage and those from whom happiness was stolen. This is romance through the eyes of the real women who lived and loved in a period of history so close to our hearts.

*Chapter One*

# Spring Campaigning

ON 24 JANUARY 1809, shortly after her family's return to their London house, Lady Sarah Spencer sat down in the wintry gloom to write to her brother Bob. 'I have no sort of objection to a slackening of our zeal for routs and parties,' she told him, filling him in on their intention of going into society with far more moderation than in the previous year. 'But I promise you,' she went on, no doubt with a smile, 'I will pretend, when it is proper to do so, to regret all such pastimes, for fear of giving room for conjectures and suppositions that I must be making Greek verses, or perhaps magical spells at home, as a substitute.'

A veteran of four London seasons already, Sarah was well aware that properly fashionable young women professed a slavish adoration for the metropolis and its springtime social whirl. Born into the upper echelons of the aristocracy and counting two of its leading ladies, Georgiana, Duchess of Devonshire and

Harriet, Countess of Bessborough, among her aunts, she might have been expected to share their enthusiasm. But Midshipman Robert Spencer, the grateful recipient of her reports from the frontline of the fashionable world, knew it was something his home-loving sister had struggled to muster from the start.

The 2nd Earl and Countess Spencer had introduced their eldest daughter into the *ton* in early 1805, six months shy of her eighteenth birthday. She attended her first ball that January – 'a most capital ball, every one said' – but it wasn't until May that she made her official debut. As for a great many other girls born into the beau monde, her move from schoolroom to society was formally marked by a pilgrimage to the palace, to be presented to Queen Charlotte. 'I cannot say I recollect very much,' she reported, responding to her Grandmama Spencer's anxious enquiries about the ceremony – which 'thank Heaven, I may now say is over,' she wrote, 'and even better over than I expected.'

Her presentation took place at one of the royal Drawing Rooms, afternoon receptions then held at St James's Palace roughly once or twice a month, and open to as many of the nobility as cared to attend. At approximately 2 p.m. on the advertised day, the Queen would take up her position between two of the full-length windows in the palace's unpretentious inner drawing room and receive – in a 'most gracious' manner – a succession of newly married couples, newly appointed or promoted officials, and young ladies making their entrance into the world.

It was by no means a necessity for a well-born young woman like Sarah to be presented before she could participate in a London season, or be considered officially 'out' – sometimes eligible families simply found the costs involved prohibitive.

Purchase of a court dress was certainly expensive. As they were usually made of the finest silk, satin or crape, ornately embroidered with silver thread or lavishly trimmed with lace, and boasted an elegant train to the rear, the bill for their creation generally ran into the hundreds of pounds. At one end of the scale, a suitable but relatively plain gown was conjured for as little as £50 (roughly £3,700 today); while at the other, a young heiress was advanced £1,500 by her trustees to kit herself out ahead of her court presentation – five times as much as many clergymen then earned in an entire year.

The dresses were not only costly, but incredibly uncomfortable. Before the Prince Regent officially acceded to the throne as King George IV in 1820, court protocol demanded that ladies appear in the wide hooped gowns that had long since fallen out of fashion for ordinary evening wear. Heavy and hot, the voluminous dresses were also ludicrously difficult to manoeuvre, and made it tricky to sit down. 'When they sat in a carriage the hoop came up nearly to their shoulders so that their hands with the fan, could only be seen,' recalled one woman, taken as a child to see the ladies arriving at court. Another observer commented cuttingly on their 'preposterous' headdresses – the tall plumes of feathers that demanded they throw their head back and hold it motionless the whole way to the palace.

Squashing themselves, their hoop and their headwear into the carriage was the first challenge for a debutante about to be presented – something they usually did as early as noon, since the streets of Mayfair were liable to become choked with the sheer number of coaches and sedan chairs heading to court. On the day of her own presentation in 1805, Sarah, her mother and her Aunt Georgiana travelled by chair to St James's, the liveried footmen who accompanied them wearing matching white feathers in their hats for the occasion.

Awaiting them were rooms similarly fit to burst with aristocrats, dripping in jewels and jostling for space. Overcrowding was a perennial problem at court, the apartments in use at St James's, and later at the Queen's House (as Buckingham Palace was then known) being much smaller than comparable public spaces – a situation that only worsened in the 1810s when the aging and ailing Queen held as few as three or four Drawing Rooms in a whole year, and sometimes none at all. It was not unusual for several ladies to faint away in the crush – something Sarah dreaded doing in company – and complaints about clothing 'literally torn to pieces' were commonplace.

'In we went, in such a crowd, we were like a pack of cards, one leaning on the other, till we got near the Queen,' Sarah told her grandmother. Thankfully she avoided knocking her Majesty down as she had feared she might. Despite the throng behind her, pushing her almost onto the Queen's nose, she managed to kiss her proffered cheek and execute a suitably deep curtsey. The Queen was glad to see her mama looking so well, and the assembled princesses made some gracious remarks, too, but nerves had got the better of her by that point. 'I fear they must have thought me dumb,' she admitted, 'for I don't think I ever attempted an answer.'

Shy and lacking in self-esteem as she was, it seems unlikely that Sarah enjoyed herself any better when, eleven days later, Lady Spencer hosted what the papers graciously called 'one of the most splendid balls and suppers of the season' in honour of her eldest daughter. No expense was spared for the occasion: covers were laid for nearly 400 supper guests on the ground floor of Spencer House, where a selection of the choicest fruits were served on silver plate; while upstairs in the grand ballroom that looked out over Green Park, five magnificent chandeliers blazed, the air was perfumed by a 'profusion of odoriferous pots of flowers' and the floor was chalked with elegant patterns.[1] It was here, a little after 11 p.m., that a teeming mass of fashionables – among them the Prince Regent, no less – had their eyes fixed on Sarah as she led off the dancing with one of her cousins, either Lord Duncannon or his brother, Captain Frederick Ponsonby, depending on which paper you read the following day.

'She is not handsome,' Mrs Calvert, one of those watching her, reflected later, 'but has an interesting, pleasing countenance, a good figure and sweet, unaffected manners.' Sarah herself was well aware that she could not be described as a beauty – unlike her mother. The Earl Spencer had confessed to being 'out of his senses' over his future wife at the time of their engagement in 1780. She did share Lady Spencer's intelligence and satirical wit, but unfortunately had none of her (sometimes haughty) self-assurance. Yet daunting as the very public performance at her 'come-out' ball might seem, it was a moment that girls like Sarah had long been preparing for.

Work on appropriately feminine behaviours tended to start from an early age. Mrs Calvert, the handsome wife of a Hertfordshire MP, part of the Prince Regent's set, and the writer of a private journal in which she diligently recorded news of both her family and the fashionable world at large had felt 'obliged to lecture' her own eldest daughter, twelve-year-old Isabella, when she visited her at school in the year of Sarah's debut. 'The

---

1 Chalking the floor served a practical as well as decorative purpose: the chalk helped to prevent guests slipping over in their smooth-soled dancing shoes.

love of talking is so strong in her,' she lamented, 'that I think it necessary to check it whenever I can.' Young women like Sarah and Isabella were instructed in good posture and graceful movement as teenagers, and, of course, comprehensively drilled in dance steps before they first dipped their toe into the world of the *ton*, but they were also shown, from a relatively young age, exactly how the season worked. When in town, children were taken to see female relations dressed for their presentations at court, given glimpses of rooms laid out for grand balls and suppers, and provided with opportunities to practise both their dancing skills and company manners at children's balls.

Certainly both Sarah and her younger sister Georgiana (known to the family as Gin) spent long spells in town with their parents long before emerging into the fashionable world. Sarah generally preferred it when they were all ensconced at Althorp, their seat in Northamptonshire, where they usually spent the winter, or their villa at Wimbledon. Earl Spencer's political career, however, necessitated lengthy stays at their frankly palatial residence in St James's Place. Then, all the Spencer children would be treated to trips to the theatre and enjoy walks in the parks, where they might see the fashionable company promenading. Both girls also received instruction from music and drawing masters during their time in the metropolis to supplement the education superintended by their Swiss governess, Mademoiselle Müller.

When the time came, neither of them made their entrance into Regency society ignorant of the underlying purpose of it all: to find themselves a respectable husband, if not immediately, then certainly eventually. Thus it was no surprise to them – or to any of their contemporaries – that from the moment they were officially 'out' their London stays were focused on mingling with as many eligible men as possible.

Daytime hours for a debutante usually followed a fairly predictable pattern: 'arranging the teaching geniuses, making the usual purchases and visiting the usual set; walking in Hyde Park, and watching the people in the Square,' as Marianne Spencer-Stanhope (no relation to the Earl Spencer) described it for the benefit of her older brother in 1806. Paying calls, not just on friends and family but also on more distant connections, was important, as they might help to secure admission to London's best ballrooms. A diligent mama would want to ensure her chimney-piece was swarming with cards of invitation for the season's most popular parties, just as Lady Spencer's habitually did come April, when the gay world began to wake for what her daughter dryly called 'spring campaigning'.

A typical season would see the well-connected take up invites to everything from grand balls and outdoor breakfasts for 1,500 guests, to smaller card parties and concerts, dinners and impromptu dances. Equally important, however, was to see and be seen in more public venues. Indeed, for many young women, part of the excitement of 'coming out' in their late teens was the opportunity to enjoy to the full London's dazzling array of evening entertainments; from the famous pleasure gardens at Vauxhall, with their glittering illuminations and firework displays, to the Shakespearean dramas on offer at the Drury Lane Theatre.

'Anne relishes London vastly, and hitherto the little going out she has had agrees with her,' Marianne Spencer-Stanhope reported of her sister, just out in 1806. 'The Opera is her delight.' Sarah, meanwhile, liked nothing so much as the theatre and 'if the other amusements of this dirty town were but half as good, I should be as fond of it as anybody,' she told her grandmother. The Spencers subscribed to a box at Covent Garden, which like Drury Lane was licensed for serious drama, but they were not above enjoying a farce at the Lyceum during the season. They were also regulars at the King's Theatre, Haymarket, home of Italian opera and one of the main arenas of the so-called 'marriage mart'.

The performances at the opera on Tuesday and Saturday evenings throughout the season attracted a primarily aristocratic audience, for whom the socialising was a much greater enticement than the singing. Like the rest of the horseshoe-shaped auditorium, the row upon row of gilded boxes in which the beau monde settled themselves stayed brightly lit throughout the evening, sometimes more brightly than the stage itself, making them the perfect place for mamas to show off daughters of marriageable age (and also, ironically, for high-class courtesans to display their charms). Men of rank and fashion could wander from box to box as they pleased, prevailing on friends to introduce them to ladies (or 'light-skirts') who had caught their eye, and visiting those with whom they were already acquainted – a practice helped by the fact that the opera had more of the feel of a private club, with affluent subscribers like the Spencers renting the same box season after season.

Like other heiresses, Frances Winckley's opera box was 'always so full of *prétendants*' that the man she would go on to marry 'could hardly ever penetrate beyond the door'. He took advantage of the other opportunity offered to would-be suitors and was invariably, she remembered, 'there at the right moment, to take me to the carriage; which was then an affair of passing at least an hour together in the Crush Room' – the space into which the company squeezed to continue their chatter while they waited for their carriages to make it to the door.

There was, of course, one other venue at which marriage-minded women of the Regency made regular appearances: the assembly rooms. London's Almack's has acquired almost legendary status, but it had a rival in the early part of the nineteenth century. With a 'superbly ornamented' ballroom of blue and gold and tiers of scarlet-covered benches for the chaperones, the Argyle Rooms were as popular then for dancing, as well as for masquerades and concerts. By the 1810s, however, tickets for the Almack's balls had become the hottest in town. Every week on a Wednesday night during the season, the club's own ballroom, on the first floor of a spectacularly un-majestic building on King Street, would throng with married couples and singletons alike, galloping down the dance floor together, idly gossiping on the sidelines or flirting over cups of almond flavoured orgeat, lemonade or weak tea, which together with bread and butter and stale cake constituted the club's famously 'wretched refreshments'.

As a space for sons and daughters to meet and mingle with prospective marriage partners, Almack's was particularly ideal from a parent's perspective, since the apparently public venue had all the exclusivity of the private ballroom. Only those men and women whose application was approved by the aristocratic female patronesses were eligible to enter its hallowed halls, and obtaining a voucher of admission was acknowledged to be 'very difficult' for any individuals who did not 'belong to the very highest or most modish world'.

But what was it like for those who did? For the young women

in their late teens who flitted from opera box to Almack's ballroom and back in search of a suitable spouse?

Above all else, the season demanded serious energy and enthusiasm. The established mode was to attend two, or even three, different events in a single evening, and to repeat the feat several nights in a row, each and every week, something Marianne Spencer-Stanhope discovered when she, like Sarah, first plunged into society in 1805. On 18 March she began her evening at a concert at Mrs Methuen's, from there went on to an assembly at the Townshends', and by midnight was at a ball at the Duchess of Bolton's home a few doors down from her own in Grosvenor Square. There she remained until after five in the morning, dancing with an amiable guardsman by the name of Cooke. 'Marianne is quite well,' her mother cheerfully reported the next day, neither of them apparently suffering from the lack of sleep and planning to sally forth for an airing in the carriage. In fact, Marianne was 'very well disposed to go to Almack's' that evening; and on Thursday, they planned to be at another ball at Lady Le Despenser's house.

Like the rushing from one venue to another, late nights were an accepted part of the season. When in town, as satirists and overseas tourists never failed to observe, the *ton* had almost a time zone of its own. Balls seldom began before ten in the evening and the best of them didn't break up before 5 a.m., meaning few aristocrats rose from their beds before midday, and even fewer stepped out to begin the round of morning calls and shopping expeditions before two or three in the afternoon. 'At six in the evening, the *morning* ends,' an American ambassador noted dryly, observing that the streets and parks of the West End were soon after all but empty, as the beau monde's carriages rumbled homewards so they could dress for dinner and another round of evening entertainments.

'No people upon earth have less benefit from the light of the sun than the people of Fashion,' one sardonic pamphleteer agreed, 'so that if it were not for torches, candles, and [oil] lamps, they would scarcely ever see each others' faces.' That so much of their social life was conducted in candlelight was not considered a particular disadvantage. After seeing near 800 members of the *ton* gather in the afternoon sunshine for a breakfast at their Wimbledon house, Sarah discovered – somewhat to her surprise – that 'several don't bear the daylight well,' and indeed, 'one could hardly believe they were the same as one had admired at night.' The ambient lighting was a blessing, in fact…

The real inconvenience of the social whirl was the insufferable overcrowding at each and every ball. 'This last week we have been very gay – that is, we have been almost squeezed to death at sundry grand crowds,' Marianne wryly observed to her brother in April 1807. Her sentiments were echoed by Sarah, who in May 1808 expressed to her brother Bob a devout hope that they would avoid Lady Lonsdale's assembly 'where everybody is to be – crushed to death, I take it.'

The crush typically began before guests even reached the ballroom, as American tourist Louis Simond discovered in 1810: it was only 'after waiting your turn to arrive at the door, [for] perhaps half an hour, the street being full of carriages' that you could at last alight and join the party. On one occasion, Marianne and her mother waited in the string of vehicles lined up in the street outside art connoisseur Thomas Hope's house for a full hour and a half before admitting defeat at 1 a.m. and turning the carriage around for home.

Though houses were commonly 'stripped from top to bottom' on the inside, with all but the ornamental furniture carried out to make room for the hoped-for hordes, only the stateliest of London residences – the likes of Egremont House, with its 'seven large rooms opening one into the other' that won Lady Sarah's approval – had apartments commodious enough to comfortably accommodate the 1,000 or so fashionables who might descend on the very best balls. With only a sultry summer night's breeze from open windows to provide air, at most assemblies the heat was uncomfortably oppressive, and the 'odour of perspiration' unpleasant. Lady Spencer typically resorted to 'grunting and elbowing' her way through the crowd, while her daughter was usually trying desperately to keep her composure. 'I was quite giddy and sick with the heat,' she sighed to Bob after another crush at Lady Essex's in 1808, 'and as I had much rather dance a hornpipe on my head than faint in an assembly, I was heartily glad when we got away from that one.'

There was little that Sarah relished about the endless round of balls and parties that were supposed to offer the Regency debutante their best chance of making a match. The stuffy ballrooms and succession of late nights, coupled with the physical strain of dancing for hours on end, disagreed with a constitution her mother described as delicate; and being well educated, fond of reading and pretty well informed when it came to current affairs, she found the insipid small talk on offer unbearably boring. The conversation, as she explained to Bob, was unlikely to stray beyond 'the shape and size of [the] rooms, the heat of the weather, the crowd of the doorway,' and she dreaded hearing over and over and over 'those hated phrases' – 'How suffocating!' and 'What a squeeze!'

18

With a sensible head on her shoulders, a decided preference for the company of her family and little appetite for gossip, Sarah was more inclined to roll a cynical eye towards her counterparts than enter into their excited chatter. Her humorous observations she saved up for Bob's amusement. 'I danced… the two last with Lord Percy, who, being to be one day the Duke of Northumberland, is of course the best partner in London, by the unanimous consent of all the young ladies, who agree that he is the most charming, interesting, bewitching, fascinating youth that ever trod with the light fantastic toe the chalked floor of any ballroom in Europe,' she joked in 1808, adding 'whether I agree with them is another question'.

But then Sarah – 'as yet perfectly heart-whole and quite happy' – seems to have been in no hurry to find herself a husband, nor under any particular pressure from her parents to do so. The 'slackening of our zeal for routs and parties' that she reported – almost gleefully – to Bob in January 1809 came after the doctor positively forbade her from going into hot, crowded spaces. Against their own inclination, the Earl and Countess Spencer agreed to spend most of that season in the country, and by the time the family returned to town the following year, Sarah was apparently excused from making appearances at the balls and assemblies that were the major arenas of the London marriage market. At the grand age of twenty-three, she began to talk of those days 'when I *went out*' – though she was still happily attending the play, the opera and various dinner parties and small soirées, charming the company with her 'beautiful' singing voice.

However, not all parents could afford to be as relaxed as Sarah's about their daughter's marriage prospects. Participation in even one London season was an expensive business. A short-term rental of a furnished property in a sought-after West End square could by 1818 easily cost more than £60 a *week* – equivalent to almost £20,000 a month today. Of course, the Spencers owned their grand residence next to Green Park, just as Marianne's parents owned their house in Grosvenor Square, but maintaining a permanent establishment in the heart of Mayfair was not an option for everyone. In the early 1810s servants, horses, carriages and stabling, taxes and other household expenditure set owners back anywhere between £2,000 and £10,000 a year, depending on the luxuriousness of their lifestyle. Those who rented their London home could expect to add anything from £400 to £1,000 a year to that figure to cover their annual rent.

It was a significant outlay. Mrs Calvert was the daughter of a viscount, from whom she inherited a respectable fortune of around £20,000, but in 1810, the year she brought Isabella out, she and her husband were obliged to exchange the roomy rented house in Albemarle Street that had been their London base for over five years for a smaller and cheaper one in Hanover Square. By 1815, the family's finances were so stretched that they had been forced to give up leasing a house in town altogether – though by a stroke of luck Mr Calvert inherited one before their second daughter Fanny came out, albeit in Wimpole Street, rather more remote than his wife would have liked.

In addition to a house for the season, there was the overwhelming array of outfits required by a debuting daughter. Even if she did not need the budget-busting court dress for a presentation at the palace, a sufficient quantity of morning gowns for paying calls and promenading, and evening gowns made with expensive materials like satin and lace still required a considerable investment. The cost of evening entertainments added up, too. In 1807, the Duke of Devonshire provided his youngest daughter, Sarah's cousin and close friend Lady Harriet Cavendish, with an allowance of £400 a year. Harryo, as she was known to her family, probably had to cover the cost of her clothes, and certainly paid for her own share in an opera box – an expense often split between several subscribers since hire of a six-seat box for the season cost a couple of hundred guineas.

A night at Vauxhall was a far more affordable two shillings, and balls at Almack's a reasonable seven shillings and sixpence each. The cost of hosting a come-out ball for a daughter at home, however, was anything but reasonable. A London guide published in 1818 told its readers that one nobleman spent a staggering £1,500 on a single large ball – over £100,000 in today's money. It put the cost of procuring a supper from a caterer or confectioner like the *ton's* man of choice, Mr Gunter – along with the necessary hire of chairs, glasses and plates – at anywhere between £400 and £1,000. On top of that were probably the costs of the wines, along with the flowers for decoration and the band for the dancing.

Clearly not all girls could be given the kind of lavish launch into society that Sarah had. But there was a presumption that those who attended private parties during the season would reciprocate with invitations of some kind – especially those with money and family mansions at their disposal. 'I find it is expected from us,' Lady Spencer wrote to her husband in June 1807, seeking his approval for a small dance and supper at Spencer House, adding, 'we shall wipe off all scores and answer our acquaintances' expectation.' In the event, they hosted a party of magnificent proportions just the following month: the breakfast for 800 guests at Wimbledon, with several different bands spread around the gardens and dancing until dusk. Mrs Calvert was there when they hosted a similar event the following year, observing the 'immense concourse of people all walking about gaily dressed', though she could not attempt anything of the kind on her more modest budget. For Isabella she seems to have stuck to evening parties, with a fiddle, and just twelve couples dancing.

For less wealthy families, each London season was an opportunity not to be wasted, and Isabella Calvert was no doubt just one of many young women who had a great deal to put up with from parents anxious for them to make a good impression. Men might have thought her so beautiful she 'shone like the sun', but her mother was preoccupied with the 'want of height' that she judged such a disadvantage for her eldest daughter, and nagged at her constantly to improve her posture. She was far from satisfied on the day of Isabella's court presentation in 1810, declaring that upon the whole, her expectations were disappointed: 'Her manners were very good and very composed,' she noted in her diary, 'but she did not hold herself well.'

It wasn't only parents who were casting critical glances at the daughters they launched into society. As Mrs Calvert was well aware, teenage girls were suddenly on display almost everywhere they went: their beauty assessed and behaviour observed; their conversations overheard and dance partners discussed. Crowded around the edges of every ballroom were not only young men openly ogling the figures of the female dancers, but a score of society matrons and seasoned debutantes, many of them fond of a gossip. Smiles, blushes, locked eyes or lingering glances could be all that was needed to make them suspect a partiality or potential match. At the opera, too, the auditorium's dazzlingly bright lighting turned the tiers of boxes into a second stage. The number of male visitors to a debutante's box, their identity and her reaction to them were every bit as visible and as interesting to the assembled company as the performance itself. Comings and goings – or, indeed, the lack of them – quickly morphed into *on dits*, as when Marianne Spencer-Stanhope professed herself surprised at the rumours of an engagement between Viscount Primrose and the younger (and less beautiful) Miss Bouverie in 1808. 'He has never given the slightest hint & did not go near her at the Opera, not even in the crush-room,' she reported to her brother. She suspected a rejection from the elder sister, adding that the viscount was gone to Bath, 'probably to avoid the talk & gossip of London till it is publickly declared.'

A certain amount of gossip and speculation was the unavoidable consequence of conducting courtships in such a public arena, since Mayfair, with its teeming ballrooms and theatres, resembled nothing so much as a gilded goldfish bowl. Not only did ladies in town for the season take it upon themselves to share in their letters to friends and family news about flirtations and expected engagements, but the papers printed the latest rumours for the benefit of all their readers. 'Lady Harriet Cavendish, it is said, has agreed to bestow her fair hand on the Hon. Mr Burrell, who has so long been sighing for her smiles,' the *Morning Post* reported in March 1804, just one of many times that Sarah's poor cousin Harryo would find herself the subject of totally unfounded speculation.

And it wasn't only gossiping guests at the season's great assemblies that young women like Harryo had to worry about; the bevy of servants bustling around the grand households of the West End were just as partial to a bit of matrimonial tittle-tattle. Harryo laughed incredulously in 1807 when her maid Walker reported – with some indignation at her lady's conduct – that not only her fellow servants at Devonshire House but those in every house where she visited firmly believed that her mistress meant to marry the man she suffered to 'dangle after her wherever she went' – her cousin William 'Willy' Ponsonby. He had developed a boyish *tendre* for her, and his leaping upstairs to her room or leaving their grandmother's house the very moment she did – behaviour Harryo had struggled to know how to quash without the appearance of 'affectation and Prudery' – had not gone unnoticed by the extended family's numerous staff, who were, she learned, inclined to lament the connection. 'Was ever… disengaged person so eternally engaged, proud person so perpetually humbled?' she complained to her sister after listening patiently to Walker's reproaches. 'In high life supposed to be promised to Frederick Byng, in low life to Willy!' she added, exasperated.

Town talk and the ever-watchful eyes of the *ton* simply made navigating the marriage market that much harder for all involved. Inevitably, it impeded otherwise promising courtships. After young ladies began to speculate in May 1818 about an understanding between Lady Elizabeth Leveson-Gower and Lord Belgrave, heir to the then Earl Grosvenor, he went out of his way to avoid her at Almack's and 'danced with every pretty girl in the room excepting Her,' – or so Lady Williams Wynn reported to her daughter-in-law. The pair did eventually marry, but not until over a year later. 'It is very tiresome that a young man cannot dance often with a girl without people's thinking of matrimony,' Mrs Calvert was inclined to think, after one of her daughter Fanny's regular partners was similarly scared off by a rumour of their impending marriage.

If an attractive acquaintance did take fright and began to studiously ignore her, the unwritten code of female propriety meant there was little a woman could do about it, just as there was very little she could do to indicate her interest in a handsome stranger. Propriety prohibited a young lady from initiating a conversation with him; she had to wait to be introduced. She could not stroll about the auditorium at the opera as her brother might; she had to sit and wait for a man to come to her. Nor could she ask a man to dance; she had to wait for him to do so; and unless she wanted to sit out for the rest of the evening she had to accept *any* man who requested her hand, whatever she thought about him or his dancing prowess. She could *encourage* a would-be suitor, though to flirt too obviously, or be too familiar with a man, was to risk the sharp-tongued society ladies – or worse, the lady patronesses of Almack's – branding her forward or fast.

Esther Acklom, sole heiress of her father Richard, a Nottinghamshire landowner, had a style that was such as to earn her a reputation as a determined flirt. 'There is no getting by any men, and she shakes hands and is so intimate,' Mrs Calvert said frowningly after spending a fatiguing evening as her chaperone at a ball in 1809. The array of conduct books and etiquette guides that proffered advice for young Regency women on manners and morals likewise disapproved of this form of friendliness in a female. 'A touch, a pressure of the hands' was one of few ways a woman could express a particular regard, said 1811's *Mirror of the Graces*, so to lavish it 'upon all comers' was 'an indelicate extravagance'. It recommended its readers frustrate any attempts by a suitor to shake hands 'with an air so declarative of displeasure' that they would 'not presume to repeat the offence'.

When it came to the marriage market, however, the flirtatious and frank-speaking Miss Acklom had a strong hand. Any woman who combined respectable birth with a handsome fortune would find small lapses like her's more easily forgiven. Indeed, the prospect of an attractive inheritance, or the possession of a sizeable marriage portion, was arguably the greatest asset to any young woman looking for love. It undoubtedly compensated not only for any indecorous behaviour, but also for a lack of beauty or charm. At least one assumes that's what Mrs Spencer-Stanhope meant when she remarked of a Miss Shuckburgh that 'the [parliamentary] Borough and Twelve Thousand a year must be thought of, by anyone disposed to think of her.'

Young women known to have handsome fortunes generally found themselves besieged from the moment they set foot in a London ballroom, if not before. And particularly if they possessed not only great riches but raven locks and an enviably creamy complexion, like Lady Sarah Fane. Her debut at court 'attracted thither all the young beaux of family and fashion,' the *Morning Post* declared in February 1803. The report name checked a viscount, an earl and two marquises before adding, 'her Ladyship is heiress to 45,000l. per annum, and consequently is a *dear child*.'

Lady Sarah's father was the 10th Earl of Westmorland, who had famously eloped in 1782 with her mother, Sarah Child, the daughter and heiress of the banking mogul Robert Child. Furious at the couple's conduct, Child had sworn that no future earl would benefit from his vast fortune, so under the terms of his will it went to Sarah, his notoriously talkative eldest granddaughter, rather than her older brother, Lord Burghersh. She stood to inherit an annual income estimated at close to £60,000 when she came of age, along with Osterley Park, an estate in Middlesex.

To be studiously courted and complimented was the lot of any woman who stood to be so obscenely wealthy, and Sarah's suitors followed her not just to court but to country house parties; they haunted her box at the opera and battled for her hand in the ballroom. Such a fortune also made her one of the *ton's* favourite topics of conversation, as they watched her try to work out which beaux had fallen in love with her, and which with her healthy bank balance. Two serious contenders emerged. George, Lord Villiers was the Earl of Jersey's son and heir, reckoned incredibly good-looking, a bruising rider and 'really and truly in Love' with Sarah. His chief rival was the diplomat Lord Granville Leveson-Gower, the Adonis-like younger son of the Marquis of Stafford. Speculation about which admirer had the upper hand, and critiques of the heiress's behaviour towards them, filled the letters of society hostesses and jealous rivals. 'I never saw anything so coquettish as Ly. S.F's manner to Ld. G. Wednesday night,' Harryo, for one, muttered. In the end he lost out to Lord Villiers, to whom, it later emerged, Sarah had long ago formed an attachment.

If it was provoking for her contemporaries to have to vie for attention with one of the era's greatest heiresses, it must have been worse for two of her sisters, Lady Augusta and Lady Maria Fane, just one and two years younger. At least both had handsome fortunes of their own: £10,000 apiece from their grandfather, with another £30,000 each to follow from their sister when she turned twenty-one. While it was possible to make a match with an eldest son of a titled or landowning family with a dowry closer to £5,000, and £10,000 was an eminently respectable portion, those women who had two, three, or even four times as much to bring to a marriage inevitably had a better chance. And the Fane sisters were not the only ones who did. The younger Spencer children seem to have been at least promised portions of £20,000 each; while their uncle, the Duke of Devonshire, gave both Harryo's older sister Georgiana and her illegitimate half-sister Caroline £30,000.[2]

Yet as an heiress Lady Sarah Fane had the definite advantage over the average well-portioned woman. Not only did she have a whole host of handsome men dangling after her, but also a bigger pool of prospective husbands from which to choose. The average younger son did not tend to look so eligible to a nobleman's daughter with only a lump sum of £10,000 to her name. The income he derived from his profession and his own portion would probably be nowhere near enough to support her and any future children in the style to which she was accustomed, even if it was combined with the £500 interest her own capital might produce. But a woman with £10,000 *a year* to her name – let alone £60,000 – could well afford to marry a man without an inherited house or rent-roll of his own. She need not shy away from dashing military men yet to make their mark, or impecunious MPs without a lucrative government post. Indeed, in 1814 Harryo's troublesome cousin 'Willy' Ponsonby, an idle younger son, without means but nevertheless yet to make any real inroads in a career, was the choice of heiress Lady Barbara Ashley-Cooper.

---

2 Harryo herself was given just £10,000 when she eventually married in 1809. Fully alive to the injustice, her brother 'Hart' ensured that as soon as he acceded to the dukedom on the death of their father in 1811, her portion was topped up with another £20,000.

It was, unfortunately, a sad reality that the more potential spouses she had, the better a woman's chances of making a match, since the London marriage market was nothing if not competitive. At the same time that Mrs Calvert was sighing over Mr Foley's retreat from her daughter Fanny's side in 1818, for example, Lady Williams Wynn was gossiping with her daughter-in-law about his having 'for the last three or four Balls returned to his old habits' with a 'Mary F'. She was not inclined to attach any particular significance to his renewed passion for partnering Miss F, however, as 'every now & then,' she said, 'He takes just the same dose of Pratt'– referring to one of the daughters of the Marquis of Camden.

Of course, the competition only increased for those who remained unmarried at the end of each season, as a host of younger, and perhaps prettier and richer, women entered the fray every year. Given all the advantages of wealth, it's hardly surprising that some parents decided to cultivate an air of mystery about their daughter's expectations – or, like the Moncks, to brazenly indicate that her fortune was larger than they ever intended it to be. Lady Uxbridge was aggrieved to discover that her future daughter-in-law's parents had misled her son Captain Charles Paget, writing crossly to his brother in 1805 that they had behaved very shabbily over the marriage settlements, 'considering that they gave out last year that she was a large fortune, which they have now frittered down to seven thousand five hundred pounds.'

Lady Spencer reportedly had another idea for putting her girls ahead of the competition. A run of peers taking actresses up the aisle caused her to quip that if her daughters didn't go off, she had a mind to bring them out on the stage. Her daughter

Sarah, meanwhile, was apt to indulge from time to time a notion just as fanciful: of getting away from the metropolis with its monotonous assemblies and swirling rumours of engagements, and travelling about the Mediterranean like a rich and single young man.

Yet while it might not have been the easiest environment in which to find love, Regency romance was by no means just the stuff of fiction.

## Chapter Two

# Conquests and Admirers

THE AFTERNOON OF 2 May 1812 found the three ladies of the Spencer household distinctly lacking in energy. 'I am alive – & that is all,' Lady Spencer dramatically began the letter she dashed off to her husband before she could be interrupted by the callers who were prone to pour in on her, 'thick as hail'. '1/2 after 4 a.m. was the hour of my return home last night, or rather this morning,' she explained in mock complaint, proceeding to tell him about the suffocatingly crowded ball to which she had chaperoned both of their girls, Georgiana, at seventeen, having recently joined Sarah out in company after seven years of watching her wistfully from the schoolroom.

No doubt Lady Spencer had considered it unlikely that two daughters so far apart in age would ever be navigating the marriage market at the same time, but neither she nor Sarah seemed fazed by the fact. 'Mama and Gin go about balling very merrily, and Gin is still extremely liked and admired, nothing *particular*, however, yet,' Sarah had reported to Bob in a letter of her own just a few days earlier. As for herself, 'I will tell you in plain English,' she had written, 'that I have completely regained my free and calm prospects of continuing in blessed singleness.'

Perhaps Bob greeted that last statement with a wry smile. Though she had near enough retired from dancing and had even begun to play the chaperone herself for her beautiful cousin Liz, the family had by no means written Sarah off as a spinster. Gin might have been her mother's main focus, but Lady Spencer was gratified to find that Sarah was 'quite making a sensation' of her own – as the most 'agreeable and clever person going,' she told the earl with a hint of pride. Hopes of their eldest daughter's marriage had even been raised as recently as the start of the year, when a certain suitor began to renew his attentions towards her, most promisingly they all thought. No matter that she had refused him once already some time since, or that she was inclined to describe his latest attentions as hostilities. No matter that he was about to turn forty, was well on his way to the 17-and-a-half-stone weight that would have chairs collapsing underneath him, and was somewhat lacking in brain power. Sir Watkin Williams Wynn, dubbed the 'Prince in Wales' because of his vast Welsh landholdings, was a family friend with an estate worth somewhere in the region of £30,000 or £40,000 a year – a beau worth considering, in many women's books. In the event, however, he had thought better of offering again. 'Heaven knows I thank him from the bottom of my heart, for I have never in my life felt happier,' Sarah confessed after his tactical retreat, heart-whole as ever.

Though not for much longer. It was in July 1812, as the beau monde were packing up their London houses to post off to seaside resorts and country seats, that the Hon. William Henry Lyttelton, MP surprised the Spencers by inviting himself to stay. He suggested that he visit them on the Isle of Wight, where they were planning to while away the whole summer at their new villa at Ryde, a quiet sea-bathing spot.

The presumptuousness of it utterly astonished Sarah, but, as she admitted to Bob, she was curious, too, and faintly pleased. Mr Lyttelton was a man she had met many times before. A friend of her eldest brother Lord Althorp. Witty. Handsome. Unfortunate tendency to dance out of time. Though what he was out of a London ballroom she didn't know. But she had a notion – not entirely unwelcome – that his self-proposed seaside stay was intended to remedy that.

The idea had come from a mutual friend, Mary, Lady Hood, who had engaged in a little matchmaking of the kind that greased the wheels of the Regency marriage mart each and every season. Noticing that the usually high-spirited William had been down of late, she had persuaded him to confide in her. When he told her he had proposed to a lady and been turned down, she urged him to offer for Sarah. 'I know she likes you and I am sure she would do it,' she told him. The words seem glib, but as an intimate of the Spencer household, it seems safe to assume, when she prophesised success it was based not on a notion that at twenty-five Sarah was anxious to settle, but that the amiable William, only thirty and more scholarly than sporting, might set her heart fluttering in a way that Sir Watkin had not.

It was far from the only Regency romance to begin with such a suggestion from a well-meaning friend or relative. Society might have turned against overtly arranged unions but there were all sorts of reasons why a softer sort of matchmaking still made sense; the most obvious being that neither the social whirl of the season nor the era's strict social conventions offered much scope for couples to properly get to know one another.

With the company coming and going all night long, passing through hot, noisy and uncomfortably crowded rooms on their way to or from another soirée, the balls and rout parties where Sarah and William had hitherto crossed paths were hardly conducive to anything more than an exchange of pleasantries. Of course, in some cases that was an advantage. 'When you have no time for conversation, you fancy everybody is agreeable,' the cynical Marianne Spencer-Stanhope told her brother, 'and in fashionable life, trust me, imagination is always preferable to reality!' When it came to courtship, though, it was far from ideal. William, as far as Sarah was able to make out, was simply a good-looking and entertaining rattle: 'the most extraordinary mixture of brilliant wit, childish nonsense, frivolous small-talk, and a universal sort of scrambling information, which seems all to come out, whether he will or not, from an incessant flow of wild spirits,' as she put it. However, the fact that he was a friend of her brother Althorp – the model against whom she measured most other men – was a strong point in his favour. It led her to suspect there was more to him than the high spirits and good conversation that characterised his public persona. 'I am glad to grow really acquainted with a London *beau*,' she mused ahead of his visit, 'it is a gratification I never had before.'

The *Lady's Magazine* preferred to call it an absolute necessity rather than a mere 'gratification', urging its female readers to obtain a proper knowledge of a potential husband's disposition before making a firm choice. The difficulties with getting properly acquainted, however, had as much to do with the rigid rules of propriety as the brief encounters to be had in a ballroom. The warm and overfamiliar style in which heiress Esther Acklom greeted young men might have been forgivable, but there was one far more inflexible rule: no virtuous young lady of marriageable age should be entirely alone in the company of a man who was neither a relation nor a close family friend. That meant that if a suitor called on her at home, any conversation would be conducted in company with her mother or chaperone; likewise if he stepped into her box at the opera to pay his compliments. If she accepted an invitation to go riding with him or drive out in his curricle, a groom went too. If he engineered a chance meeting as she walked in Hyde Park of an afternoon, or sauntered up to the circulating library, propriety stopped her shaking off completely the company of the maid, friend or sister who went with her. When one writer complained that men and women were 'as carefully watched and spied as if the one was an article to be stolen, or broken, or eaten up, and the other the thief and spoiler,' he was only half-joking.

Dancing was the most socially acceptable opportunity for a woman to spend time one to one with a man – to talk to him and flirt with him, and all under cover of the music, and at a comfortable distance from the all-hearing ears of her chaperone. As such, anyone on the lookout for their life's companion wanted to be confident with everything from the steps of the cotillion and the quadrille to the various combinations involved in the country dances.

The latter – in which partners stood opposite one another in two lines running longways down the room – were still the mainstay of any large ball or public assembly at the time Sarah and William were navigating the marriage market in the early

1810s. While a couple literally 'stood up' together, waiting for their turn to perform the steps, they were not just encouraged but expected to make conversation, albeit on light topics. Since men engaged their partners for the two simultaneous country dances that comprised a set, a couple might have anywhere between half an hour and an hour together, depending on the number of other couples who joined in.

Of course, the real thrill of dancing wasn't in the talking. It was in the endorphins that flooded the body as a result of the exercise, and in the uncommonly close proximity to a member of the opposite sex: the standing face to face, looking directly into one another's eyes; the constant touching of hands or entwining of arms; the glimpse of a delicate ankle as a woman showed off how gracefully she leapt and stepped. To a twenty-first-century eye the country dances might seem straitlaced, but with most forms of physical contact between unbetrothed couples being otherwise prohibited, dancing could – with the right partner – be a sexually charged affair. Even more so after the arrival of the waltz, of course – a dance that required a whole new level of physical intimacy, couples coming much closer together, clasping each other by the elbows or even with a hand on each other's waists.

It was the potent combination of physical thrill and rare tête-à-tête that made dancing so key to Regency courtship. Despite the fact that propriety demanded a lady not dance more than two dances (or two sets) with the same gentleman in one evening, it remained pretty much the only way for a woman to test the chemistry between herself and a prospective husband, and one of only a few ways for her to get a feel for his manners, tastes and opinions, even his intelligence.

That's not to say that no debutante felt confident about finding the one after just a handful of the short, chaperoned and relatively superficial meetings to be had during the season. Quite the reverse. Not long after seventeen-year-old Isabella Calvert had been presented in 1810 she lost her heart to a man she had known for mere months. Their courtship had seemingly commenced in earnest after a visit to Vauxhall Gardens, when Sir James Stronge was one of a small party formed by Isabella's aunt. The baronet proposed just three weeks later.

The romance of Harryo's sixteen-year-old niece, the Hon. Harriet Howard, and her 36-year-old cousin George, Earl Gower was even more fast-moving. He proposed exactly a week after they danced together for the first time at her 'come-out' ball in April 1823, and they married a month on from their first whirl around the dance floor. It was love, though even their contemporaries, more used to swift courtships and sizeable age gaps than us, struggled to believe it.

Since marriage determined the whole course of a woman's life – not just her future happiness, but her prosperity, her social circle, the part of the country (or the world) she would call home – if she was considering accepting the hand of a man she knew through only a series of brief and very public encounters, it must have felt much less of a risk if she knew that someone she loved and trusted thought highly of him. Frances Winckley, possessor of such a handsome fortune that her opera box was routinely overflowing with admirers, seems to have thought so. In 1806 her most appealing suitor was a man fifteen years her senior with an 'alarming reputation' – baronet and boon companion of the Prince Regent, Sir John Shelley. Since her guardian was intent on marrying her off to his own son, and her half-brother was determined to deny his sister's profligate pursuer entry to his house, Frances was able to meet him far less than she would have liked before he proposed. With society gossips and rival fortune-hunters pouring tittle-tattle about his expensive gambling habit and married mistress into her ears, she was grateful for the glowing endorsement of his close friends, her Lancashire neighbours Lord and Lady Sefton. They believed Frances was 'the wife most likely to suit, and to *steady*' the careless, warm-hearted Sir John, while at the same time saving him from impending financial ruin. With so much evidence weighted against her favoured suitor – whom she personally thought 'the most entertaining of any man I ever conversed with' – it was these 'dear people' and their wholehearted approval of him that gave Frances the confidence to follow her heart, trust in her ability to reform a rake, and become his wife.

The Seftons were, in fact, the ones who first introduced Frances and Sir John, at a dinner party at their house in Arlington Street. It was the kind of practical matchmaking effort that was as much valued by besieged heiresses and near-bankrupt baronets as those struggling to make an impression on the marriage market. If, like Sarah and William, your best qualities were hidden behind your public persona, or you preferred not to frequent packed ballrooms, a matchmaker might bring you together with the perfect partner in a more intimate environment – over the dinner table, perhaps, or at a country house party.

Of course, William Lyttelton didn't wait for Lady Hood to engineer such a meeting, but the outcome was the same. As a self-invited guest of the Spencers at Ryde, seeing Sarah around the breakfast table every morning, and sitting in the same drawing room with her night after night, he had a far better opportunity to get to know her than anything the season could offer. When he followed her family across the Solent to Westfield, the earl's spacious new-build overlooking the sea, he was no doubt invited to join in with all their usual summertime schemes – everything from excursions on the water to boat-building with the two youngest boys, 'my two little sons' as Sarah affectionately described 'Fritz' and George, whom she revelled in mothering and tutoring. Perhaps William also trotted forth with her on one or two of the 'romantic' rides referred to in the Isle of Wight's principal guidebook.

He was certainly unmistakeably attentive to Sarah during his stay. So much so that Lady Spencer – closely observing what she described as 'the Lyttelton romance' – began thinking seriously of him as a son-in-law. 'I am willing to believe that if this one takes place happiness will be the result,' she wrote to her husband, reassured not only by her own son's partiality for him, but also all that she had seen herself of his 'never failing good temper' and good sense.

What exactly her daughter felt was less clear. The letter she dispatched to her Grandmama Spencer as William's stay drew to a close at the end of August was almost studied in its indifference. 'He has dropped the character of a mere buffoon with a very good grace, which makes him much the more agreeable as a constant companion, and we all begin to think him a very amiable person,' she told the dowager. 'A perfect stranger among one's most private family circle in a small house is, however, on the whole, not entirely a comfortable thing,' she added, 'and I don't think our gay guest will be very much regretted.'

The outward nonchalance was perhaps a ploy to prevent the kind of talk that had rippled around the family circle earlier in the year when Sir Watkin had renewed his attentions, only to stop short of proposing again. In reality, she was a fair way to falling in love with William already. Their greater intimacy had revealed a warm heart and intelligent mind and, to her gratification, he shared her religious piety and moral values too. But she was trying not to indulge the idea that he felt the same about her. He was a younger brother and not rich, she told herself, not likely to be thinking seriously of marrying anybody, much less marrying her. In actual fact, William stood to inherit a house and title from his half-brother, an inheritance that seemed likely as the current Baron Lyttelton was unmarried at forty-nine and struggling with a mental illness, but Sarah was obviously reluctant to place too much reliance on something that might be many years away yet.

It could be difficult for women faced with an attentive admirer to find out what exactly he was thinking without being thought forward, it being entirely improper for a lady to make her feelings known first in the hope that he might be encouraged to reveal his own. And, of course, neither uncommon attentiveness nor gallant compliments could be relied upon as a sign that a man had matrimony in mind. In her years on the marriage market, Sarah had seen plenty of men engage in conspicuous flirtation that progressed no further – men like Lord Henry Petty, whom her cousin Harryo did not scruple to label 'a gay deceiver to more than one' when she learned of his engagement in 1807. 'I hope it will not make Lady Maria unhappy or Miss Napier, or Miss Crewe, or Miss Beckford,' she wrote to her sister, 'for if report is to be believed one's compassion must take a very wide range upon the subject.' Matchmakers could, again, prove invaluable as go-betweens in the tricky business of turning an apparent admirer into something more. They could – subtly, of course – enquire into a suitor's intentions, or drop a hint in his ear that any romantic overtures might be favourably received.

Often it was a mother who took on the task, but she, too, had a delicate path to tread. A few discreet efforts on a daughter's behalf were perfectly acceptable, but anything too pushy, or anything that might be mistaken for manipulation, was to be avoided. Likewise anything that gave the impression that rank and riches were of greater importance to her family than romance. In an age when affectionate unions were valued more and more, the 'matchmaking mama' with her mercenary schemes to ensnare rich and titled men for her daughters was increasingly treated with scorn. She had also become a target for satirists, females of a managing disposition being problematic no matter what their field of operation. The Duchess of Gordon, an outspoken matriarch with a broad Scottish accent, was repeatedly vilified by contemporary cartoonists for her determined pursuit of dukes for her five unimpressively dowered daughters. Her so-called 'exertions' extended over a period of fourteen years in all, but perhaps the most notorious of her manoeuvres came in 1802, after the 5th Duke of Bedford died suddenly, before his anticipated engagement to her youngest daughter Georgiana could be announced. Undeterred, the duchess simply dressed Georgiana up in mourning clothes and sent her to sympathise with his widowed brother John, the new duke, sowing the seeds for their marriage the following year. He was to be the last of three dukes she welcomed into the family in total, along with a marquis and a baronet.

Though they might criticise the duchess's method of finding husbands for her girls, in a world where marriages mattered to the whole family, and it was so hard for daughters to stand out from the crowd, few mothers would criticise her motives. Or few fathers, in fact. For in spite of the emerging stereotype, patriarchs of titled families were just as apt to try engineering advantageous matches, and for offspring of both sexes. The Marquis of Abercorn reportedly worked hard to throw together the young and wealthy Earl of Aberdeen and his eldest daughter Lady Catherine during amateur theatricals at his country seat in 1805; and in 1807, so intent on stealing a march on rivals was he that after an embarrassingly short acquaintance he wrote to an heiress who was 'but 17' to offer for her hand on his eldest son's behalf. 'They say [it] was like the K[ing] of England proposing the P[rince]. of W[ales]. to some little German Electors, and setting forth the honour he was doing them,' said an amused Lady Bessborough, relating the tale of his inevitable rejection to her lover.

Her Ladyship had not laughed, however, when her own son had been embroiled in a matchmaking scheme taken straight from the Duchess of Gordon's rulebook. It was in 1802 that the Countess of Jersey had embarked on a quest to lure Lady Bessborough's eldest son, Lord Duncannon, away from his cousin Harryo – with whom a match was looking very promising – and win him for her own daughter, Lady Elizabeth Villiers.

Her long-running campaign first began when the two families were sojourning by the sea: the Jerseys in Margate and the combined Devonshire–Bessborough clan five miles away in Ramsgate, near enough for the two parties to socialise together. It very soon revealed that constancy was not the 21-year-old Duncannon's strong suit. He was immediately receptive to Lady Elizabeth's flirting and flattery. 'She is so very pretty and her manner so pleasing that Ly. Jersey need not take half the pains she does to make poor John in love with her,' his mother had noted with more than a little unease.

The decampment of Duncannon to France with his family had been a temporary setback, but the countess had resumed her manoeuvres in 1803, the year that Harryo, with whom Duncannon still seemed equally smitten, made her curtsey to the Queen. Her tactics were always undeniably clever. She took the box next door to the Devonshire and Bessborough tribe at the Covent Garden Theatre, wangled invitations to dine with Harryo's father in order to get Duncannon and Elizabeth round the same dinner table, and, if Duncannon refused her invitations to the Jersey house, she teased him for being under his mother's thumb – something he was acutely sensitive about. Certainly his mother violently opposed the match, and saw that trick for what it was: an attempt to goad her son into being particular in his attentions, thus providing Lady Elizabeth with 'a right to complain if it goes no further.'

In reality, Lady Jersey had little success with her scheme. For two years, Duncannon – 'this weathercock cousin of mine' as Harryo growled in her letters – blew hot and cold towards Lady Elizabeth, while an indignant Harryo refused to give him up without a fight. Her own machinations earned her a trimming from her former governess, who suspected that without caring especially for her cousin she had made him in love with her, simply 'to enjoy the triumph of having supplanted Lady E.'

Harryo – witty and lively, but in looks no match for her rival's radiant beauty – appears to have been undecided about how she felt about Duncannon. He was 'uncommonly handsome, good-tempered and affectionate' on the one hand, but she did '*not* think him clever' and she had no desire for the sort of fickle, unfaithful husband he was bidding fair to become – as she was inclined to tell him, much to his annoyance. But both her mama and his were all for the match and had counselled time for reflection. It was neither illegal for first cousins to marry, nor all that uncommon in aristocratic circles. It had the benefit of keeping money and influence in the family, though to their credit, the Duchess of Devonshire and her sister seem to have been driven chiefly by a desire to keep Harryo and Duncannon in their tight-knit Whig circle.

In the end, however, despite continuing to bristle with jealousy whenever Harryo attracted the attention of another man, Duncannon spurned both Lady Elizabeth and his cousin. After conducting another desperate flirtation with the 'coquetish' (and married) Mrs Payne, he turned his attentions towards the adoring and undemanding Lady Maria Fane and her share of the Child fortune, and in 1805 suddenly presented his parents with the news that she had done him the honour of accepting his hand. The family's congratulations came with a certain measure of surprise and scepticism. 'I began to think you were vying with Don Juan in the list you meant to produce of broken hearts & plighted vows,' his sister Lady Caroline Lamb said laughingly. Yet the couple were married later that year, and from then on habitually observed 'in a broad grin' and sitting hand in hand, or walking arm in arm. Harryo was not much disappointed. Her letters indicate that she had lost all patience with Duncannon and his roving eye, and she could not help but like Maria, whom she saw was 'really and sincerely attached' to him. But it seems that like her aunt and Grandmama Spencer – who had gently rebuked her grandson for his 'careless but dangerous attentions to young women' – she felt a slight niggle of guilt where Lady Elizabeth was concerned. Duncannon's public flirtation had ended for her in an equally public rejection, and few things were more damaging to a young lady's reputation.

If a formerly eager suitor failed to make a proposal – and particularly if they soon after married someone else – then naturally it must have been she, not he, who had been found wanting. That was partly why girls were encouraged to maintain a feminine reserve in public, avoiding any behaviour that might advertise their partiality for a particular gentleman. It was also the reason why corresponding with a suitor during courtship was usually discouraged. Few things implied that a match was imminent like an exchange of letters, and while there was still every chance that a proposal might not materialise, not too many parents wanted to risk making a budding romance the talk of the town – or, indeed, to risk the existence of love notes that could stand as evidence, of either their daughter's failed courtship or her caprice in leading on a man she subsequently refused.

Plenty of couples did nevertheless embark on a correspondence. In 1807 Harryo learned that her illegitimate half-sister Caroline St Jules was writing to George Lamb, the man she hoped to (and eventually did) marry, but it was 'to be kept a profound secret,' she told their other sister Georgiana. So, too, was Eleanora Campbell's correspondence with her preferred suitor. Their private communication had begun with a note, slipped to her by a friend of his as he handed Eleanora her shawl on the way out of Almack's one evening in 1817, and was only revealed to her mother after her nosy younger sister caught sight of one of his heartfelt missives. Perhaps conscious that it was the family's financial difficulties that were behind the decision to leave for the continent as soon as the season was over, or perhaps aware that a correspondence would be the best way to keep Eleanora in her noble admirer's heart while he did battle for his father's consent, her mother gave permission for it to continue – provided, that is, that it was conducted openly, with any letters carried through the post.

Despite concerns, it was perfectly possible to make a happy marriage in spite of an intense courtship that never led the parties to church. The slighted Lady Elizabeth Villiers, for example, was linked with at least two other men and received a respectable proposal in 1807, though she turned it down and was still unmarried when she died a little over two years later. The behaviour of heiress Esther Acklom, meanwhile, had been everything young women were advised against, but it still didn't stop her making a brilliant match.

'She has a way of encouraging men, without meaning to have them,' Mrs Calvert had complained, having watched her make conquests of her brother-in-law Charles and two of her nephews. By the time her father died at the end of 1812, Esther had not only turned down numerous proposals, but had one broken engagement behind her and would soon jilt her current fiancé. She was no longer just an heiress but a very wealthy woman. With £10,000 a year at her disposal (an income likely to be closer to £26,000 after her mother's death), she decided to ditch the unfortunate Mr Maddocks before she was out of black gloves, soon trading him in for another man – specifically Lady Sarah's brother Lord Althorp, who had caught her eye.

Much to his mother's dissatisfaction, Lord Althorp had never been interested in doing the niceties in a lady's drawing room. Rendered shy and undemonstrative by Lady Spencer's sarcasm and sharp tongue, he was far more interested in chasing foxes than females. 'Althorp as he is, no reasonable woman can for a moment think of but as an eager huntsman,' sighed Harryo in 1807, after the family tried to convince her that yet another cousin was seriously interested in marrying her. She could see very little attraction in a man who did not care 'for anything on earth but that noble animal, a horse'.

By the time his sister Georgiana was 'out' and seeking a spouse, however, Althorp was growing mindful of his own duty to marry, and even more mindful that with mortgages on the family estates, it would be best if the lady was a rich one. He hardly knew Esther, the rather plain, slightly stout heiress six years his junior, whose warmth, vivacity and confidence had won her so many male hearts. But when she – daringly – made it known that she would enjoy life as the future Countess Spencer, Althorp felt duty-bound to think about making her an offer. The chattering chaperones of London society, seeing what was in the wind, thought it a strange match. Althorp might not have had the grace, striking good looks or polished manners of a man of fashion, but he had plenty beyond his title to recommend him – not least an unusually high level of achievement at Cambridge University and a benevolent temper. Esther by comparison had a very chequered romantic history, and her connections were nothing compared to his. Yet, after roaming around the family's estate for an hour or two's hard soul-searching, Althorp resolved to make a classic marriage of convenience. He would bring the title Esther wanted; she would bring the money he needed.

At least that's what he thought he was doing. Esther, he discovered, was more in love with him than his rank, and as they began to spend time in each other's company in the wake of their engagement in spring 1814, familiarity fast turned to fondness on his side, too. By the time they came back from their honeymoon, theirs was shaping up to be a marriage capable of rivalling any made from purely romantic motives. The flighty, flirtatious Esther would never be a favourite with the Spencers – even gentle Sarah went so far as to call her 'a vulgar person and a spoilt child' – but they did readily admit that 'never was there a happier marriage, never more sincere and deep affection on both sides.'

Esther, as it turned out, was absolutely right to risk denting her reputation by leaving a trail of disappointed lovers behind as she sought a marriage that offered everything she wanted, emotionally and economically. But female writers of the Regency period were entirely correct to point out that for the majority of women, the power of accepting or rejecting, rather than selecting, was their only privilege. Yet it was still power of a sort. Provided, of course, that an admirer did at last come to the point, revealing that he had secretly adored her for months and felt an ardent desire to make her his affianced wife.

Traditionalists still preferred a man to seek permission from a woman's father before making a declaration of love, as the future Lord Jersey did when he first sought the hand of heiress Lady Sarah Fane in 1802, the year before she was brought 'out' into society. He sent an elegant missive to the Earl of Westmorland, spurred on, he said, by the hope that his 'sentiments had made such an impression on her mind as to want only the sanction of your Lordship's approbation'. As the resident agony aunt at the

*Lady's Magazine* reluctantly acknowledged, however, this was the 'ancient mode' by 1818. Most young men were choosing to make their proposals first and tackle their beloved's parents afterwards, as Sir James Stronge did in 1810.

Mrs Calvert's nerves were left all a-flutter after the 24-year-old offered her daughter Isabella his hand in the moonlit surroundings of Vauxhall Gardens, perhaps having taken the opportunity to separate his young love from the rest of their party during a stroll down one of its romantically leafy, lantern-lit walks, or having drawn her apart for a whispered conversation under cover of the fireworks. However it happened, having no inkling whatsoever of his intentions, the first Mrs Calvert knew of his proposal was the arrival at her Hertfordshire home of his stepfather Mr Holmes the following day, Isabella having behaved like a perfect model of maidenly propriety and returned a favourable answer, subject to her parents' approval. 'It has flurried me so I scarce know what I am doing,' her mother confided in her diary after their unexpected visitor had departed, noting down what he had said about Sir James's fortune and 'angelic' disposition.

Not only did Vauxhall provide an undeniably picturesque backdrop for a proposal, it probably held an added significance for Isabella and Sir James, their romance having blossomed in the three weeks since they had last spent the evening there together at the end of June. Exactly where and when a man chose to make his offer appears to have been ungoverned by etiquette. It was entirely proper to propose in writing. Or a gentleman might seek a private conference with the object of his affections, as the Hon. Emily Lamb's first serious suitor did in 1803, returning again the following day to offer 'a great many oaths... taking heaven & earth to witness that he could love only [her]' in an attempt to change her nay to a yay. If a man preferred to be more spontaneous, musical evenings seem to have been ideal for a covert, unchaperoned conversation. Lord Grantham was known to have proposed to Lady Henrietta Cole at Lady Salisbury's concert in June 1805, and it was at a concert at Lady Jersey's in June 1811 that Esther Acklom had become engaged to the first of her three fiancés. Another contemporary, meanwhile, mused over how often 'the guardian abigails in the cloak-room' at Almack's – the maids waiting patiently for their mistresses – had overheard a whispered exchange as the question was popped.

As for Mr William Lyttelton, not a word about matrimony had crossed his lips by the time he ended his seaside stay with Sarah and the Spencers in late August 1812. Though still waiting expectantly as the year drew to a close, Lady Spencer obviously remained hopeful. William was invited to spend Christmas with the family at Althorp, Sarah fizzing with anticipation as he sprang out of the coach on 21 December, a day that would be marked on her heart for many months to come. By then it was clear to all her nearest and dearest that she had fallen for her exuberant admirer. For her aunt and closest confidante, Lady Anne Bingham, known to the family as 'Nan' or 'Nanette', Sarah had promised to scribble down a journal of sorts as she waited anxiously to see if he would, finally, speak. And whether it was from worry about another rejection, or a desire to see some of the other house guests depart first, he did keep her waiting.

'He has been here a fortnight, and at last, the day before yesterday, it all came out,' Sarah was finally able to write to Bob just after New Year 1813, still struggling to believe that she was going to be *married*. 'Papa and Mama are perfectly delighted, so is Althorp, so is everybody who loves me and knows him,' she wrote jubilantly. It was true. Her Grandmama Spencer – not over-pleased with all of her grandchildren's matches – was quick to send congratulations. 'Her sweet steadiness with his brilliant vivacity will I trust suit remarkably well,' she wrote to her son, this letter swiftly followed by a second, urging him to tell her 'when & where is Sarah to be married & what will they have to live upon.'

On William's part there was no sign at all that he was pining for the one who got away. He talked of Sarah 'in terms of rapturous admiration' according to his sister. 'Ever since she had consented to be his, he had felt quite another man,' he had told her. For Sarah, it was simply perfect happiness 'to respect, and admire, and love with one's whole heart, a person whose warm affection one is sure of possessing'. Even more so because, on the verge of turning twenty-six, she was convinced that she knew herself well enough to be sure that what she approved now, she would always approve. This time, there had been no question of her exercising her power of refusal.

*Chapter Three*

# The Power of Refusal

A T THE TIME of her own betrothal the previous year, Sydney Owenson could not have sounded any less jubilant than Lady Sarah if she tried. 'I have been battling off, from day to day, and hour to hour, and have only ten minutes back procured a little breathing time,' she wrote to a friend of her attempts to stall the wedding preparations. Seemingly determined to wriggle out of an engagement contracted in haste and now being repented at leisure, the author of a famous novel of high romance and Irish nationalism would spend the next three months 120 miles away from her fiancé, giddily going to parties, hosting gentleman callers and flirting determinedly.

The reluctant bride owed her regretted engagement to the kind offices of her noble friends and patrons, the Marquis and Marchioness of Abercorn, in whose household she had been a semi-permanent resident for the past two years. Encountering her in London, where she was flitting between high-society parties, basking in the success and celebrity that had followed the publication of *The Wild Irish Girl* – the novel that had made her name – the Abercorns had encouraged her to join them as a sort of companion-cum-court jester. Accompanying them as they revolved between their homes in Mayfair, County Tyrone and Middlesex, Sydney had leisure to write new novels, luxurious surroundings in which to do so and a glimpse of the political intrigues that occupied the elite. In return, she was simply required to be high-spirited and witty, entertaining both them and their frequent guests with her Irish jigs, ballads and harp recitals. It was not a bad bargain, especially for one who thrived on theatrical display and delighted in mingling among the beau monde – into whose orbit she had definitely not been born.

Fiercely independent, having towed herself and her family out of poverty through her writing, as far as anyone could tell she was contentedly unmarried in her mid-thirties – or thereabouts; her petite frame allowed her to be deliberately evasive on the subject of her age. Lady Abercorn, however, had a habit of meddling in the affairs of those she took up and had seemingly decided that a young(ish) and lively woman possessed of sufficient money to marry on must be in want of a husband.

Possibly it was simply an idle quest for amusement; a vicarious longing for romance. Possibly a concern for Sydney's reputation. One observer thought that Lady Abercorn had become afraid that 'her lovely *protégée*' – so fond of exhibiting – 'might get herself into a scrape, if she did not make some effort to have her respectably off her hands.' Possibly it had something to do with Lord Abercorn's roving eye and tender friendship with their flirtatious companion. Whichever it was, she had concocted a plan with her husband to set Sydney up with his doctor, Charles Morgan.

Her matchmaking had begun some weeks before Sydney even met Charles for the first time in the summer of 1811. He was then a new addition to the Abercorn household, appointed as physician in residence, a lucrative post he owed more to his likeable manner and numerous accomplishments than his medical capabilities. He had arrived at Baronscourt, the couple's Irish residence, while Sydney was away in London overseeing the publication of her latest novel, and the Abercorns had swiftly furnished him with a glowing account of the wit and genius of their absent friend, Miss Owenson the authoress. She, in turn, had been persuaded to welcome their amiable new employee by sending him some comic verses. So it was, said Sydney, that when she and Charles did meet face to face, it was 'under circumstances... too favourable to the romantic feelings peculiar to his character,' which, she added, it was her 'lot to excite and feed.'

At first, she had been amused by Dr Morgan's evident awkwardness around her and more than willing to oblige the Abercorns with a harmless dalliance. Flirtatious to the point that even her dearest friends called her a coquette, Sydney took an 'evident delight in her powers' – the charisma, confidence and humour that won her so many admirers, despite the fact that she could not be called a beauty. At least not according to contemporaries, who pointed to her lack of height, lopsided shoulders and large, uneven (though expressive) eyes.

To one who so relished attention, Charles Morgan's bashful reserve was, as she later admitted, a challenge she could not resist. He was of a different breed to the majority of her former conquests, of which there had been many among the lawyers, clergymen and soldiers of Dublin's smart set. 'Sydney's Army of Martyrs,' her sister Olivia called them, because though she basked in their flattery, none had seemed to enjoy her reciprocal regard. Or none except barrister Sir Charles Ormsby – a cynical, witty but unattractive widower with whom she had been inexplicably romantically entangled for a time. Like Ormsby (and Lord Abercorn), her admirers tended to be older, knowing men, who gratified the 'clever little soul' with their lavish compliments. But the idealistic Dr Morgan was no expert in the art of romance. Married and widowed despite being only just thirty, he was quiet and sensitive, 'too honest to trifle with truth' and not 'especially qualified to shine in society'. Generally reckoned handsome, to Sydney's fastidious eye his looks were 'too indicative of goodness' – there was not enough of the rogue in either his appearance or his manners to make her 'wild in love with him'. He was certainly the epitome of respectability; born and bred in London, educated at Eton and Cambridge, he spoke several languages, played the piano and sang, and was well read on all matters of science and philosophy. To add to his virtues, he had a comfortable private income of £500 a year, on top of his salary from the Abercorns.

Frivolously embarked upon her flirtation with Charles might have been, but Sydney very soon began to describe him as a friend. In fact, she began writing of him to her regular correspondents with an almost lover-like enthusiasm, calling him 'a person of extraordinary talent' and 'a most amiable and benevolent person'. Evidently they were spending plenty of time together. He had improved her Italian, she reported, and she was able to admire his 'bold and singular opinions' and to confirm that he 'thinks upon every subject of importance with us'.

For his part, Charles had quickly decided he wanted to be

more than friends. Barely a month after their first meeting, spurred on by the Abercorns, he had proposed. Apparently all astonishment at the turn of events, Sydney had written to her father. 'My dearest Dad,' her letter of 20 August began, 'I am… at a loss how to begin to tell you what I am going to ask you – which is, your leave to marry Doctor Morgan, whom I will not marry if you do not wish it. I dare say you will be amazingly astonished; but not half so much as I am, for Lord and Lady Abercorn have hurried on the business in such a manner, that I really don't know what I am about.'

There was no mention of her part in the affair. According to the various letters she dispatched on the subject, she was every inch the reluctantly courted maiden, bewildered by the ardour she had 'most unwittingly inspired'. But then, as her biographers never fail to note, Sydney was fond of editing and arranging the facts of her life for dramatic effect, sometimes in a way that bore little resemblance to reality. Certainly by 1 September she had detached herself even further from the whole thing. 'A man has fallen in love with me… and almost married me, before I know where I am or what it is all about,' she told one friend, adding, 'I have refused and denied him over and over again.' Reading between the lines of her letters, however, she knew that she had encouraged him to think his feelings were reciprocated. And though she never actually confessed to being in love, what she did tell her confidants betrayed a decided partiality for the accomplished and besotted Charles: 'barring his wild, unfounded love for me, the creature is perfection,' she gushed in another letter. 'The most *manly*, I had almost said *daring,* tone of mind, united to more goodness of heart and disposition, than I ever met with in a human being.'

The one thing that was crystal clear to her correspondents was her alarm at the speed with which her unexpected, totally 'unlooked-for' romance had progressed. The next they heard of the matter, she had engineered an escape from the gilded cage that Baronscourt had become, buying herself some breathing space. Ostensibly retreating home to attend to her sick father, she had bolted back to Dublin at the end of September, with a promise to Charles to be back in two weeks' time. But weeks had turned to months, and there she had still been in December. Not indulging in a period of quiet reflection, but revelling in freedom: flirting and partying, while her affianced was stuck with the Abercorns, growing ever more jealous and frustrated by the day.

Was it deliberate coquetry, as some suspected? Was it an attempt to goad him into calling off the engagement? Or simply a reluctance to commit, given everything becoming a wife meant, and everything it meant giving up? Sydney would later try to defend herself to Charles by saying, 'there was so much of FORCE in the commencement of this business, that my heart was frightened *back* from the course it would *naturally have taken*.' If she was struggling with the idea of marriage, Lady Abercorn's manoeuvring must certainly have been suffocating. Before Sydney had even written to her father for permission, she and her husband had not only obtained the marriage licence and the ring but overseen the settlements too. In their most outrageous manoeuvre of all, they had even prevailed on the Duke of Richmond, then Lord Lieutenant of Ireland, to knight Dr Morgan as a favour to them. Lady Abercorn had seemingly 'no idea that the ceremony in real life could be anything more than the last page in a novel, or the last words in a play'. Sydney, on the other hand, had been 'almost out of [her] mind between contending feelings'.

Putting love and companionship aside, marriage was not an overwhelmingly inviting prospect for a woman in her situation. A Regency-era husband would be automatically entitled to all her property and her earnings, unless the marriage settlement said differently, and he could dispose of them as and when he liked. He could restrict her movements, punish her for disobedience with violence, refuse her a separation or divorce – even have her confined in an asylum. And the problem was that Sydney (to borrow a phrase) had none of the usual inducements to marry. She did not want for money; she did not want for something to occupy her time; she did not want for male attention.

Admittedly, she had sometimes felt that something was missing from her life; had wondered why she still felt 'sad and miserable' when she had good health and all the fame she had ever hoped for. But to look for happiness in marriage was a risk: a probable surrender of both her hard-won financial independence and her literary career. Sydney had her critics – many more, in fact, than other female authors, who had become strangely fixated on exposing her real age – but her novels were popular, and she had worked hard for the kind of money and success that did not come easily to women of her background. The product of an elopement between an Irish actor and theatre manager and the daughter of an English merchant, in her teenage years her life – or so she said – had been one of 'scrambling poverty and discomfort'. With her mother dead and father almost bankrupt, only her 'good conduct and good sense' had 'kept her out of all sorts of mischief, to which her exposed and unprotected situation left her open', according to her memoirs. She and her sister Olivia – provided in less straitened times with tuition at genteel boarding and finishing schools – had been forced to take work as governesses. But instead of sinking into obscurity, as many a penniless governess had done before her, Sydney had begun to write, and then to seek publication for her works. And she had managed it well. She had not only whipped up competition between rival publishers for *The Wild Irish Girl*, but had also created a buzz around the novel – and herself – by becoming the living image of its heroine, Glorvina.

Her £5,000 earnings to date were very respectable – Jane Austen, by comparison, earned less than £700 in her lifetime. The profits of her literary endeavours also provided her with a tolerably good income for a single woman, particularly one living in Dublin. The prospect of that transferring into the hands of a husband the minute her vows were exchanged must have been galling. Not to mention the thought that her writing – and her socialising in the Abercorns' glittering circle of aristocrats – might have to take second place to duties as a wife, a housekeeper and, perhaps, a mother. 'I give up my career of pleasure and vanity to sink into privacy and oblivion; and the ambition of the authoress and the woman is lost in the feelings of the mistress and the wife,' she tried to explain to Charles.

There was also, Sydney said, the parting from both her father and her sister Olivia to consider: 'the dreadful certainty of being parted… from a country and friends I love, and a family I adore,' as she put it. The plan sketched out for the couple was a return to England with the Abercorns, where it seemed likely they would then settle in their own home. However, since Charles had readily offered to make his home in Ireland instead, and had also assured her that he – most unusually – wanted to be equals in marriage, there was possibly another, less worthy thought responsible for her reluctance: that she could do better.

The Abercorns had not been entirely wrong to think that a title might convince Sydney to enter the married state. There is 'nothing in it very gratifying to my *ambition*,' she had confessed after Charles proposed, adding, 'it is not in worldly circumstances a very good match for me.' Secretly, as the Abercorns knew, she had cherished hopes of making a brilliant marriage; but this was real life, not one of her romances, and she was not the unacknowledged daughter of an aristocrat. However captivating her personality, the former governess with a 'worldly shrewdness' about her and an unfortunate habit of peppering her conversation with inexpert French was not likely to snare one of the bachelors who graced the guest rooms at Baronscourt. As Lady Abercorn condescendingly reminded her, she 'had no place in the society upon which she now looked but that which whim had accorded or charity bestowed.'

There was, as Sydney said, 'much *pour et contre* on the subject' and it must have been hard to think it all through at Baronscourt, with Lady Abercorn eagerly pushing her towards a wedding ceremony – a feeling no doubt familiar to many a Regency debutante whose family and friends were caught up in all the merits of a brilliant match. One of Sydney's trusted correspondents had been more understanding of her fears. 'Who can be married without such attendants?' the 69-year-old Lady Stanley had assured her, counselling that 'in the main, establishment is good… since the delights of youth, of friends, of range, and frolic, are but passengers.'

No doubt she sympathised with her young friend fleeing to Dublin for some space to think, though Sydney's behaviour there had seemed more self-destructive than anything else. 'You use Sir Charles very ill indeed,' was the opinion of Lady Abercorn, no doubt well aware of the increasingly irritable letters that had been flying back and forth between the couple during the stormiest weeks of their courtship, filled with accusations of cruelty and neglect from him and plentiful excuses from her. 'I recommend you to play no longer with his feelings,' she advised.

Sydney's rollercoaster romance eventually reached a climax in late December 1811 when the now *Sir* Charles, sick and tired of being kept dangling on a string, sent an ultimatum to his wayward wife-to-be. 'The love I require is no ordinary affection… I must have a large bank of tenderness to draw upon,' he wrote. 'If, then, your love for me is not sufficiently ardent to bring you freely to me at the end of a three months' absence… do not let us risk a life of endless regret and disappointment,' he begged. There must be no further 'delay and trifling'.

Her choice was a simple one. Return to Baronscourt and marry a man who was besotted with her, or break off the engagement for good, secure in the knowledge that she could continue to support herself as a single woman. She need only marry if it was what she wanted. In the end, she did not deliberate for long. She chose Charles.

Sydney's was an enviable situation to be in. Yet despite what fiction would have us believe, marriage was not always a fait accompli for the aristocratic debutantes the author sometimes encountered in Lady Abercorn's drawing room. We're quick to assume that a need for financial security or parental pressure gave them no real choice in the matter, but when it came to those born into the upper echelons of society, it wasn't actually quite so black and white.

There were certainly incentives for upper-class women to marry. Marriage was the universally accepted sign that they had reached adulthood: it transformed their status, freed them from parental authority and, perhaps most significantly, cut the ties of constant chaperonage. For the average genteel woman, unaccustomed to the liberty that Sydney had enjoyed since her late teens, marriage at least *promised* a degree of freedom only dreamed of in her debutante days. Married women could make friends of their own choosing, converse more freely, and more privately, with members of the opposite sex – even dress more daringly. Marriage also offered them a sense of purpose that could be harder to find in their childhood home. As the mistress of a large house, the figurehead for a noble family's charitable endeavours, or the sounding board and supportive hostess of a prominent politician, women could obtain the stimulation and personal satisfaction that, with her writing, Sydney probably felt less need for.

Marriage no doubt appeared more financially attractive to the average Regency debutante, too. It was undeniably her best hope of replicating the lifestyle she knew, and enjoying the luxuries she had become accustomed to under her parental roof. If she stayed single her standard of living was likely to be reduced, in her later years at least. Though usually on a par with the sum allotted to younger sons, a genteel woman's marriage portion was never intended to make her comfortably independent – the clue, after all, was in the name. What's more, the portion was not usually paid unless or until she married. She could expect to receive the income it generated, at least once her parents died, but a highly respectable fortune of £10,000, invested to provide £400 or £500 a year (at the most), was totally insufficient to cover the rent of a house in a smart part of town, a retinue of servants, a frequently refreshed wardrobe and a means of transport.

Making her own money to supplement what she earned on her inherited capital was more of a challenge for a young lady born to rank and riches than it had been for the resourceful Sydney. Among the upper classes there was, as writer Priscilla Wakefield lamented, a general prejudice that acted 'like an insurmountable barrier' against a woman 'employing her time and her abilities' to maintain herself. It was only those employments that women could pursue 'without endangering their virtue, or corrupting their manners' that were reluctantly accepted. A post as a governess or paid companion would fit the bill, but no elite family was likely to countenance a female relation taking such a job as Sydney and her sister had done – not unless they had already fallen in wealth and status. But salaried positions at court, akin to being a companion to a royal, could be accepted with perfect propriety. The wages were attractive, at £300 per annum for a maid of honour and £500 for a lady of the bedchamber, and court posts provided a welcome boost to a single woman's consequence: cast-iron evidence of a contribution to society and to her family's standing, and a role almost as socially valid as that of wife and mother. But court posts were not an easy option, as Lady Anne Hamilton, unmarried daughter of a duke, found out during her two stints as lady-in-waiting to the Prince Regent's estranged wife, Caroline of Brunswick. The inflexible court routine was not conducive to maintaining an independent social life, and ladies-in-waiting had to be as resilient to snubs as any other put-upon paid companion. The Princess of Wales was frequently observed mocking her virtuous 'virgin' attendant, nicknaming her 'Joan of Arc' and vowing to find a husband to take poor Lady Anne off her hands.

A paid post as 'lady housekeeper' at one of the royal palaces might have been the more attractive option. The Hon. Miss Georgiana Townshend, daughter of a viscount, took up the appointment at Windsor Castle in 1801; and Lady Elizabeth Seymour-Conway, daughter of a marquis, filled the role at Hampton Court Palace between 1813 and her death in 1825. At that time, the position at Hampton Court boasted a basic salary of £250 a year but was actually worth somewhere between £650 and £800 annually, on account of the tips collected from visitors wanting a tour of the palace. It came with free lodgings, too, and in exchange for such largesse demanded no exertion likely to offend a woman's noble relations.

Regrettably, though, bank-account-boosting positions of either kind were few and far between, and with competition fierce, single women tended to be forced to make some sacrifices. Not being able to 'keep a carriage the year round' was one of the things that Lady Louisa Stuart, daughter of the 3rd Earl of Bute, regretted most about her single life. She was able to live fairly centrally in London's Gloucester Place on her budget, but without an extra £300 a year, a carriage was utterly unaffordable. It was a privation that curtailed her movements, sometimes meaning that she stayed at home (chiefly alone) for as many as ten days at a time.

There was one other sacrifice a single woman couldn't avoid, no matter how much money she had. Staying single meant committing not just to a childless life, but to a celibate one, since enjoying liaisons of a romantic nature as an unmarried woman was out of the question, unless she wanted to be a social exile. Aristocratic men might have as many lovers as they liked before becoming 'leg-shackled' but for a woman, going to bed with a man before marriage was totally incompatible with her continued membership of polite society. Getting married was the only respectable way for her to have a family of her own.

It was, of course, a glaring double standard. 'Man may commit an hundred deviations from the path of rectitude, yet he still can return, every one invites him; in sober truth, he gains an eclat by his failings, that establish him in the Ton, and make him envied, instead of pitied or despised. But woman, when she makes one false step… becomes a mark for the slow-moving finger of scorn,' Julia Johnstone, the niece of an earl, purportedly observed in the 1820s. Whether the words were really hers, Julia – who joined the coterie of courtesan Harriette Wilson and embarked on a lacklustre career after treading off the path of righteousness with a married man – certainly knew the truth of them. And she was not the only well-born woman who did.

The 'seduction' of Miss Harriet Spencer was a scandal that rippled through polite society at the beginning of 1818, a story made all the more gossip-worthy by the fact that the lady was a distant cousin of some of the fashionable world's most prominent peers: the dukes of Marlborough and Devonshire and the Earl Spencer.

Harriet, whose mother was a far less zealous chaperone than the likes of Mrs Calvert, had as a debutante acquired a troubling reputation, thanks to the loose lips of a group of fast-living young libertines whose company she had been permitted to keep. While it might have been possible to bury a few rumours of a less-than-virtuous character with a respectable marriage, her fate had been sealed when she was caught in a compromising situation with one of them, Mr Henry de Ros. It was soon common knowledge that Miss Spencer, only just turned twenty, was pregnant, and de Ros, unquestionably a rake, was widely condemned as the author of her misfortune. He, however, emphatically denied it; and he was justified in doing so. The father of Harriet's child was actually her second cousin, the eldest son of the Duke of Marlborough, George Spencer-Churchill, Marquis of Blandford.

It must have been mightily convenient for the Marlboroughs that his name was kept out of the frame by the intense focus on de Ros. Battling a mountain of debt, the duke and duchess could ill afford for their son and heir to wed a penniless cousin purely to smooth over a scandal. The lack of money on both sides no doubt persuaded the two families who knew the truth not to force a marriage on the pair, but George's disorderly private life surely had something to do with it, too. At the time that Harriet's pregnancy became the talk of the town, the duke's errant son was living under the name of Captain Lawson with a sixteen-year-old merchant's daughter named Susanna. Having been deceived by a mock marriage ceremony at which her lover's younger brother had played the clergyman, and her apparently trusting parents had acted as witnesses, she claimed to be his lawful wife. And just like Harriet, she was due to give birth to his child in March 1818.

With marriage off the table, Harriet's extended family had stepped in to help her salvage her broken reputation. Lady Bessborough, a cousin of her father, generously agreed to become the guardian of her namesake's baby, whisking little Susan away to her house at Roehampton shortly after she was born. While the detestable George was disentangled from the merchant's daughter – who was left with only an annuity of £400 a year in compensation for her ruin – and sent up the aisle with a wealthier cousin, Harriet was taken abroad to meet her mother's German relations and encouraged to think romantically of one of them. She and Count Charles von Westerholt married in October 1819, the pair of them 'so much in love', according to her mother.

Yet despite her apparently happy ending, Harriet discovered exactly what Julia Johnstone had done before her: that after a 'false step' there was, for a woman, no way back into her world. By the time she returned to London in 1820, Harriet was married to a social equal and, just as propriety demanded, had sacrificed any relationship with Susan. As far as is known, mother and child never saw one another again. But it was still not enough. A lavish ball given by the Duke of Devonshire in April that year in a valiant attempt to persuade society to welcome her back into the fold failed spectacularly. 'No one spoke to her,' noted one of his guests, adding that the very reason for the ball's being given had kept many people away. To those who did come, said another, Harriet, her husband and her new in-laws were the objects of 'universal curiosity, commiseration, [and] contempt'. Even with one of the leaders of the *ton* on your side, the stigma arising from a very public loss of virtue was impossible to shake off.

Celibacy was thus non-negotiable for any unmarried woman who wanted to maintain her place in the polite world. Yet even if she toed the line of propriety and vigorously protected her maidenly virtue, an unmarried woman was probably not a complete stranger to the contempt of her acquaintances.

Spinsterhood itself carried a social stigma of the kind that contemporaries were firmly convinced had young women hastening to the altar at speed, simply to avoid it. Indeed, to be unmarried when the blush of youth was gone (allegedly in your thirties or forties) was to be a valid object of scorn in the Regency: an unnatural, unwomanly, selfish and sour creature, 'the pest of society' according to a male writer and, even in the eyes of a female one, prone to 'inordinate self-love'.

The negative stereotyping of single women was near-impossible to avoid: it was to be found onstage in the theatre, in the pages of novels, and in the print-shop windows, seemingly so ingrained that a middle-aged singleton might as easily suffer jibes behind her back from her social equals as from disrespectful schoolgirls. Even in high-society circles, where unmarried women were far less likely to be living in the 'forlorn and unprotected situation' that was so widely said to be their lot in life. 'I can't help laughing in my sleeve at Charlotte's beauty, airs, and dress,' Mrs Calvert guiltily confided in her diary about one of the Misses Grimston – 'nearly an old maid but don't think herself so,' as she (quite generously according to the standards of the day) described the 45-year-old sister of a viscount.

Even conduct manuals and magazines for young ladies, though generally aiming for a more sympathetic portrayal of the spinster, sometimes painted a pretty bleak picture of her life. Priscilla Wakefield, advocate of female employment, struggled to write with any optimism about living with a parent as an unmarried adult. Her readers were counselled that 'cheerfulness, good temper, and an obliging resignation of [their] will to that of others' would be both their duty and their interest. There would be little pleasure, she unhelpfully observed, in dealing with the infirmities of mind and body in a parent's declining years. With writers who did put a more positive slant on the single life tending at the same time to drip-feed debutantes the mantra that women were 'unquestionably… created to be the wedded mates of man' (lest celibacy begin to look *too* attractive), and friends and family like Lady Abercorn taking it upon themselves to push potential husbands their way, it seems little wonder that, in spite of all the legal handicaps of matrimony, the majority of young women did not hesitate quite so long as Sydney before walking up the aisle.

That said, the Misses Grimston, whom Mrs Calvert acknowledged lived in 'a very pretty house' in Chesterfield Street, were not complete anomalies. Despite what TV scriptwriters would have us believe, in and around Regency Mayfair could be found high-society ladies successfully living the single life, with the blessing and support of their families. They represented, in fact, a sizeable minority of aristocratic women: according to some estimates, in the late Georgian era as many as 20 or 25 per cent were destined to remain unmarried, whether they wanted to or not.

Partly, at least, it was down to a lack of men of suitable birth and fortune. Mothers like the Duchess of Gordon, who managed not only to marry off all their daughters, but to pair nearly all of them with men of similar rank to their father, had every reason to be self-satisfied.[3] It was no mean feat in a world

---

3 The duchess herself took considerable pride in her matrimonial achievements. So proud was she, in fact, that she requested that the names of all five of her sons-in-law – three dukes, a marquis and a baronet – be engraved on her tombstone.

where for every duke – and there were still only twenty-five of them by the end of the Regency in 1820 – there were several dukes' daughters seeking a spouse. With the younger sons of peers frequently earning too little to support a wife and children, and parents (particularly those from ancient and titled families) apt to think staying single a far better fate for a daughter than marrying outside her social class, it was a limited market. And it was thus a simple fact of life that some women, especially those with small portions, plain looks or a lack of feminine charm, would be condemned to spinsterhood.

The Hon. Frances Arden looked for many years as if she would be one of them. In her case, it was not so much that the man she wanted to marry was unsuitable, but that the money side of her much-wanted match did not stack up. It was reportedly owing to the profligacy of her older brother, the affable dandy Lord Alvanley, that her two-year courtship with Mr John Warrender, the son of a baronet, stalled in November 1814. 'We have heard that [he] has lost her 10,000£ which is the preventative,' one lady wrote in a gossipy letter from Brussels, where Frances, her mother and sister were then living, possibly for reasons of economy. 'If this is a true report she has cause to be unhappy,' the acquaintance went on, as the star-crossed lovers seemed to her to be 'very much attached' to one another.

Lord Alvanley was certainly expensive: as extravagant as his close friend Beau Brummell, he was as fond of gaming and as frequently in debt. 'He was to the last degree reckless and profligate about money,' remembered another of his intimates. 'He cared not what debts he incurred, and he made nothing of violating every sort of pecuniary engagement or obligation.' Indeed, not six months after the report about Frances and her disappointed hopes, he was joking with fellow dinner guests about having exhausted his credit with London's Jewish money-lenders. The following year, he was joining with Brummell and Lord Worcester to take out yet another loan, of £30,000.

Unfortunately for his sister, as a second son – whose own brother was both healthy and lately married – John was in no position to disregard any deficiencies in her fortune. He went on to marry another woman, coincidentally (or perhaps not) in 1823, the year that Alvanley first began selling off lands to meet his burgeoning debts. That he still harboured feelings for Frances, and that their split was down to practicalities alone, is clear from the couple's eventual union in 1831, at the respective ages of forty-five and thirty-nine. John had been widowed early, and his financial prospects had taken a turn for the better, too, his older brother being without children, permanently separated from his wife and determined to bequeath all his property along with the baronetcy. Frances thus became one of the lucky ones, saved from an unwanted spinsterhood, and in time to have a family of her own.[4]

It was not only inadequate dowries or a suitor's inadequate prospects that dashed women's hopes – there were daughters tied to their families by caring responsibilities or by their own ill-health, and suitors lost in the era's long-running war. And of course, those women single by circumstance are only one part of the story. Among the sizeable minority of upper-class singletons there were undoubtedly those who simply had no inclination whatsoever to marry: no desire for an intimate relationship with a man, no wish to be governed by a husband or saddled with

---

4   In a satisfying turn of events, her daughter and son-in-law eventually inherited what remained of the Alvanley estates.

children, or simply no taste for any of the suitors who offered for their hand.

A power of refusal existed, and it appears plenty of upper-class women were prepared to exercise it – and seemingly without fear of parental displeasure, if the experiences of Lady Sarah Spencer and Lady Elizabeth Villiers, Esther Acklom and Emily Lamb are anything to go by. Even mamas with high hopes for their daughters seem to have tolerated indifference to matrimony. On her second daughter Fanny's twenty-third birthday in 1822, Mrs Calvert expressed in her diary a vague hope that she would yet find a good husband, as her sister Isabella had done. 'I have one in my eye for her, but I fear, should he choose her she will not have him, though amiable and excellent,' she wrote, with surprising indulgence. Fanny had been a regular attendee at Almack's, and much admired according to her fond parent, who devotedly recorded all her illustrious dance partners. But if Mrs Calvert made any attempt to remonstrate with her daughter when she gave up dancing a month or two later, she made no record of it in her journal. Fanny's days of playing the marriage mart in earnest were apparently over, and with little or no complaint from her mother – perhaps because 'darling Fan' had become her favourite companion.

Whatever the reason for their lack of a wedding band, unlike those lower down the social ladder well-born women rarely had anything to *fear* from spinsterhood. Certainly their single life might entail some sacrifices, like Lady Louisa Stuart and her lack of a carriage. Quite probably it would entail a few snubs from smug married friends now and again, too, but there was very little chance that their families would see them sink into either poverty or a state of pitiful loneliness.

The trade-off for their staying single appears to have been a tacit agreement to reside under the parental roof for as long as that was possible. Not only did it cause the minimum strain on the family finances, but it was the most socially respectable residence for an unmarried daughter – particularly one still of marriageable age, who still required chaperonage according to the rules of polite society. Certainly Lady Caroline Bruce and her younger sister Lady Frances had found their father, the Earl of Ailesbury, violently opposed to the idea of their setting up home together in 1793, when, at the ages of twenty-seven and thirty, they had expressed a 'desire to withdraw' from his house and, more specifically, from the presence of their stepmother.

On account of the gossip that their removal from his household would give rise to, the earl had firmly rejected his daughters' pleas. The sisters had been forced to accept a compromise, agreeing to reside on a near-permanent basis at his London house instead of travelling back and forth with him and his wife to his seat in Wiltshire. His opposition had been no less fierce when Caroline renewed her requests for a home of her own six years later, after Frances married. 'There is no act of Kindness you may not have under My roof,' she was told by her father, but if she continued in her 'rooted aversion' to living at home, he warned, she would be 'drove to live in a way not creditable' to herself or her kind.

A courageous Caroline, however, had proved impervious to all such thinly veiled threats, and had eventually, begrudgingly, been granted a fairly liberal allowance of £150 a quarter, or £600 a year – a little bit more than her anticipated portion of £10,000 could be expected to earn in interest. At the age of thirty-six, she was able to rent for herself a villa with a walled garden in

Brompton, then on the outskirts of London. It was close to her sister's marital home, Chelsea Park, but – crucially – was her own space. She was still living there in apparent contentment when her father died in 1814, her allowance by then £900 a year, with £25 to cover the property tax. Three times what the average physician or surgeon was estimated to earn in a year, it was probably just enough to afford a carriage, as well as three or four servants.

Caroline's independence was hard-won, and she does, indeed, appear to have been unusual in achieving a home of her own while one of her parents was still alive. Perhaps not so many women actually craved it; a sense of familial duty, appropriately feminine behaviour and pure affection must have tied many of them to their family home, while others surely valued the company. Yet after a woman's parents passed away she could seemingly expect a much more independent life, with wealthy families apparently feeling an obligation to ensure that it would be both feasible for her, and fairly comfortable. For as Caroline's story shows, financial provision for unmarried women could, in reality, be more generous than the few hundred pounds their marriage portion would earn in interest.

Enlightened parents of means like the Marquis of Downshire certainly recognised the difficulties for daughters when compared to younger sons, and were inclined to see that the family resources were allocated accordingly. 'My boys will serve their country and have many ways of providing for themselves,' he wrote, whereas 'the dear girls have not such opportunities but must patiently wait the caprice, the love or perhaps the avarice of some man to obtain a settlement.' He consequently directed that the £40,000 set aside for his four younger sons and two daughters be divided at a ratio of 7:10 in favour of his daughters, presumably intending for the portions of Ladies Charlotte and Mary Hill to be pushed up from their equal share of around £6,500, to over £11,500 each. Such a boost would have nearly doubled the amount of income they could expect to receive on the capital if they remained unwed. In the event, the sisters lived with their mother until their untimely deaths (probably from consumption) at the ages of twenty-seven and thirty-three; but, had either or both needed to strike out on their own, the extra income would have made an appreciable difference to their standard of living.

Somewhat surprisingly, Lord Downshire does not seem to have been so unusual. As the only unmarried daughter of her family, Lady Sarah Spencer's favourite aunt, Lady Anne Bingham – 'Nanette' – benefited from generous bequests from her father, the 1st Earl of Lucan, when he died in 1799. Generous enough that in 1802 the 35-year-old was able to buy a four-storey townhouse mere steps from Spencer House as a residence for herself and her widowed mother, and to employ a fashionable architect (probably Henry Holland) to renovate it for them. When she sold it to her brother-in-law in 1819, she was able to take out a lease on a larger property right on the River Thames at Richmond. The Ladies Louisa and Elizabeth Clements, meanwhile, were so lavishly provided for when their mother died in 1817 that, in a surprising reversal of fortunes, it was the men of the family struggling to make ends meet. The sisters, daughters of the 1st Earl of Leitrim, had an income of £3,000 a year, along with the right to go on living (seemingly rent-free) at the family's house in Grosvenor Square, and also at a villa they had shared with their mother, opposite Hampton Court Palace.

Even in families where there was less money to go round, single women seem to have been consistently supported to create comfortable lives after their parents died. When the Dowager Countess of Portarlington passed away suddenly in 1813, a wealthy female cousin stepped in to top up the pensions of £200 apiece that her two unmarried daughters, then eighteen and twenty-nine, inherited from her. The Ladies Louisa and Anna Maria Dawson were able to take a lease on number 61 Grosvenor Street, rather than become permanent guests in the homes of one or other of their aunts or sisters. Likewise, when Mrs Spencer-Stanhope died, her four unmarried daughters were offered Banks Hall, a house close to the family seat in Yorkshire, rent-free by their brother; while Lord Auckland was just one bachelor heir who invited his two unmarried sisters to keep house for him after their mother's death.[5]

Of course, it would be wrong to suggest that life was easy, emotionally or financially, for all the upper-class women who either could not, or chose not to, wed. The Dawson sisters, who moved out to the village of Banstead in Surrey in 1823, can't have been the only ones who found Mayfair rents tricky to manage. 'The lowness of rent… will set them more at their ease and enable them to make excursions if they like,' reported their aunt and fellow singleton Lady Louisa Stuart, herself no stranger to low spirits and a sense of regret about her situation. If an unmarried woman did have regrets, unfortunately she was constantly reminded of them in day-to-day life, given that in every social situation even a sixteen-year-old wife took

---

5 Not all high-society singletons lived with siblings. Some women shared their houses with companions, who may have been relations, friends or paid employees, but could potentially have been something more. For women in the Regency, same-sex relationships were fairly easily cloaked in a veneer of companionship; two unrelated women making a home together was not an especially shocking idea.

precedence over a single woman two or three times her age. What is clear, however, is that women from wealthy families had a viable alternative to marriage – and not the miserable one that men were apt to imagine for them. While they might have been technically dependent on fathers or brothers, the bulk of their income often paid from the family estates, their lives were certainly not ones of duty and drudgery.

While the five Spencer-Stanhope sisters lived with their widowed mother in London's Langham Place, for example, they had their own servants and carriage at their disposal. When they weren't busy studying a new language or learning a new instrument (or, in Marianne's case, penning a satirical roman à clef about Almack's that set the *ton* astir when it was published anonymously in 1826), their carriage was whisking them off to meet their beaux in the park or to call on friends with invites for parties – a far cry from the existence that Priscilla Wakefield had prophesied for her female readers. Lady Louisa Stuart was another singleton who devoted her time to writing, from poetry to biography, though she never sought publication. She, her two Dawson nieces and 'Nan' Bingham all had similarly active social lives, too: attending assemblies during the season, staying with friends and family at their country seats, and travelling to spas and seaside resorts in the summer, where they formed new acquaintances.

Travel was most definitely not the sole preserve of the married woman. The very fact that Lady Emma Edgcumbe was still single nearly five years after making her curtsey to the Queen meant she was able to accept an invitation to accompany her aunt, Lady Castlereagh, to the continent in December 1813, where her uncle, the British Foreign Secretary, was to 'enter into negotiations with Bonaparte' in an attempt to bring to an end the long war with France. While her younger sister Caroline stayed at home with a spendthrift spouse and a growing brood of babies, Emma spent six months watching history being made: travelling through war-ravaged towns, talking to Allied war heroes and European royalty, and witnessing the triumphant restoration of the French monarchy in the wake of Napoleon's eventual abdication in April 1814.

At home, Lady Emma's life was no less busy. She acted as household manager and hostess for her father, who had been widowed when she was just fifteen. She and he jaunted around the country paying visits, jointly hosted royals at their Cornish seat and even enjoyed days out at the races together. Emma was clearly a treasured companion – much like the bachelor Lord Auckland's sisters, Emily and Fanny, who were in charge of all his domestic affairs. Where single women stepped in to provide such practical and emotional support, not just to parents, but to aunts, siblings and sisters-in-law, in times of sickness, bereavement or absence from home, it was seemingly from a sense of affection rather than obligation. So far from being unattractively self-sufficient, aristocratic single women's family relationships seem to have been exceptionally strong. Lady Sarah Spencer's aunt Nanette was her favourite person to gossip with, and a frequent companion of the Spencer family at Althorp and on the Isle of Wight. And Sarah was by no means the only niece to form a close and lifelong bond with an unmarried aunt.

In fact, it was surely thanks to the presence of positive role models like Nanette in their lives that continuing in so-called 'blessed singleness' was nowhere near as repulsive to young aristocratic women as we tend to think. Contrary to what fiction might lead us to believe, they don't seem to have been in any particular hurry to marry in their first season, nor to accept the first offer of marriage that came their way. Emily Lamb, for one, was clear that nothing but true love would tempt her into matrimony, standing firm when the ardent suitor who had struggled to process her rejection of his proposal returned for his (exasperating) second interview. 'I plainly told him... I never would marry unless it was to a man whom I loved better than all the world besides,' she reported to her brother. 'On some occasions I can sacrify my happiness to that of others,' she explained, 'but this is too serious.'

The very idea that Regency women either married in their first couple of seasons or started a slow descent into the oblivion of the old maid is belied not only by the average age of marriage for an aristocratic woman in the period – twenty-five – but by the stories of those who walked up the aisle long after making their entrance into society. Taking time to find the right partner was even something that magazines and conduct books were apt to recommend, endorsing the idea that those who 'lived single till the age of fancy is over' were most likely to find happiness in the married state.

Certainly, enjoying the single life for some years was no barrier to marrying eventually. Fittingly for a granddaughter of the Duchess of Gordon, Lady Georgiana Lennox's youth had been full of 'matchmaking and manoeuvre' – flirting obediently with the wealthy, parent-approved Lord Hotham and Lord Rous, and less obediently with hardened rakes like Charles Greville, whose diary reveals that at a country house party he came to her room at night, only to be 'fool enough to go away without doing anything'. Yet her eleven-year stint on the marriage market and series of aborted flirtations did not stop her 'going off in romance at eight and twenty' with Lieutenant William de Ros, two years her junior. The impecunious soldier was the better-liked (and much more honourable) younger brother of the Henry 'de Rot' believed to have 'seduced' Harriet Spencer, and a man some secretly thought too good for the flighty Georgiana 'Georgy' Lennox. She was pretty, admittedly, but still a 'beggar' with no dowry to speak of.

Wed at the age of twenty-eight, Georgy actually looks like a relatively young bride when compared to some of her contemporaries. Lady Emma Edgcumbe, who accompanied her aunt Lady Castlereagh to Europe, was almost ten years older when she eventually married, becoming Lord Brownlow's third wife in 1828. A match of quiet affection rather than overwhelming passion, it was nonetheless a marriage of choice and not circumstance. With a doting father and fond, unmarried brothers, the 36-year-old Emma had no apparent need to seek out a spouse simply to secure her future comfort. Similarly, Marianne Spencer-Stanhope, also from a well-off family and surrounded by four unmarried sisters, had no pressing reason to wed. Yet she, too, made a pragmatic union, hers with a Surrey landowner named Robert Hudson at the age of forty-one.

It's quite clear that for all the unpleasant stereotyping, women in their thirties and forties were not considered too past it to be of interest to an eligible Regency bachelor. Nor was a later marriage necessarily an indication of a prior lack of attention from suitable men. Looking 'a little thin' in 1816, Lord Clive had been suspected of 'a tender passion' for Lady Emma Edgcumbe; while Lady Louisa Dawson, who set up home with her sister in Grosvenor Street, had been eagerly pursued by an unnamed suitor before her mother died. She, too, went up the aisle eventually, becoming the second wife of the Reverend Walter Davenport at the age of forty-five. Their stories are satisfying proof that far from *having* to marry, plenty of Regency women born into wealthy families wed only if and when they *wanted* to. Self-sufficient Sydney was not alone in that.

One group of women, though, usually found that marriage was not a matter of choice. For heiresses, in whose hands rested great riches, the pressure to choose a husband was normally particularly acute, as Lady Frances Anne Vane-Tempest discovered.

When her father died without any other legitimate children in 1813, she became one of the wealthiest heiresses in Britain. She had only to come of age to take possession of a country seat, swathes of coal-rich land and several collieries in County Durham, together with a considerable fortune. She was worth, according to contemporary reports, £35,000 a year – probably something of an exaggeration, but indicative of the huge earning potential of her property. It was the kind of inheritance that most women could only dream of, thanks to the aristocracy's determined prioritisation of male heirs, with whom the family title and fortune could remain united – a course that noble families tended to pursue even if it meant passing over a daughter for a nephew, cousin or even more remote relative. Mrs Calvert's father, Viscount Pery, had no sons either, but his Irish property was entailed on his nephew, and she and her sister received just a lump sum of £20,000 each – and that only because her father had amassed considerable personal wealth that was not subject to the entail.

Sir Henry Vane-Tempest's will had granted his daughter far more than a mere marriage portion; she was given the means to be independent of a man her whole life long. More than that, she was given the ability to reign sovereign over her affairs in great splendour. Not for her a small house on the outskirts of the capital. She need not scrimp and save to fund excursions, nor beg and borrow a carriage. By the age of just fifteen, she had been granted the sizeable sum of £5,000 a year to fund an establishment of her own in London's Cadogan Place, with a full complement of servants and a governess for a chaperone.

Unlike other women living alone in the capital, she was not, in fact, an orphan. Frances Anne's mother, Countess of Antrim in her own right, was still very much alive; and, under the terms of her late husband's will, her daughter's joint guardian, alongside his sister, Mrs Taylor. But Frances Anne and her mother had an uneasy relationship. Lady Antrim had been an emotionally remote and sometimes harsh parent, and it was Mrs Taylor who had supplied most of the affection in her niece's childhood years. Since she cordially disliked her sister-in-law – a feeling entirely mutual – she had been only too happy to support Frances Anne when she voiced concerns about her mother's treatment of her. Partly owing to that, and partly to the discord between the two women, Frances Anne had been made a Ward in Chancery – a decision that meant that both she and her property were placed under the protection of the court for the remainder of her minority.

It was the court that had ordered that she have her own establishment, and Frances Anne knew that, whatever else they disagreed on, neither of her guardians entertained the possibility of her heading a household of her own for too long. Her duty was to find a suitable man and produce a son so that her inherited property could descend through the family line. It was certainly the firm intention of her father that she should do so; his will stipulated that his daughter was to retain her own surname on her marriage and her husband to adopt it as his own. That her future lay in becoming a wife and mother was also abundantly clear from her own mother's behaviour. Whenever she had her daughter under her roof there were male visitors, who clearly dropped by simply to become better acquainted with the heiress. Some made love to Frances Anne – paying audacious compliments and no doubt attempting to engage her in a little flirtation – while others she heard being talked of as a potential match for her. Irish earl, Lord O'Neil, was a frequent caller at Lady Antrim's London house – 'every one told me he went there for my sake,' Frances Anne later remembered, but she was still very surprised when her mother discreetly drew her governess out of the room, leaving him to propose. Undeterred by her forthright refusal, Lady Antrim had simply said she might do better. Next thing her sixteen-year-old daughter knew, she was being introduced to the Duke of Leinster – though Mrs Taylor had put a stop to the talk of their union. She was, she said, too young to marry for a year.

In a pragmatic sense, there were certainly good reasons for Frances Anne to marry, and not to delay too long about it. Aside from anything else, while an heiress remained single she ran a safety risk. Though it had become the stuff of sensationalist fiction, 'heiress stealing' still posed a real threat, with kidnappers prepared to go to great lengths to abduct wealthy young women and force them into marriage, often using extreme violence. And while not quite so traumatic, Lady Sarah Fane, heiress of her grandfather's banking fortune, had been troubled by a stalker who took up lodgings near her father's house.

*Left*: William Henry Lyttelton, later 3rd Baron Lyttelton.

*Right*: Lady Sarah Spencer.

© National Trust Images

*Below*: Spencer House in London, seen from Green Park in a print of 1815.

*Inconveniences of a Crowded Drawing Room*

*Above*: The auditorium of the King's Theatre, Haymarket, home of Italian opera in Regency London. The bright lighting meant the occupants of the boxes were almost as visible as the performers on stage.

*Below*: In this cartoon of 1818, George Cruikshank poked fun at Queen Charlotte's increasingly infrequent and thus notoriously crowded Drawing Rooms.

*Left*: Heiress Lady Sarah Fane, later Lady Jersey, a prominent member of Regency society and a patroness of Almack's.

*Right*: Lady Harriet 'Harryo' Cavendish around the time of her marriage in 1809.

The GORDON-KNOT, – or – The Bonny Duchess hunting the Bedfordshire Bull.

*Below*: James Gilray was among those who lampooned the matchmaking manoeuvres of the Duchess of Gordon, depicting her pursuing 'the Bedford Bull' with her daughter Georgiana in tow.

*Left*: Sir Charles Morgan.

*Below*: Sydney's friends and patrons, John James Hamilton, the first Marquis of Abercorn, and his third wife, Anne.

*Right*: Charles, Lord Stewart, painted in his cavalry officer's uniform by Thomas Lawrence in 1812.

*Above*: Satirists were quick to spot an opportunity in the dispute over Lord Stewart's eligibility. In this cartoon from 1819, the boat in which his Lordship sails, buffeted by hostile gusts from two 'Guardian angelos' above, is towed towards the 'Harbour of Matrimony' by the Lord Chancellor.

*Opposite page*: Frances Anne Vane-Tempest, also painted by Thomas Lawrence c.1828 By then Marchioness of Londonderry, she is pictured on the steps of Wynyard Hall, her County Durham seat, with her son and heir George.

*Right*: Harriet Fane, in a portrait by Thomas Lawrence from 1817.

*Left*: One of few surviving images of Charles Arbuthnot, aged 82.

It was no doubt partly for her protection, and partly to stop her running off with an unsuitable man of her own volition, that Frances Anne was living a relatively claustrophobic life as she waited to be presented at court. Her mother and aunt had to approve visitors to her house; every trip, every stay at a seaside resort, had to have their blessing. Even as she walked to church her governess followed close behind her, stopping strangers (and especially handsome ones) from engaging her in chit-chat. The court had to authorise any expenses over and above the maintenance she had been granted. While Sydney had wistfully talked of being 'free as air' before Charles came into her life, from where Frances Anne sat it must have been marriage that looked like freedom.

In her case there was another incentive to wed, too. The older she grew, the more aware she became that her estates and finances were being mismanaged – partly because of the incompetence of the court, and partly because her mother was a little too ready to treat her daughter's inheritance as her own. Frances Anne wanted some kind of control; to act on her own ideas, to maximise the potential of her property and to reap the monetary rewards. Marriage to a man she could trust – with sufficient entrepreneurial nous – was a way of making that happen. But she had to find him first, and then she had to win the approval of her guardians.

*Chapter Four*

# Objections

As ENGAGEMENTS GO, Frances Anne Vane-Tempest's had a wretched beginning. It was with justifiable trepidation that she tripped up the steps of her aunt's townhouse to break the news of her betrothal to Charles, Lord Stewart in early April 1818. As expected, Mrs Taylor reacted furiously. Emphatically refusing to give her consent, she freely abused the widower as a fortune-hunter and philanderer. He was forty – old enough to be her father. And she had it on good authority that there was insanity in the family, too. No, she would sooner see her favourite niece in the grave than let her marry that man.

It was not the first time Mrs Taylor had voiced such opinions on Lord Stewart and his suit, and it would definitely not be the last. Within just two days of his Lordship's proposal she had lodged a petition in the Court of Chancery to prevent him marrying Frances Anne, telling anyone who would listen why he was a man 'wholly unfit to be connected' with her.

Her niece had only met her betrothed for the first time nine weeks earlier, when her mother Lady Antrim had invited them both to dine with her. Frances Anne was not even officially 'out' in society then, her entrance into the fashionable world having been delayed by her mother's own whirlwind romance the previous year. To the delight of the gossipmongers, after less than a month's acquaintance the widowed countess, still only thirty-nine and with no son to inherit her title, had married a comparative nobody: one-time professional singer Edmund Phelps. The marriage had caused quite a rift between mother and daughter, not least because Frances Anne had been forced to postpone the court presentation she had long been anticipating, which was deemed unthinkable by Mrs Taylor so soon after her mother's 'degrading' alliance. Frosty relations between the pair had only just been thawing as they had sat around the dinner table with Lord Stewart that evening.

Below average height but reckoned to be good-looking, the former general with a reputation for gallantry, who had been gifted a barony on his appointment as Ambassador at Vienna in 1814, was an old friend of Lady Antrim's. At first, Frances Anne had been distinctly underwhelmed by him: 'he seemed finniken and looked as if he had false teeth' was her only response when prompted by her mother for her impressions of his Excellency. Yet he had grown on her the more they met – as Lady Antrim had seemed determined they would. Frances Anne had begun to encounter him at Bruton Street when she called on her mother of a morning. He 'took care' of her when she was finally presented at court on 26 February, amusing her with his conversation and escorting her to her carriage. And, his Lordship being a diligent attendee of the various assemblies in those early weeks of the season, they danced together at Almack's and elsewhere.

Inevitably, rumours had soon begun to ripple around town that a match was on the cards, but they only reached an almost oblivious Mrs Taylor's ears via the first of a series of anonymous letters, delivered to her home in Whitehall by the two-penny post. Perusing the contents of the unexpected communication, she had been considerably alarmed. The anticipated match with Lord Stewart she did not like. There was the considerable age gap between him and eighteen-year-old Frances Anne, the presence of a son and heir five years her niece's junior, and the stories of insanity in his family, which she well remembered circulating at the time of his sister's engagement. Her anxiety had only increased when the first letter was followed by three more, each of them carrying disturbing intelligence. To Mrs Taylor's own objections, the anonymous correspondent was able to add others of an even more colourful nature. His Lordship, the letter-writer told her, was not only a man of loose morals and dissipated habits, but was at that very moment in a state of pecuniary embarrassment.

Mrs Taylor had been inclined to agree with her informant that, seen in that light, his brisk courtship of her niece looked very much like a determined campaign to catch an heiress. When a 'lady of high rank' then visited her in her box at the theatre one evening, seemingly just to press Lord Stewart's case with his young paramour's guardian, she had become almost certain of it. And when she then recollected Lady Antrim's pivotal role in bringing them together, she had been left with no doubts whatsoever in her mind. Mrs Taylor was firmly convinced that when her sister-in-law had invited the Duke of Leinster to visit her daughter two years previously, not only had it been made plain to his Grace that, should Frances Anne prove to his liking, the countess would be perfectly content to arrange a marriage of convenience, but also that her niece had been kept completely in the dark about the negotiations that were going on. To her objections to the match, she had thus added deep suspicion that this was a scheme to marry off Frances Anne to her mother's advantage – before she had time to see anything of the season, or to receive the addresses of any other suitors.

She had hastened to her niece's house in Norfolk Street with anonymous missives in hand in an attempt to counter her sister-in-law's influence by sharing everything she knew to Lord Stewart's discredit. 'A scene ensued,' said Frances Anne, who had been forced at that point to confess to her aunt that she liked Lord Stewart. In fact, she had started to feel 'restless and discontented and more interested about him' with every day that passed. Having been entreated to read the letters, however, she promised Mrs Taylor that she would 'endeavour to conquer' her feelings. 'There were objections which I could not get over even if our years were more *assorti*,' she remembered telling her. The two had parted with Frances Anne promising to pass a week or two in Tunbridge Wells with her companion, and Mrs Taylor no doubt fervently hoping that by the time they returned, the objectionable Lord Stewart would be on a boat back to his embassy in Austria.

Of course, her prayers had not been answered. Frances Anne had simply been afforded time to reflect on how much she was missing her attentive suitor. 'The result of my cogitations,' as she herself put it, 'was a determination to accept Lord Stewart if he was still in London' – which he was, and she had, leading to the furious confrontation at her aunt's house. 'I was overpowered by the most unseemly abuse from Mr Taylor, and reproaches from my aunt who accused me of duplicity and art,' said Frances Anne. This some considered to be Mrs Taylor's crowning blunder. No wonder, they said, that the girl was 'madly in love' with Lord Stewart – the Taylors had 'nailed the marriage by their abuse' over it. Whether or not that was true, the abuse had certainly left Frances Anne in no doubt that she would have a fight on her hands for permission to marry him.

By law it was only those who, like Frances Anne, wanted to wed by licence while under the age of twenty-one who required the consent of their father or guardian, but most aristocratic offspring sought it even after coming of age – not merely out of respect, but because parents so often had it in their power to make life financially difficult if they disapproved of a marriage partner. In the absence of consent they might be able to withhold a marriage portion, significantly reduce the promised sum, or wreak even greater revenge. When, in 1817, his daughter Margaret married the Comte de Flahaut – an illegitimate Frenchman, a Catholic and, most shockingly of all, a former aide-de-camp to Napoleon, who had fought against the British – Admiral Lord Keith was reportedly so enraged at her choice that he cut her out of his will. She was said to have 'given up an inheritance of 30,000*l.* a year' on her wedding day – and all for 'a bald headed man, without fortune, character, or birth,' according to a bemused Mrs Calvert. Morally, parents might no longer be able to pick and choose their children's spouses, but practically, they still had a good deal of control.

Even where a hopeful bride considered her choice unexceptionable, permission was not always immediately forthcoming.

Mr and Mrs Calvert kept their daughter Isabella in a state of suspense for two or three days while they deliberated over her match with Irish landowner Sir James Stronge. Hastening to town from Hertfordshire, where they had received the surprising news of his proposal, the couple had quizzed their daughter about her feelings for him, and her maternal aunt Mrs Knox, who had chaperoned the lovers at Vauxhall, was consulted at great length about his character. The following day, as a suitably atmospheric summer storm raged outside, an 'awkward meeting' with his mother had been endured by Mrs Calvert, while Mr Calvert interrogated his stepfather over the possible settlements, and the prospective groom himself about his plans for married life. Only after that had Isabella, at last, been called to her father's study and given her parents' blessing. The invitation subsequently extended to Sir James to make a visit to them in Hertfordshire, however, was no doubt intended to give them leisure to observe his temperament at closer quarters before Isabella was irrevocably committed, a good temper being one of the most sought-after qualities in a prospective son-in-law given the legal power that husbands had over their wives.

Whether there were struggles or not, however, most young women had only a parent to convince of the eligibility of their match. When Mrs Taylor lodged her petition – countering an overhasty application by Lady Antrim for the court to advise on a financial settlement for its ward (made within just thirty-six hours of Lord Stewart's proposal) – she kick-started litigation that, ultimately, meant Frances Anne's fate rested in the hands of one of the most senior lawyers in the land. It would be for the Lord Chancellor to decide whether her proposed marriage was a fit and proper one. Not only that, but the debate over her prospective husband's suitability would happen not behind the closed doors of a family home, but in a courtroom sometimes so packed with curious onlookers that the barristers involved in the case struggled to reach their benches.

The legal proceedings rumbled on for three months in all, the lawyers beginning by combing through Mrs Taylor's accusation that the proposed marriage was a conspiracy, along with her personal objections to the prospective groom: essentially, that no less a personage than his Majesty's ambassador to Austria, a decorated soldier and the half-brother of the Foreign Secretary, was in fact too old and too poor, not to mention a man of dissipated habits and from a family with an unfortunate history of mental illness.

However uncomfortably public the forum might be, Lord Stewart was forced to put up a thorough defence on all points. As regards a matrimonial plot, any such scheme would 'have been equally an insult to Lady Frances and an eternal dishonour to himself,' his affidavit for the court read. It was his betrothed herself and not her fortune – 'her excellent understanding & the personal qualities with which she is gifted' – that had made a strong impression on him, he stressed. On that point, however, fine words were never going to be enough. Both the Court of Chancery and conscientious guardians up and down the country were apprehensive about credible, well-connected fortune-hunters – and with good reason.

In 1811, for instance, the whole of the *ton* had watched Mr William Wellesley Pole, a dashing nephew of the Duke of Wellington, win the affections of the richest heiress in the kingdom, Catherine Tylney Long; and they had watched him bleed her bank accounts almost dry in the seven years since.

Like Frances Anne, Mrs Long Wellesley (as she was known after her marriage) had been deaf to the misgivings voiced by her family and friends. Even a set of anonymous letters, which condemned her chosen spouse as a 'peevish, vain, self-sufficient profligate young gentleman' and carried tales of his debts and amorous indiscretions, had failed to kill her passion for him. But she was paying dearly for her folly by the time of Frances Anne's Chancery hearings. It was clear that she had acquired nothing more than a spendthrift, unfaithful husband, who was barrelling headlong towards bankruptcy.

To firmly quash the allegation that pecuniary embarrassment had prompted his own pursuit of an heiress, there had been no choice but for Lord Stewart to authorise his lawyers to itemise his various sources of income in open court. The exercise revealed that Mrs Taylor had been misinformed. Admittedly, Lord Stewart was a younger son, so some of his prospects were precarious, but he could hardly be compared to the perennially cash-strapped Wellesley Pole. His current income stood at almost £18,000 a year: £15,700 in salaries from his diplomatic, military and royal household appointments, and £2,000 from the estates of his father, the Marquis of Londonderry. Furthermore, he stood heir to land worth at least £8,000 a year, and, since his half-brother, the Foreign Secretary Lord Castlereagh, had no children, heir presumptive to estates worth another £18,000 annually. And if that wasn't satisfactory enough, he 'possessed personal property to the value of 26,000*l*. exceeding his debts.' Was it probable, his lawyer humbly submitted, that a nobleman with such a fortune should be 'induced to pay his addresses to a young lady merely for lucrative motives?' The Lord Chancellor was inclined to think not.

The one thing his Lordship had no power to rebut was his age. Though his lawyers, deliberately or not, shaved a year off in their submissions to the court, he was about to turn forty the following month. The age gap between him and Frances Anne was thus almost twenty-two years – a disparity that the Lord Chancellor viewed almost as unfavourably as did her aunt. And, indeed, other observers. 'Did you ever hear anything so horrible?' one matron asked her sons. 'An old profligate old enough to be her grandfather,' she wrote with a shudder, relaying the news of the engagement (with some exaggeration). Not everyone would have agreed, however. When it came to an acceptable age gap for a married couple opinion tended to vary pretty wildly – not only from parent to parent and daughter to daughter but, more surprisingly, from parent to daughter. It was 24-year-old Harriet Williams Wynn who set her heart on a match with her 43-year-old neighbour, and her mother the one who was anxious to avoid it on account of his advancing years. Similarly, it was not the Hon. Mary Townshend's parents who pushed her, at twenty-nine, towards a match with Mr George Cholmondeley – 'tottering' at the age of seventy-three 'between the Grave & the Altar' according to astonished observers, and a full twelve years older than her father, who seemed simply bemused. There were really no hard and fast rules.

The age gap between Frances Anne and Lord Stewart was, nevertheless, an aspect of their romance that satirical commentators found particularly amusing. Young ladies were mocked for going so mad 'as to marry old Dandies that might be their daddies' and his Lordship was described with heavy irony as 'the best lover we have – *of his years*'. If a 'matrimonial speculation' was what the courtship had been, Charles certainly paid handsomely for it. Not only was he the butt of every journalist and satirist's jokes, he was also the talk of the *ton*. Mrs Taylor had failed to provide any detail in her court documents about what exactly his 'dissipated and irregular habits' were, but plenty of his peers knew stories, which were undoubtedly shared over the port in the gentlemen's clubs of St James's. Indeed, a flurry of bets on the subject at White's in April and May 1818 suggests that his chances of marrying Frances Anne were a matter of particularly lively debate among its members.

Lord Stewart, said those who had encountered him on the continent in recent years, had a reputation for vanity and excess. Fond of parading in his uniforms, heavily embellished with his various military and civil honours, he was nicknamed 'the golden peacock' and 'Prince Charles'. He was also known to be fond of spending. In fact, so extravagant was his nature that the Foreign Office had had to warn him on at least one occasion to keep the expenses of his ambassadorial household within the amount of his salary.

Then there were the stories of his romantic dalliances. Philandering in a man's past – or even present – did not necessarily render him unsuitable as a husband in the eyes of either parents or society more generally. Sir John Shelley was known to have been embroiled in a twelve-year affair with the married Lady Haggerston (sister of the Prince Regent's morganatic wife, Mrs Fitzherbert) at the time he proposed to heiress Frances Winckley, but his close friends Lord and Lady Sefton, who encouraged her to accept him, seemed to think nothing of it. Likewise, the fact that Lady 'Harryo' Cavendish's favoured suitor Lord Granville Leveson-Gower (the 'uncommonly handsome' younger son of the Marquis of Stafford) had fathered two illegitimate children – and with her aunt, Lady Bessborough, no less – drew forth no objections from her father. The couple were married with the blessing of both her family and his in 1809. Harryo was even to become one of a number of Regency women who welcomed into their marital home the 'natural' children of their husband – something that must have been far easier to do with a smile and open arms if, as in her case, their conception pre-dated the marriage.

In fact, the young women whirling through the season in search of a spouse were much less naive about such matters than the starchy Victorians have led us to believe. Home from a shooting party in 1808, the Earl Spencer had not scrupled to regale an unmarried Lady Sarah with the details of his fellow guests: his host's mistress and her long-suffering spouse, a former courtesan who was accompanied by her late husband's 'natural' daughter by another woman, and a bevy of children whose parentage he didn't like to enquire into. 'There's a set of people for you!' had gaily remarked his daughter, passing the anecdote on to her brother Bob. Harryo, meanwhile, was certainly well aware of Lord Granville's fifteen-year affair with her aunt long before she married him, even if she did not approve.

That being so, it wasn't so much that Charles had enjoyed one or two amorous liaisons in the six years since he had been widowed, but that some of his dalliances had been more than usually indiscreet, and his general conduct not always considered fitting for a diplomat. His affair with the Duchesse de Sagan had been common knowledge on the continent – and the nights he spent in her apartments of interest to the Austrian secret police – and on one occasion, he had excited dissatisfied comment back in Britain after supposedly taking advantage of the crush in exiting a theatre to grope the daughter of a comtesse. There were tales of brawls in the street with Viennese hackney coachmen, and heavy drinking – after one bout he had managed to sleep right through the robbery of most of his possessions. There were also reports that the British mission under his supervision had been turned into 'en bordel et en trîpot' – a brothel and a gaming house. If these were the habits hinted at to Mrs Taylor by her anonymous letter-writer, no wonder she condemned them as 'irregular' – others preferred 'disgraceful'.

On the subject of his character his barrister put up a spirited defence, remarking on 'the most arduous and distinguished offices' in which his Lordship had been employed, and the honours he had received – and it was not actually mere courtroom swagger. His Lordship was famed for his bravery on the battlefield and his military career had, indeed, been a particularly distinguished one. And while his half-brother's political influence was partly responsible for his more recent diplomatic roles, even the Duke of Wellington – 'not particularly partial to the man', as he put it – was forced to admit that Charles made 'an excellent ambassador, procured more information and obtained more insight into the affairs of a foreign court than anybody'. Certainly Lord Castlereagh reposed complete confidence in his younger sibling's abilities, even if some of his actions left him exasperated – his courtship of a young heiress included, perhaps.

The prospective bridegroom's family did not relish the unfolding drama into which they were all catapulted by the sudden fancy Charles had taken to Frances Anne. The whole thing was an inconvenience, not to say embarrassment, with the Tory Prime Minister urging his Foreign Secretary to make sure that both he and Charles stayed away from the court hearing. Lord Castlereagh's own wish was to avoid any further 'misrepresentations and possibly fresh mortifications' – particularly as regards the lingering suggestion of 'insanity' in the Stewart line. Mrs Taylor's belief was that it had required more than one family member to be restrained, and she argued that the Stewarts had been confronted on the very same issue five years previously, before the marriage of Lady Octavia, one of the brothers' younger sisters.

It was a common enough concern when it came to consenting to a match. The merest hint of hereditary disease was something that tended to trouble families with dynastic ambitions; naturally, even more so if an heiress like Frances Anne was marrying for the express purpose of producing a male heir to continue her line. In their submissions for the court, the family attempted to suppress the allegations, which centred on another of their sisters, Lady Caroline, once and for all. New medical opinion ruled out any hereditary affliction, and an affidavit from their brother-in-law confirmed a mere 'temporary affection' of his wife's mind in 1807; attributed it to childbirth followed by bathing in the open sea; and attested that since her complete recovery she had been 'in no respect mentally affected or her judgment in any [wise] impaired'. They were details she can't have enjoyed being shared with the reading public via the court reports that were published at length in the press.

The entire family must, indeed, have wondered if Frances Anne was worth the intense scrutiny that accompanied the Chancery case. 'She is not a beauty, but she is extremely well looking,' Lord Castlereagh wrote to their father, Lord Londonderry, a couple of days after Charles had proposed. Not only did he think her intelligent, but 'for her time of life, she seems to have a great deal of decision and character,' he said – before adding with accurate foreboding, 'the situation in which she is placed will require a large scale of both.'

Frances Anne had committed herself in the most public way possible to a man whose very character was in question, and she later wrote of being 'harassed to death by all the painful histories which were daily put before me respecting him' – some of them, no doubt, from the Lord Chancellor. He insisted on conducting several private interviews with her, anxious 'to state all the objections that had been made with all the force with which they had been stated to him'. Like Mrs Taylor, he seems to have felt that she ought to have spent a little more time on the marriage market. That, indeed, was a factor that influenced numerous other parents when it came to deciding whether to consent to a particular match. Lady Jerningham's niece was encouraged at seventeen to refuse a suitor on account of the disparity in their fortunes, but the very same man was warmly welcomed into the family several years later. With no more wealthy bachelors having offered their hand in the interim, the match had no longer looked so unfavourable. Similarly, the Duke of Bedford was, at first, reluctant to permit his son and heir Lord Tavistock to rush into a marriage with a lady six years his senior when he was yet to reach his twentieth birthday and was, in fact, still up at Cambridge.

But whatever her aunt had to say, Frances Anne had far more experience of men and matrimonial schemes than most girls beginning their search for a husband at eighteen. She had fancied herself strongly attached to a real fortune-hunter at fifteen – the younger brother of one of her mother's many flirts, and already engaged to another heiress. She had received and calmly refused a proposal from an indebted Irish earl at sixteen. She had paraded for the Duke of Leinster, heard various other titled men 'talked of for [her]' and been followed around seaside resorts by handsome younger sons. She had also spent time with eligible beaux under Mrs Taylor's chaperonage during the year before she was officially 'out'. What's more, however much Lady Antrim had sung the praises of the men she invited into her house, in every previous instance her daughter's views had been decided ones. She did not love the Irish earl and was sure that no time would change that. She thought the duke was dull and was not sorry when talks of an engagement were scotched by Mrs Taylor. The attentions of Lord Forbes were not disagreeable to her, but she was afraid of the satirical Lord Beauchamp and his lovemaking. In fact, she hated him.

All in all, it seems fair to assume that she had reached her own conclusions about Charles, too. He talked to her a good deal at court, she remembered – showing an interest in her opinions, perhaps, that her other suitors never had? Maybe he offered sympathy that thanks to her warring guardians, she was without an impartial adviser, and her only settled home was with her former governess. Charles himself had been no stranger to loneliness and attacks of the 'blue devils' during his time abroad, and was a man with 'a great deal of feeling', according to one of his female admirers. Pushing forty he may have been, but he was still considered fairly handsome – too vain about his 'pretty' face, according to his detractors, but popular with the ladies, who thought his appearance 'taking'. And as for his only being a younger son, very recently raised to the peerage, one suspects that it would not have suited Frances Anne – instilled from a young age with a strong sense of her own consequence and the value of her inheritance – to marry a high-ranking peer or head of an ancient house, to whom her land and collieries would be a cash cow, never valued like his own ancestral acres, and simply awaiting a second son to take them on. With a reputation for energy, astuteness and efficient organisation, particularly when it came to his military career, Charles was a totally different prospect – perhaps just the person to help her overhaul her underperforming estates. She might not have been unexpectedly swept away like Sydney Owenson, or fizzing with love and a sense of her own good fortune like Lady Sarah Spencer, but, in each and every interview, the Lord Chancellor found her adamant that Charles was the man she wanted to marry.

By the end of June, the time for his final judgment was drawing near. On the morning appointed for it, the court was heaving; every seat was occupied a full hour before time, and the passages to the barrister's benches completely impassable. Spotted among the crowd was Mrs Long Wellesley, who knew better than anyone what hung in the balance for Frances Anne. When the Lord Chancellor emerged he struggled to deliver his judgment, so rowdy was his audience. Several times he had to pause while the public benches, mounted by some animated onlookers, were set upright again. It was, however, a spectacular anticlimax. There were a few further points on which he wanted clarification, he said, and he still wanted one last interview with Frances Anne.

It was another three weeks before she at last got her answer. It was not 'the most eligible marriage the young lady could contemplate,' the Lord Chancellor declared to the 'great concourse' again gathered in court, yet, as the press reported, 'he could not see any principle upon which he could determine that it was an improper match.' Hardly a ringing endorsement of Lord Stewart, who must have been at least slightly embarrassed to think of friends and colleagues opening their newspapers the following morning to read an admission from a senior law lord that he had repeatedly attempted to draw Frances Anne's mind towards the various objections to a match with him. It was altogether clear from the judgment that as regards the eligibility of the marriage, the Lord Chancellor's personal views very much chimed with those of Mrs Taylor. Both seemingly felt that with her wealth and personal charm, Frances Anne could have snagged a younger man with less baggage; a peer possessed of a more ancient and illustrious title than Lord Stewart's brand-new barony, and someone who had a courtesy title ready and waiting to be bestowed on her firstborn son. Indeed, the Lord Chancellor would later remind her that he had not so much made a judgment in favour of her marriage, but rather found that 'he could not refuse his assent to it.'

While a union with Lord Stewart might not have been a spectacular match for an heiress, it could hardly be described as a *mésalliance*. It could have been much, much worse – had Frances Anne's eye alighted on her music master, or a showy soldier with little more to recommend him than his commission, for instance. Generally, however, young women caused their parents fewer headaches over their choice of spouse than did their brothers, for the simple reason that they had much less chance of meeting the sort of marriage partner who would be deemed totally unsuitable. As debutantes, their social lives were closely managed. The whole point of Almack's and the private parties where the guest list was strictly controlled was to ensure that they encountered only those partners who met the minimum acceptable criteria. Mothers were careful when it came to making introductions and inviting men into their house, and might manage matters even more by seating favoured suitors advantageously at the dinner table or soliciting their company more regularly than others. Young women were encouraged to go looking for a love match – but there were usually only suitable fish to be found in the sea of possible suitors.

Young men, on the other hand, were permitted to roam about the capital – and the country – at will. Free of the shackles of chaperonage, they had every opportunity to make friends from outside their parents' social circle, and to mingle with men and women of other social classes. Not surprisingly, they pushed the boundaries of suitability more often than their sisters. While Lady Georgiana Lennox's match with Lieutenant William de Ros had made her ambitious mother frown (the groom lacking money and a title, and possessing a rakish older brother widely believed to have seduced Miss Harriet Spencer), the Duchess of Richmond was made far more unhappy by the marriage of Georgy's younger brother, Lord William Lennox. The droll army captain met singer Mary Anne Paton behind the scenes at the Covent Garden Theatre and, finding her unwilling to become his mistress, took her up the aisle in 1824, to a chorus of disapproval. It turned out far less happily than his sister's more conventional match – something *The Times* did not hesitate to blame on both parties choosing spouses 'from a different class of society'. While his glamorous wife continued to perform, her star firmly in the ascendancy and her earning power undiminished, William's reputation suffered and his military career faltered. He sold his commission in 1829, reputedly after the Duke of Wellington dropped a hint in his ear about the incompatibility of his army rank and service with his wife's profession. In the end, amid insinuations of his indifference to everything but her income, Mary Anne left him for her leading man and, to the delight of the scandal-peddlers in the press, the marriage ended in divorce.

The true value of the London season, with its socially exclusive events and inflexible code of propriety, was only discovered by one aristocratic mama, Lady Caroline Capel, when the absolute necessity of retrenchment forced her and her expensive husband to take their vivacious daughters to Brussels in the summer of 1814. John Capel having incurred debts of over £20,000 at the gambling table, the couple (both the offspring of earls) could no longer afford to live in England, let alone bring their eldest girls, Harriet, Georgiana and Maria, 'out' in the capital. They repaired to Brussels, site of a British military garrison, soon after the long-running war with France was declared officially over in 1814, and were relieved to find everything 'above half as cheap' as at home. The one thing that troubled Lady Caroline was the thought of her girls' heads being turned. Tourist hot-spots on the continent having been so long closed to British visitors by the war, and the army's officers so long employed on arduous campaigns, Brussels was fast developing a '*ton* on tour' atmosphere. A more relaxed set of social rules prevailed among the wealthy British set, as did more daring European fashions. Dissipation surrounded the Capel girls in the form of picnics and parties – along with a host of dashing military officers, ready and willing to waltz all night with them. Regrettably, far too many of them for Lady Caroline's comfort lacked the fortune that her daughters, with their negligible (possibly non-existent) dowries, needed.

She was delighted when the sensible and respectful General Sir Edward Barnes proposed to Maria, but had accepted with good grace her daughter's decision to refuse him. 'I think a *Veto* we have a right to, If Unfortunately it ever becomes necessary,' she told her mother, 'but I am afraid of *persuasion* because if the thing did not turn out happily I could never forgive myself.' Interestingly, the fact that she had overcome strong parental opposition to her own love match – her father saying at the time that 'he had rather see Car dead than married to Capel' – had not left Caroline in favour of her children having a totally free choice. Perhaps because twenty-two years on, with eleven children and an income reduced to just £1,200 a year thanks to her husband's gambling habit, she could see the sense in their objections.

As it turned out, she was entirely justified in having reserved a veto for herself. Not all the Brussels beaux were as unexceptionable as Sir Edward; and her daughters, revelling in the heady freedoms of Brussels, were not so demure as London debutantes. Conspicuous flirtations conducted by Maria and Georgiana – of which their grandmother back in London even seemed to have heard disparaging talk – had to be scotched on account of the officers in question having '*every thing* to recommend [them] but that detestable article, *Money*.' It was Harriet, though, drunk on Byron's poetry, who embarked on the most undesirable and improper affair – one that called for more than a mere veto of the match.

The man who utterly beguiled the eldest Capel sister was forty-year-old Dutch aristocrat and aide-de-camp, Baron Trip.

Said to combine the impeccable dress sense of the dandy with all the athleticism of the soldier, he had a reputation for being dangerously captivating. 'I can't conceive his shewing the *slightest degree* of preference for any Girl, without her feeling a most *lively* one in return,' had mused one of the British ladies in Brussels, and so it had proved with Harriet. At first, the baron had held her at arm's-length, telling her they could never be more than friends. 'Friend! What a cold word for what I feel,' Harriet had written to him, professing her adoration in a passionate note that, along with the intensity of her crush, she successfully concealed from her parents, whom she felt were unduly prejudiced against him. It was soon after that, or so one or two of her later letters hint, that they became far more than friends. 'I am writing this, Ernest, *from* the room *on* the couch where you *once* promised to be *Mine* for ever,' she scribbled in one. 'This dear couch where I passed three *such* hours!' Sifting through one of his open drawers as she wrote it, she found a hair comb of her own, 'left in your room myself on that never to be forgotten night!'

Her parents uncovered the intrigue when they intercepted another of her love letters in spring 1815, by which time Harriet's missives had started going unanswered by the baron, who had seemingly also declined to have the 'decisive conversation' about their feelings that she had pressed for. Whether the pair's affair had actually been anything so scandalous as a seduction, or simply a couple of unchaperoned meetings, a few snatched kisses, a clandestine correspondence and idle talk (from her) of an elopement, what the Capels learned made them sufficiently angry at the baron's conduct towards their daughter that John felt obliged to call him out. 'You may suppose what the blame must have been to have induced so peaceable a nature as Capel's... to have taken such a step,' Lady Caroline wrote, informing her mother of the duel. She contented herself with denouncing the baron as both 'villainous' and devoid of 'every honorable principle!'

Their infatuated daughter was, nevertheless, desperate to be his wife, and 'so little *troublesome* a wife', as she had put it to her paramour himself, but the Capels were resolutely opposed to it – if, indeed, the baron had ever put matrimony on the table. His being a long-time friend and former comrade of Lady Caroline's eldest brother Lord Paget, Harriet's parents were in possession of sufficient information about not just his finances but also his amorous career to be convinced that this had never been a serious courtship on his part. What Harriet never knew was that she was one of several young women similarly driven to distraction by the baron over the years. Like her, all had sent him love notes and locks of their hair; one her self-portrait. All were safely stored in his dispatch box, almost like trophies.

On the day of the duel, reported Lady Caroline, 'they *both* fired,' – her husband's shot sailing 'within a Hair's breadth of his Antagonist's Ear' – but no blood was spilled. A promise was extracted from Trip that he would not contact Harriet again – a promise he faithfully kept, to her dismay. She received no response to her letters, not even when she made a proposal that would have had her unflappable mother reaching for the smelling salts, and probably seen her grandmother carried off in a coffin, had either of them known of it, begging that he let her come to him and share his life, with no obligation whatsoever to make her his wife. The intoxicating liberties of life in Brussels had only served up heartache at the hands of a practised rake who her parents were seemingly right to be prejudiced against – not to mention the sort of stain on her reputation that a woman like Harriet, whose lack of fortune made marriage more of a necessity, could ill afford.

Of course, it would be wrong to think that no such similarly ineligible bachelors were to be found in London's lavish ballrooms during the season. Naturally they were, and, however hard they tried, it wasn't always easy for parents to identify those men to whom they ought to object until it was too late, as Laura Manners found out to her cost. It was only having married Captain John Dalrymple, nephew and heir to the Earl of Stair, that she discovered not a trail of broken hearts left behind him, but a wife.

Her married bliss was shattered just a matter of weeks after her wedding in June 1808, when a Miss Johanna Gordon, having learned of the union, burst into Laura's life declaring that she was Captain Dalrymple's lawful spouse. It was a claim that would later be upheld in court, rendering poor Laura's marriage null and void on the grounds of bigamy. 'An innocent lady has been betrayed into a marriage, which conveys to her neither the character nor rights of a wife,' the judge lamented when the case, after many delays, reached a conclusion in 1811. Laura, who had loyally continued to reside with Dalrymple as his wife, despite Johanna's shocking claims (perhaps even risking falling pregnant with a child who would have been doomed to illegitimacy), was robbed of both her husband and her virtue by the decision. 'She and Lord Stair should marry and have children in mere revenge,' one Scottish writer quipped on learning of her fate, no doubt thinking that it would serve

Captain Dalrymple right to be cut out of the line of succession to his uncle's earldom.

The romantic career of the man at the centre of the scandal served as both a cautionary tale for Regency bucks who revelled in the pulling power of their redcoat, and for trusting young women who had little knowledge of their bridegroom. It was in 1804, four years before he had taken Miss Manners to the altar, that John, then a nineteen-year-old cornet in the Dragoon Guards, quartered with his regiment in Edinburgh, had first met the captivating Miss Jacky, as she was known, daughter of a prosperous local gentleman. Regrettably for the young soldier, the Victorian song 'The Tourists' Matrimonial Guide through Scotland' had not yet been written. A celebration of the differences between Scottish and English marriage law, the catchy ballad would have told him much that he needed to know before he embarked on his amorous affair. 'Suppose that young Jocky and Jenny,' it went, 'Say, "We two are husband and wife", The witnesses needn't be many – They're instantly buckled for life.' In a later verse it warned specifically against Dalrymple's particular folly: 'You'd better keep clear of love-letters, Or write them with caution and care; For, faith, they may fasten your fetters, If wearing a conjugal air.'

Unfortunately, a smitten John had gone beyond mere love letters. In haste, one assumes, to claim the privileges of a husband, he had set his signature to various documents declaring Miss Gordon to be his lawful wife and promising to acknowledge her as such the minute he could. It was these, along with a collection of passionate missives addressed to his 'dearest sweet wife', that he had left behind when his father, suspicious of an undesirable liaison, had borne him off from Edinburgh and had him packed off to a new posting in Malta. Along with the nights spent with

Miss Gordon in her bedroom, he had striven to forget them in the years that followed. As a family friend told the court, he had 'cautioned [Mr Dalrymple] in the most anxious manner' that it would be dangerous to disregard his connection with his Scottish lover, who had, through him, kept up a regular if one-sided correspondence with her spouse, but John had still wooed and wed Laura all the same. It was an arrogant course of action that he came to bitterly regret. 'What the Devil will he do with his *Spare-rib?*' Lord Byron wondered in the wake of the judgment in 1811, which confirmed that a marriage had taken place in 1804, albeit an irregular and clandestine one. Following the story as it unfolded in the papers, he joked with a friend: 'he is no beauty, but as lame as myself. He has more ladies than legs, what comfort to a cripple!'

Successive appeals from both Laura and John failed and, in the end, Dalrymple simply had to divorce Jacky. Afterwards, he tried several times to persuade Laura to marry him again, visiting her in the house near Richmond where she was living in semi-retirement with a companion, but she would never agree to become lawfully his wife – unsurprisingly, given that she had not only been publicly humiliated by his arrogant and reckless behaviour, but also left in an invidious social position, neither chaste debutante nor respectable widow. Both died single and childless.

Laura's was an exceptional case, but it was certainly true that an upper-class woman had more to lose by marrying the wrong man than vice versa. Marriage had a far greater impact on her wealth, status and way of life than on his – something parents kept firmly in mind when weighing up potential matches. One of the Calverts' principal objections to Sir James Stronge, for instance, was his 'belonging to another country' – his seat being in Ireland meant that seventeen-year-old Isabella was likely to be spending most of her time at a considerable distance from her nearest and dearest. Would there be the money for her to return regularly? Would Sir James be content for her to leave on prolonged visits? Once all was settled, his mother in-law cheerfully reported that he had promised they would 'come often to England' after their marriage, a promise that might even have been a condition of his future in-laws' consent.

With a daughter usually only entitled to a limited share of the family money (and rarely able to earn anything for herself), it was more often the ability or otherwise of a suitor to ensure her future financial security that made parents pause. But when it came to objections over the plumpness of a suitor's pockets or his lack of a landowner's rent-roll, what we might think was pure greed or snobbishness on their part could arguably have been judicious concern for a daughter's welfare. Few members of Regency high society felt that 'love in a cottage' was a good idea beyond the pages of a novel. Lord Abercorn, for one, had made clear that he wanted his daughters to be 'maintained in the style of splendour [they] had always been us'd to, which was proper for [their] rank in life.'

Parents like his Lordship knew full well that if a daughter contemplated living on an income much lower than her father's she left behind more than her family on her wedding day. There might be no house in town for the season. There might be insufficient funds for her to make regular visits to family and siblings around the country; not to mention for the coterie of servants that she was used to relying on; for the fashionable wardrobe she would need if she wanted to continue participating in the *ton*'s social events; and for the reciprocal hosting of balls and parties. It was not something that women themselves were inclined to disregard, either. When, in 1800, she was encouraged to refuse her suitor on account of his unsatisfactory fortune, Lady Jerningham's niece Charlotte had certainly seemed to see the sense in it. 'She feard the difference of fortune, would make an unpleasant change which might not enable her to supply to her future Husband the chearful activity which would be expected from Her,' according to her father. A blend of romance and realism, passion and practicality was generally what both parents and children navigating the marriage market wanted.

The benchmark for titled parents like Lord Abercorn (who possessed an annual income of well above £40,000) was probably somewhere in the region of £5,000 to £10,000 a year – considered the minimum on which a fashionable life, split between a seat in the country and a house in town for the season, could be afforded. But many parents were clearly not unreasonable in their expectations. When in 1820, the Duke and Duchess of Rutland were asked by their daughter Lady Elizabeth to consent to her marriage to Andrew Drummond, a partner in his family's bank, their financial demands of him were certainly not outrageous ones. Lady Elizabeth came from a household where the annual income was in excess of £100,000, but all that her parents asked was that Andrew have £3,500 a year at his disposal, with £500 of that to be set aside for her pin money. Parents like the Countess of Portarlington, meanwhile, whose four daughters had 'little to bring to a family', merely wanted to know that their suitors would have sufficient to provide for a wife and children. It was only on account of his being a mere curate, whose earnings were possibly as little as £50 a year, perhaps topped up by a small annuity from his father, that prevented her consenting to her daughter Harriet's marriage with the Reverend Henry Erskine. They were eventually permitted to wed on £1,000 a year.

Nor can we dismiss objections about a suitor's rank as simple snobbishness (though, of course, there was both social cachet and advantage for the family in marrying off a daughter to a titled or exceptionally well-connected man). Living in a hierarchical society, aristocratic parents were attuned to the practical implications for a daughter of marrying a man of lower rank than herself. While a peer's son would see his wife raised to his status on marriage (thus singer Mary Anne Paton was transformed overnight into Lady William Lennox, entitled to the precedence and privileges due to the wife of a duke's younger son and suddenly outranking both viscountesses and baronesses), it was not the same for a peer's daughter. She retained her own courtesy title and place in the order of precedence – styled Lady Elizabeth Drummond, rather than plain Mrs Drummond, for example – but her husband's status remained unchanged, and it was his, not hers, that would dictate that of any children of the marriage. The next generation, and the next after that, would each be a step further outside the inner circle of the aristocracy, with all the consequent disadvantages of that remoteness for their future careers and courtships.

Banker Andrew Drummond, while he worked for his living, was not actually so radical a choice for a duke's daughter as he might sound. His mother was the daughter of an earl, and he had been raised in a manner befitting a man of fashion: educated at Eton and Christ Church College, Oxford and then sent on a grand tour of Europe. He had the entrée to Almack's and was often on the guest list for the balls and parties given by the bank's wealthy clients. He was set to inherit a property in Hampshire, and even hunted near the Rutlands' seat in Lincolnshire. He certainly had the connections in fashionable society that meant marriage to him would not have the impact on Lady Elizabeth's social life and circle of acquaintances that could be the result of marrying a man of lower rank.

It was a risk that Sydney Owenson had taken seriously, when Lord and Lady Abercorn had argued for her marriage to Charles Morgan by forcefully reminding her that they could never acknowledge 'a *Dublin husband*' whose status was so far below their own. A husband who was acceptable company for the Abercorns guaranteed Sydney's continued relationship with them – with all the benefits their patronage gave her in terms of introductions and the social invitations she craved – and for an aristocratic debutante, a husband of a similar rank guaranteed her continued membership of the elite world into which she had been born, and access, in due course, to its marital arena for her own children.

In the end, the Rutlands had asked their daughter to wait two years to see if her affections remained unchanged, doubtless wanting to be absolutely sure that if she was going to snub the kind of match that would have placed her at the pinnacle of society, what she felt for her less conventional suitor was a true and lasting love. Finding the feelings of the couple unchanged in 1822, they had eventually compromised, allowing them to marry on an income of £2,500 a year, with a further £2,000 promised by Andrew's father as a wedding gift.

For those who despaired of ever convincing a parent to consent, one option did, of course, remain: an elopement. Choosing love over daughterly duty, however, was not something to be considered lightly. A runaway marriage was a determined flouting not just of parental authority, but also of the code of propriety and society's courtship norms. There was certainly nothing so disgraceful in Mrs Calvert's eyes. 'Oh, my dear girls! May you never do a thing of that sort!' she addressed her daughters, with a rare and emphatic use of exclamation marks.

Nevertheless Miss Maria Petre agreed to elope in late February 1805, when her parents began to talk of finding her paramour a new position, having discovered with dismay the existence of an attachment between their eldest daughter and Mr Phillips, their son's tutor. Before Phillips could be sent packing, however, Maria ran off with him from her family's Norfolk house, leaving one night under cover of darkness. When they were missed at breakfast the following day, Lord Petre reportedly set off in search of the runaways, successfully tracing them to Whitechapel but not beyond. The couple had, said the newspapers, switched to a hackney carriage on reaching the City, in an attempt to 'elude the vigilance' of their suspected pursuers. It later turned out that, finding no one willing to marry them in Lambeth, they had travelled on to Oxford and been united there by an unsuspecting Catholic priest, before going into hiding at the house of a friend of the groom.

Of course, the most undesirable thing about an elopement was that it triggered a great deal of talk. Maria's flight made her family the *ton*'s 'chief subject of conversation' that March. 'They can do nothing but get her married to the man at

Church,' remarked a sympathetic Mrs Spencer-Stanhope, referring both to the fact that Maria's reputation had been ruined beyond repair, and that a Catholic marriage – though acceptable to the Petres – was an invalid one under English law. Her daughter Marianne, like the press, was more preoccupied with the disparity in status of the two parties. 'He is a very low man, quite another class, always dined with the children, never associated the least with the family, a sort of upper servant,' she told her brother, her comments no doubt echoing those of Lord and Lady Petre themselves when they had made it clear to Maria that Mr Phillips had to go. Quite possibly they came from the mouth of the 'inconsolable' mother herself, since she added that 'Lady Petre thought him rather forward'.

While the Hon. Miss Petre had chosen London for her 'matrimonial excursion', Scotland was the more obvious destination for minors desperate to marry. Since it had refused to adopt the provisions of the Clandestine Marriages Act of 1753, English couples under the age of twenty-one could marry over the border without permission from parents or guardians. In the now-legendary Gretna Green, the first Scottish village to be reached via the main coach road, young runaways could be united quickly, no questions asked. Its famous marriage ministers kept registers, provided certificates for the purposes of evidence, and could even gratify the happy couple by giving their hasty wedding a quasi-religious tone. By the Regency it was a veritable 'land-mark for fugitive lovers' and welcomed many thwarted young aristocrats. Between March 1811 and March 1812 alone, a younger son of Lord Ellenborough arrived in haste with a baronet's daughter, Miss Nightingale; Viscount Deerhurst with Lady Mary Beauclerk, daughter of the Duke of St Albans; and heir to another Durham mining fortune, John Lambton, with the Earl of Cholmondeley's illegitimate daughter Henrietta.

Racing to the border at breakneck speed had, by then, become highly romanticised, appearing in countless sentimental novels. In reality, a Regency elopement was neither a glamorous nor easy option. Especially not for a woman, who was putting herself entirely in the power of her fiancé, placing her reputation in his hands. Could she trust him to take them to a parson? Having gone gadding about the country in his company, possibly shut up in a carriage alone with him for hours on end (and that perhaps the least of her crimes against propriety); for her, more things were broken than an engagement if vows were not eventually exchanged.

Practically, too, an elopement wasn't an easy thing to carry off. Spiriting away a carefully chaperoned young lady from the house of a parent or guardian, staffed by an army of watchful servants, was no simple task. Lady Mary Beauclerk was reportedly helped to escape by her faithful abigail, who, it was said, had previously assisted her mistress by delivering letters to and from her noble lover. Nineteen-year-old Mr Lambton, meanwhile, might have benefited from a nod and a wink from Miss Cholmondeley's relatives, who were thought to be 'very glad to get rid of her' since her beauty easily outshone that of her legitimate half-sister. The lovers' elopement was not, said the papers, 'looked upon as an unpropitious one at *Ch—d—y House*, the Noble Lord having... written to the *amorous fugitives*, kindly requesting that, on their return, they will make his seat, in *Cheshire an honeymoon asylum!*'

An elopement also called for a stash of ready cash to cover its numerous attendant expenses. Hire of a carriage and fresh horses at each stage was not cheap. If an impatient bridegroom opted for the speediest and most private conveyance available, a post-chaise and four, he would be looking at a cost of nearly £40 for the journey from London to Gretna – not much less than a peer paid his coachman for an entire year's work. Then there were the tolls to pay en route, and the cost of refreshments – and possibly rooms – to cover too, since travelling the distance of approximately 320 miles from the capital took well over twenty-four hours, even if the horses were pushed hard and the fugitives consistently achieved a speed above the average of 7mph. Miss Nightingale and her fiancé the Hon. Charles Law were reported to have reached it in 'two nights and a day', which seems almost improbably quick, though less so if they departed not from London but her family home in south Cambridgeshire. Finally, on arrival in Scotland, there was a fee for the presiding 'minister'[6] – a sum undefined, and usually left to a gentleman's 'honour, or their discretion, or their generosity, or, more properly, to their ignorances of the usages of Gretna'. Couples arriving at the border being a captive market and the bargain generally made before the knot was tied, 'the priests always try to get as much as they can,' confirmed a writer in 1844, chronicling the thriving marriage trade of Gretna's recent past. Fifteen guineas was the going rate for the service in 1815, according to one

---

6   Interestingly, while tradition has it that marriages at Gretna Green were usually conducted by a blacksmith, this has proved to be a complete myth. Some think that Charles Stuart's popular comic opera *Gretna Green*, in which the village's 'god of marriage' was the blacksmith, was behind the legend; while Robert Elliott, who married into the family of long-standing Gretna 'marriage minister' Joseph Paisley, and himself conducted 3,000 marriages at the Scottish border, thought that his esteemed in-law (formerly farmer and fisherman) became known as the blacksmith simply because of his quickness in uniting eloping couples. 'Strike the iron when it is hot, Joseph' was apparently the common saying. 'Parson' Laing, who married Lord Deerhurst, was certainly not a blacksmith either, but a peddler. So-called priests, they were, in fact, anything but – any Scottish person then could marry two people on Scottish soil, no qualifications required.

of his sources, but he heard tell of Georgian gentlemen paying as much as 30 guineas – about the sum that a footman in a noble household earned each year. If the newspapers are to be believed, 'Parson' Laing pocketed a staggering 100 guineas for marrying Lord Deerhurst and Lady Mary in 1811. 'He who goes there bent on economy,' the Victorian chronicler surmised, 'had better go in sackcloth, and mounted in a vehicle whose appearance shall not indicate splendour or ostentation.'

While the distance to the border meant it was entirely possible for an angry parent in hot pursuit to overtake their errant child, assuming their flight had been found out in good time; those who elected not to do so, or failed to, could do little more than accept the marriage as a fait accompli and shrug off the resulting scandal. The Duke of St Albans had it put about (truthfully or not) that his daughter's union with Lord Deerhurst had been in train for some time but that the couple were too impatient to wait for the lawyers to sort out the settlement. Lady Anne Wyndham, John Lambton's mother, let it be known that she was repairing to Cholmondeley Castle to greet the honeymooners. What she, and most other parents, insisted on was a remarriage on English soil, to be absolutely certain that there would be no questions about the legitimacy of the union in future years. Of course, what caused guardians – particularly of heiresses – the greatest anxiety in the wake of an elopement was the absence of a signed and sealed marriage settlement. An impatient or strong-willed young woman who flew to the border with her fortune risked missing out on some, if not all, of the protections that the Regency form of the 'prenup' gave her. Certainly any leverage her legal representatives had disappeared the minute she said 'I do'.

Frances Anne and Lord Stewart never appear to have considered an elopement – not even after Mrs Taylor took the opportunity to scotch any hopes they had of a swift wedding by taking more than six months to decide whether or not to proceed with an appeal against the Lord Chancellor's decision. For her part, Frances Anne appeared to repose perfect confidence that there would, eventually, be a firm decision in her favour. She simply resigned herself to a wait and rented a cottage in Putney to live in quiet retirement with her companion, while Charles returned to his post on the continent. The two of them parted with 'mutual vows of constancy' and the handover of her 'little dog Dash' as a pledge of her affection for him. At the end of March 1819, after one last spirited, but ultimately failed, attempt by Mrs Taylor to change the Lord Chancellor's decision, their patience was finally rewarded. Their marriage was given the go-ahead, and there remained only one more hurdle to clear. It was time to talk about the settlement, something Frances Anne would be much too shrewd to go without.

*Chapter Five*

# The Price of Love

THE NEWS THAT her sister had declared herself the 'mortal enemy' of her chosen marriage partner had come as no great surprise to weary bride-to-be Harriet Fane. She had fought hard for 46-year-old Charles Arbuthnot, but by the time he had received her sister's melodramatic communication in December 1813, it was clear that what she had won when she gained her family's reluctant approval for their engagement was not the war, but simply the first battle. Since then, negotiations over the terms of a marriage settlement had rumbled on and on, her affianced becoming steadily – and noticeably – more irritated with his future in-laws, and they more anxious than ever to thwart a match they had disliked from the start. The latest developments in the settlement saga had left the would-be-bride absolutely convinced that no happiness could possibly result from a union so inauspiciously begun, and she was determined to walk away – or *almost* determined, anyway.

Harriet's rollercoaster of a romance had its origins in a schoolgirl crush. Six years earlier, the gentlemanly but sombre Charles, mourning the recent loss of his cherished wife Marcia in childbirth, had cut a romantic figure in the eyes of a fourteen-year-old Harriet, who credited him with 'more feeling... than any other man in the world'. It had been only a passing fancy then, forgotten as soon as her teenage heart was set aflutter by dashing Trafalgar veteran Captain Thomas Capel (another older man), but she had remembered Mr Arbuthnot well enough when they found themselves part of the same house party at Apethorpe, home of her cousin Lord Westmorland, around Christmastime in 1812. Despite the fact that Charles had utterly failed to perform any of those courtesies she was accustomed to from her (plentiful) admirers, the joint secretary to the Treasury, trusted keeper of all kinds of political secrets and dispenser of government patronage had been the only man there who Harriet had liked. So much so, in fact, that her confidante Lady Monson had forecast wedding bells for her friend Miss Fane, grown not only decidedly pretty in recent years, with silky dark hair and a graceful figure, but also decidedly interested in politics.

The campaign for her somewhat eccentric choice of spouse, who had 'never had a moment's happiness' in his seven years of widowhood (or so he said), had begun soon after he proposed in July 1813. In the minds of Harriet's eldest brothers, the 'mild, modest, and sincere' Charles was not the husband she deserved. Lively, intelligent and playful, their youngest sister was not yet above dancing around the churchyard at night dressed as a ghost in fulfilment of one of their dares; they could 'see no prospect of happiness' for her in 'so preposterous a union' with a much-older man. They could not but dread that she would be left alone at an early age, and without any of those comforts she had a right to expect. Hearing their objections, the widowed Mrs Fane had been inclined to agree. There was 'not a creature existing she would prefer' for a son-in-law she told her daughter, but it did seem a lot like madness for Harriet to tie herself at the age of just twenty to a man so much her senior.

Harriet, however, had been adamant that she knew her own heart. 'I never have or never shall really love anyone else, & I feel quite certain with you I shall be as happy as possible,' she assured Charles, who was sensitive himself about not only his advanced years but his want of rank and fortune; not to mention the matter of Harriet having 'made love' to him – a source of great amusement for her siblings, who seemingly thought it just like her to have taken the lead, even in romance. That they would succeed in gaining approval for their marriage – once her mother had reconciled herself to the idea of her youngest daughter leaving home – Harriet had also been quite certain, but, to her dismay, the family opposition had not abated. And as she had, unlike Frances Anne Vane-Tempest, a supremely close and loving bond with her mother and nine surviving siblings, it soon became clear that she would find it very difficult to marry against their wishes – or, indeed, to condemn them for what she could appreciate were reasonable concerns. So when her mother, bowing to the pressure from her eldest son Harry (then abroad with the army), had told her daughter that she must break off the engagement, Harriet had suppressed her misery and dutifully complied, writing to Charles to tell him so.

But the engagement had not been toppled – not then, anyway. The return post had brought to the Fanes' Lincolnshire home a letter from a defiant Charles so strongly worded that it had caused Mrs Fane to keep breaking into tears. 'I can generally contrive to have things as I like best, & so it will be in this case,' Harriet soon felt able to tell her affronted lover, confident that the opposition of her tender-hearted mother was crumbling in the face of their joint determination to be wed. 'I foresee [it] will finally take place,' her brother, the Reverend Edward Fane, was forced to admit, despite still fervently praying that it would not. All indications were, however, that it would: Mrs Fane had (albeit reluctantly) made plans to take Harriet to London to prepare for her nuptials, and it was agreed that negotiations could begin for the marriage settlement. These were to be handled on the Fane side by Vere, Harriet's fourth brother, nominated by his mother on account of his being a banker.

In aristocratic circles, thrashing out a settlement was regarded as an indispensable preliminary to marriage. It was through this legally binding agreement that the happy couple – who would usually rely, at least in part, on family money for their future maintenance – were secured financially. A settlement typically specified the dowry or portion that was to be paid over by the bride's family, and the financial commitments that the groom's would make in return: the immediate income to be set aside for the newly-weds; the annual allowance the bride could expect to receive for her personal expenses (her pin money); and the annual annuity she could expect if she was left a widow (her jointure). It also fixed the inheritance rights of the next generation, including the marriage portions of any children born of the union. Charles Arbuthnot was, regrettably, heir to neither land nor title, but where the groom had expectations, the matter of inheritance was of especial importance. At the time of an eldest son's marriage, aristocratic families normally provided for the transference of the family estates to *his* eldest son in due course (i.e. entailed it) and ensured that the bridegroom himself would be a mere life tenant, unable to sell up at any time during his own tenure.

For the bride, the importance of contractual provisions for pin money and jointure was not to be underestimated. The one gave her the freedom to make purchases, to give gifts and spend on travel and entertainment, all independently of her husband; the other was, of course, her guarantee of financial security when he died. And if either were not paid, her representatives would be able to take legal action on her behalf. But what was most important of all about her marriage settlement was that it provided her with rights of property otherwise firmly denied to married women.

The common law of England and Wales said that a husband and wife were one person: a woman's legal identity was, if not suspended during her marriage, subsumed into that of her husband, 'under whose wing, protection, and cover' she acted at all times. The doctrine of coverture, as it was known, not only prevented a married woman from contracting debts or taking someone to court in her own right, but stopped her owning property. Near enough everything a single woman possessed at the time of her marriage became her husband's the moment she was lawfully declared his wife, along with almost anything she earned, inherited or was gifted thereafter.

But coverture could be circumvented – as it related to property, at least – by the judicious creation of trusts prior to a woman's wedding. When property was placed in the hands of trustees as part of the settlement process, it could not transfer into a husband's hands the minute the knot was tied because the bride did not legally own it. Instead, the nominated trustees –

usually male relatives, friends or lawyers – were the legal owners, holding the property on her behalf, for her sole and separate use. Money or assets that a prospective bride had inherited, or become entitled to on her marriage, were thus ring-fenced for her benefit, and/or that of her children: safe from plunder in later years by a spouse who had spent his own inheritance, or by the creditors snapping at his heels, and the income sometimes even at her sole disposal.

For women who inherited property that eclipsed the average marriage portion, the practice of creating prenuptial trusts had the potential to be enormously valuable, practically but also psychologically. They certainly considered capital held by trustees to be theirs alone. 'It was with real pleasure that I spent this enormous sum on Sir John's new property,' Frances, Lady Shelley remarked casually of the £70,000 outlaid on improvements to her marital home, patently aware that the usual power balance between husband and wife was tipped in her favour because their money was mostly hers. Even women of more modest means could benefit, however. Much depended on the terms of the settlement, but if capital or land set aside to fund a wife's pin money was placed into the hands of neutral trustees for her separate use, they would dispense the income directly to her, ensuring she received her allowance entirely independently of a spouse who might turn out to be forgetful or tight-fisted, frequently absent, angry or indebted.[7]

---

7   Of course, such a measure didn't stop a wife directing her trustees that income she alone was entitled to could be paid over to her husband, as heiress Catherine Tylney Long was persuaded by her profligate spouse William to do with her £7,500 pin money in the first year of their marriage. In order to foil similar attempts by a husband to 'kiss or kick' his way to the whole of a wife's separate property, the terms of a trust sometimes prevented her either selling or mortgaging her assets during her lifetime or drawing on the principal, meaning that the property did not always feel entirely hers to do with as she pleased.

It was the settlement of separate property on Harriet that became a particular sticking point in the Fane–Arbuthnot negotiations. Being the point in a courtship at which monetary interest and matters of the heart collided, discussions over a suitable marriage contract were rarely ever entirely straightforward. The terms could be complex, depending on the financial affairs of the two families involved. Debating them, running them past the lawyers, and then drawing up a mutually acceptable agreement often took weeks at best, several months at worst – and that even where both families looked on the union with a friendly eye.

Things had been much less positive where Harriet and Charles were concerned. Mrs Fane might have reluctantly accepted the need to prepare her youngest daughter for 'this wedding' (as she privately described it) but there had lingered in the minds of most of the Fanes a suspicion that the match could not, and would not, turn out well; and in Charles a (fairly well-founded) conviction that whatever they said publicly, the family remained hostile and disapproving towards him. The tension between the two sides was hardly conducive to compromise, necessary given Charles's finite funds, and the talks had quickly hit the rocks.

What the Fane family wanted in the way of financial provision for Harriet, both during the marriage and in what seemed likely to be a long widowhood, Charles declared to be 'ruinous' to his finances and 'unjust' to his four children, two boys and two girls, all under thirteen. His advisers objected strenuously to his having to settle £10,000 on his bride – to provide her jointure and, presumably also portions for any children – without being permitted to touch any of Harriet's fortune, or, indeed, receiving any other financial assistance whatsoever from the Fanes. 'It is

I believe without precedent that that burthen shd fall on the husband when no use whatever is derived from [the] marriage fortune – at least so say my Lawyer & every friend whom I have thought it right to consult,' an increasingly tetchy Charles had complained to Vere in the autumn.

It did seem 'very extraordinary' that Mrs Fane was unprepared to make any contribution, conceded Lord Westmorland, one of Harriet's guardians and a prospective trustee of the marriage settlement. It was, indeed, generally accepted that in exchange for guaranteed sums of pin money and jointure, the bride's marriage portion would be paid over to her future husband (or his father), and that (unless it was larger than average) it would be entirely non-refundable, even if the bride died soon afterwards, or without leaving any children to benefit from her money. The trustees and advisers of Frances Anne Vane-Tempest worked diligently on her behalf in the matter of marriage settlements, ensuring that Lord Stewart was tied up in a 'petticoat hold'– rendered no more than a life tenant of the vast estates that remained legally *hers*; unable to sell any of *her* property unless he replaced it with land or stocks of equal value, and at risk of having his authority suspended if he acted imprudently.[8] Yet even they conceded that, despite the splendid income that his Lordship was set to receive from his new wife's estates and collieries, a no-strings-attached lump sum should be paid over to him as part of the deal. He received £10,000 as a token marriage portion, in exchange for which Frances Anne was guaranteed a jointure of £1,000 a year, to be funded from

---

8   Interestingly, Lord Stewart also took on a considerable burden in exchange for the considerable boost his income would receive from Frances Anne's property: he was responsible not only for the repayment of her estate's existing debts (well over £100,000 at the time of her marriage) but also for provision for her mother and aunt, as well as the payment of £2,000 in pin money to Frances Anne herself each year.

his own Irish estates – though the jointure would hardly be necessary, given that her inherited property was held in trust for her, the income to be at her disposal in her widowhood.

That said, in aristocratic circles it was relatively common for the bridegroom's family to deny any interest in taking the bride's cash simply to top up their own coffers. Lord Wicklow 'does not desire one shilling of the fortune,' Lord Abercorn's representative reported after preliminary discussions between the two men over the marriage of Wicklow's son and heir to Abercorn's fourth daughter, Lady Cecil, who had a portion of £10,000. 'Let that be settled on herself and her issue,' Lord Wicklow had recommended, meaning that a trust should be created to ring-fence the money for use as marriage portions for any of the couple's younger children, to which he would also contribute a further £10,000.

To be fair to Mrs Fane, too, her demands were not deliberately obstructive. It was a vision of 'Harriet and a dozen children starving twenty years hence' that was spurring her on, both in pursuit of a healthy jointure for her youngest daughter, and in her steely determination to see that her inheritance was not simply paid over to her future husband to boost his income. Charles had done very little to convince her that such a vision was only the product of an overactive imagination. In fact, more than once he had declared, to her extreme vexation, that Harriet might 'as well marry her footman' as him.

Under no illusions as to his financial situation, the increasingly hassled Charles knew he could ill afford to take the same stance as Lord Wicklow. Having run through a £23,000 inheritance from his maternal relations in earlier years, he was now wholly reliant on, and spending (he said) almost the whole of, his £4,000 salary from the Treasury, an income that was precariously dependent on both his retaining his post and his Tory friends remaining in government. With a relatively undistinguished career to date and a tendency to overwork himself, his prospects were not dazzling, and he would in all probability be forced at some point in the marriage to fall back on the £2,000-a-year pension he had from his previous diplomatic role, which languished in abeyance as long as he held his current position. On top of that, he was carrying debts that ran into the tens of thousands of pounds, a significant proportion incurred during an expensive and much-regretted spell as ambassador in Constantinople, but some through the ill-advised purchase of his small Northamptonshire estate at an overinflated price.

He also appeared to have a woeful inability to manage what money he did have. The details of his income and expenditure over the last year, shared with Vere, had shown a fairly considerable sum under the heading of 'pocket money' – including £300 for which neither he nor his secretary were able to account. He did not seem to run with a fast set any longer, but such spending habits certainly raised unfortunate suspicions of losses at the card table or nights spent carousing, if not something a respectable widow like Mrs Fane might consider even more unsavoury.

By November, a solution of sorts had finally been agreed on, but if Harriet's hopes had soared as a result, they had come crashing down again soon enough. Charles had agreed to insure his life for £10,000, the payout from which could provide her jointure after his death. It was not an entirely unusual step where the groom was short of capital, but the problem was that this particular groom did not really have the disposable income to pay for the policy, especially if he was not to touch anything belonging to his bride (still a bone of contention). When he took into account taxes and repayment of interest, and the money needed to see his two sons through school and then a stint at Oxford, he feared, he said, that if he was to go out of office, there would be as little as £1,000 a year left to cover his and Harriet's needs. Scarce enough to buy bread for them both, he bemoaned.

That, clearly, was a significant exaggeration. Even on £1,000 a year, the newly-weds would be very far removed from the poverty line. An agricultural labourer and his family might be attempting to survive on as little as £25 a year; an innkeeper and his dependents living on about £100. But the life Harriet had been born and bred to – and more importantly, the London life she (and Charles) wanted to live – was an expensive one. She was probably exactly the sort of debutante that Jane West, the author of 1806 conduct-book *Letters to a Young Lady,* had in mind when she urged her female readers to consider that they were unlikely to be content in a situation too far removed from that which they had occupied in their single life – in Harriet's case, as a member of a household with an annual income of £6,000. 'An income inadequate to our real (not our imaginary) wants,' she counselled, 'is a calamity of sufficient weight to overthrow the fairest fabric of happiness, and to oppress the most amiable temper.'

According to contemporary household guides, £1,000 a year stretched to just a couple of maids, a cook and a footman, along with a lone carriage, a coachman and perhaps a stable-boy – not a butler or a housekeeper, and certainly nothing like the thirty or forty servants who waited hand and foot on some aristocratic households, the wage bill for which alone often topped £1,000 a year, sometimes even double that. While Charles kept his Treasury post he had an official residence at what was then number 12 Downing Street; but without it, he and Harriet risked finding themselves buried in the country for long stretches or reliant on the hospitality of friends and family, since rent of a house in town and associated costs would hardly leave any change from £1,000 a year. Even with the Downing Street pièd-a-terre, many of the trappings of metropolitan life for members of the *ton* – a box seat at the opera, an elaborate, regularly updated wardrobe, lavish dinners for a table full of distinguished guests – must have been beyond their reach had that comparatively meagre income been their only resource. £5,000 a year was a more realistic income for an aspirant to fashion, thought one contemporary writer.

Charles seems to have suggested, slightly antagonistically, that Mrs Fane cover the regular premiums on the insurance policy instead, a proposal that she declared a disgrace. 'It would have appeared that I was so anxious for [the union],' she wrote to Vere indignantly, 'that I was ready to *pay him* for marrying my Daughter.' The problem, as Mrs Fane saw it, was that her intended son-in-law was being unduly influenced by his friends, who seemed to be urging 'him on to make demands one after another in the hope of getting the better of [them]'– and none of whom 'would give themselves one moment's concern' if Harriet and her hypothetical brood of twelve children were to be poverty-stricken in later years, as she told Vere crossly.

The business-minded member of the family might have been nominally in charge of the negotiations – and it was usual for a male relative to handle them – but the rest of the Fanes had been following every development, with letters flying back and forth between the harassed Vere at his office at Temple Bar on the edge of the City, and his mother and sisters at home in Lincolnshire. Their inability to resist encroaching on his brief had only intensified the ill-feeling between the two sides. Charles had reacted with deep resentment when his affianced wrote artlessly to tell him that the objections raised by his trustees were 'nonsense' and that he should do just as her brother required. On another occasion, he had sought out Lord Westmorland 'in a great Fidget' over 'an Epistle' he had received from his future sister-in-law Caroline, which his Lordship admitted to Vere was 'not a very proper one'. Married herself the previous year to a local squire's son, Caroline had been sending plenty of epistles her brother's way, too, in an attempt to bring him firmly onto the side of the siblings ranged against the match.

For Harriet, the stand-off between her family and fiancé made for an uncomfortable time. On the one hand, she appears to have seen the sense in what her family were fighting for, telling Charles herself that she would not marry without a settlement. On the other, she was sympathetic towards her chosen marriage partner, fully conscious of his various financial responsibilities. 'I have not been able to bear up against the idea that I am your ruin,' she wrote to him as the clock struck four one sleepless night, her eyes sore from crying. For her 'subdued' spirits, Charles himself was partly to blame. His failure to spare her from his sometimes bitter reproaches over the settlement demands, not to mention his accusations that she had broken her promises, left her feeling 'thoro'ly worried and wretched'.

The weeks or months between the engagement and exchange of vows were not normally such stressful ones. The betrothed couple were usually permitted to live almost in each other's pockets, just as they had been urged not to do earlier in their courtship. Mrs Calvert was obliged not only to let Isabella's intended, Sir James Stronge, run tame in their London house in the lead-up to their wedding in 1810, but to accept invitation after invitation to dine at his own. 'I am *completely* tired of *love making*,' she confessed, longing to see a few different faces. William Lyttelton similarly haunted Spencer House in the weeks after his engagement; Lady Sarah confessed to her brother Bob that she looked forward to the moment each day when she heard his step along the passage and his voice outside the drawing-room door. For almost all couples, though, the tie between them was still a delicate thread at this stage, as hinted at by Sarah's grandmama, who expressed the hopes that all was going on as her son would wish with Mr Lyttelton. No matter how in love they continued to be, the match was never a done deal until the money side was sorted to everyone's satisfaction.

With the matter of the insurance unresolved in her case, Harriet had been forced to admit that it seemed unlikely that Charles would be able to make the settlement her family required – not without bringing his own young family to the brink, financially speaking. It was thus that she had decided – even though the very idea made her 'perfectly miserable' – that the sensible thing would be to put an end to their engagement. For the second time in almost as few months, a melancholy, though perhaps not sufficiently decisive, letter to Charles had consequently gone winging its way to London.

Their romance having gone so far, Harriet worried that she would be 'abused by every creature' for jilting him, her decision perhaps making her look mercenary. Yet she would certainly not have been the first debutante to have a match collapse for economic reasons. Esther Acklom's first engagement had foundered at the settlement stage, six months after Thomas Knox, nephew of Mrs Calvert and heir to a viscountcy, had proposed to her at a concert in June 1811. The discussions over finances had been fraught and protracted ones in their case too: the lovebirds' respective families had been at 'daggers drawing' by the autumn according to Mrs Calvert, who thought that Mr Acklom was being unnecessarily troublesome. 'He still holds to his demands,' she noted in her journal, 'w$^{ch}$ are for a much larger *present* income than Mr K. will give.' Not yet in possession of title and estates himself – these were still held by his 82-year-old father – there was probably only so much that her brother-in-law had in his power to grant his eldest son. Had he already acceded to his inheritance, no doubt it would have been much easier. The Duke of Bedford was able to settle one of his Bedfordshire properties, with an income estimated at £6,000 a year, on his son and heir Lord Tavistock when he married in 1808 – a sum that must surely have satisfied Mr Acklom, while also ensuring that the newly-weds would have no cause to resent the robust health of the present title holder.

When their negotiations had foundered not long before Christmas 1811, Esther and Thomas had simply returned the portraits and letters exchanged during their carefree days of courtship and, with no apparent angst, gone their separate ways – much to the delight of the extended Knox family. 'Never was any thing equal to the conduct of the Acklom crew – Miss at the head,' Mrs Calvert had tutted. Harriet's own attempt to break things off with Charles, however, had only caused more turmoil. Apparently acting like a wake-up call, her communication had prompted a near-total about-turn from the Arbuthnot camp.

Having previously stated 'so strongly the impossibility of making the sacrifice of annual income required' for the settlement – as an indignant Harriet recalled – he now told her that it would 'not distress him the least' to do it, that it would 'not be injurious to his children', and that he could 'easily find the security' for the insurance policy. An astonished Harriet did not know whether to be hurt, furious or relieved. Fury won out at first. He had made so many difficulties, she ranted, which he now appeared to admit were 'wholly imaginary' ones. His conduct, she decided, had been cruel.

'It is very true that I have promised to marry him,' she wrote to Vere – acting, once more, as go-between and on the receiving end of a furious missive from her – adding that if Charles insisted on her fulfilling her promise, as he seemed inclined to do, she knew she was bound in honour to do so. Yet she urged her brother to make him see that breaking it off was the most sensible thing to do. 'These pecuniary discussions have excited great irritation in his mind against my family,' she argued, not to mention that she could see their mother would be made miserable if she were to wed him now, for which she held Charles himself to blame. 'He has destroyed the cordiality that existed between him & my relations,' she seethed. Were they to have married before any of the negotiations began, 'I should have been I am sure perfectly happy he is too amiable & excellent & I am too much attached to him for me to have been otherwise,' she did, however, confess.

It was true that both Mrs Fane and Caroline were cock-a-hoop over the end of the affair, as Charles – whose dubious privilege it was to have gained a 'mortal enemy' in Caroline, thanks to his behaviour – was well aware. When Vere calmly and civilly proposed that they take the necessary steps to dissolve the ill-fated engagement – putting it about that it was 'by mutual consent & to avoid mutual inconvenience' – he appears to have felt compelled to comply, though he responded with the mournful assertion that 'I love her at this moment far more than perhaps any of you have ever been aware of.' To his sister, Vere recommended that the 'war of words' cease, and once the various letters, trinkets and love tokens were returned, she endeavour to 'bury everything in oblivion' – adding in the voice of one who knew his wilful sister all too well that there must be 'no assignations' with her former fiancé.

Suitable for a sentimental novel it may all have been, but it was not to be the end of the story. Lord Westmorland, for one, thought such theatrics totally unnecessary. When consulted by Charles, he merely laughed at the idea of his being the enemy of the family. Harriet, he was sure, did not really mean to give it all up. Despite having engineered the end of her engagement, Vere, too, seems to have been unconvinced that his sister really did want to part from her paramour. She was angry at Charles, he knew that, but he also knew that the lovers were still writing to one another. Perhaps he was moved by Charles's declaration of love; perhaps, having got to know Arbuthnot better than any of his brothers, he had come to approve of the match. Perhaps, having always hated his banking career, he liked the idea of having for a brother-in-law the government's patronage secretary – the man in charge of dispensing crown appointments. For whatever reason, he added his own encouragement to that of Lord Westmorland, recommending (to his mother's intense dissatisfaction) that Charles head up to Fulbeck Hall, the family's Lincolnshire home, as soon as Parliament rose for its recess in late December.

'In my present state of mind I will be off, to some distant place where I shall not easily be come at,' Mrs Fane had threatened her son when he issued the invitation, but come Charles did, and a reconciliation was the result. The discarded settlement documents had been picked up again by New Year's Eve 1813, and the bridegroom made good on the promises that had made Harriet so angry, having been proffered so late in proceedings. He had probably exaggerated when he told his bride that he could *easily* find the security for the insurance policy, but it was done; placed in a trust were government bonds to the value of £11,091 belonging to his incoming colleague at the Treasury, Stephen Lushington, and to Stephen's father-in-law, the income from them to pay the policy premiums until such time as Charles could replace their bonds with property of his own of equivalent value. All outstanding objections of Charles's trustees were waved aside as the Fanes had always advocated and, on the advice of Lord Westmorland, it was agreed that Harriet would receive the £10,000 insurance payout after Charles's death, since that was the only money her betrothed had brought forward for the marriage contract. Harriet's own fortune, meanwhile, was settled for her separate use, though Mrs Fane did unbend sufficiently towards Charles to make one key concession: if his income dropped below £4,000 a year, he was permitted to draw on the dividends from her daughter's capital. All that remained was to do as Vere the peacekeeper had earlier advised: to make every effort 'to banish both from thoughts & conversations all recent events'.

Finally, on 31 January 1814, a mere two days after their settlement was signed and sealed, the star-crossed lovers were married, almost certainly in the church at Fulbeck where

Edward Fane was rector. Harriet was happier than ever with her unconventional choice; Charles, 'all fire and flames and love… and so very proud' of his new wife. Dragging on for more than six months thanks to the fractious settlement negotiations, their engagement had turned out to be a long one by Regency standards. The time between proposal and procession to church was rarely more than eight weeks for most brides. Once the ink was dry on the settlement, there was not usually any reason to delay. Unless the bride was hesitant, of course…

*Chapter Six*

# Marriage à la Mode

IT WAS A cold and crisp morning in late January 1812 when Sydney Owenson was surprised into marriage – aptly, for an author, in a scene straight from a novel. One minute the reluctant bride was huddled by the fire in the library at Baronscourt, completely alone and deep in contemplation. The next, Lady Abercorn had burst in, taken hold of her arm and hurried her upstairs. For despite having returned to her infatuated fiancé in a cloud of love and remorse more than two weeks earlier, her protégée had shown very little desire to actually get the knot tied, and Lady Abercorn had decided to take matters into her own hands. Bundled unceremoniously into her meddlesome matchmaker's dressing room, Sydney had been greeted by the family chaplain, Mr Bowen, standing robed and ready, candles lit and prayer-book open. By his side, not in the least displeased by the turn of events, was the newly knighted Sir Charles, to whom a startled Sydney was duly wed, still in her morning gown, with the rest of the household's guests entirely oblivious to the ceremony. They would not in fact know of it until several days later, when Lord Abercorn stood up at the dinner table and made a toast, to Sir Charles and Lady Morgan!

If Sydney's marriage really was such a scrambling, secretive affair – and with Sydney, there's no guarantee that the storyteller in her had not spiced up a much more humdrum occasion – it would not, in fact, be so very different from the average aristocratic wedding of the age. When it came to getting married, privacy and intimacy were the *ton's* watchwords. In their eyes, the only truly genteel way to wed was without any fanfare whatsoever, in front of just a few friends and family members, and behind firmly closed doors.

If you were planning a marriage à la mode, the number one thing on your to-do list was to procure a 'special' licence. Obtained from the office of the Archbishop of Canterbury at London's Doctors' Commons, these were both exclusive and expensive: available only to a select and specified minority that included peers, peeresses and their families and MPs and theirs, and costing in the region of £14 plus duty by 1819 – roughly the same as a maid in an aristocratic household earned in an entire year. To the upper classes, however, they were worth their weight in gold, sparing a gently bred bride the indelicacy of having her name, and that of her betrothed, bandied about in open church when the banns were called on three consecutive Sundays, while at the same time conferring a certain cachet on her celebration, marking her out as a member of the privileged elite. Romantic fiction may have married in our minds the special licence and speedily held ceremonies, where the couple needed to scotch a scandal or wed in secret, but, in reality, it was favoured by the members of the fashionable world with access to it simply because of its privacy and prestige. There was one further benefit, too. Unlike banns, and the cheaper and more freely available 'common' licence, the 'special' variety allowed a happy couple to eschew altogether their local parish church, where weddings could only be conducted between 8 a.m. and noon, and marry instead at a time and place of their choosing.

Not for all members of the beau monde did that mean rejecting a church altogether. Married by special licence in March 1813, Lady Sarah Spencer – more pious than some of her contemporaries – selected the snug little chapel on her family's estate at Wimbledon, to which she could walk the 200 yards from the house on the appointed afternoon, arm in arm with her father and her future husband. The glossy parish church of St George's in Hanover Square, which boasted neoclassical ceiling work and noble church wardens, was also a popular choice, and could be a neat way for Mayfair residents to wed in a suitably smart venue while saving the cost of a special licence, provided they were prepared to wed before midday as Isabella Calvert did in September 1810. Often, though, the place of an aristocratic bride's choosing was the drawing room of her family's London house, and the time a fashionably late, candlelit hour.

When it came to choosing a date for a modish marriage ceremony, any month of the year, any day of the week would do. Often, in fact, the day of a wedding could not be decided in advance, being dependent on the successful completion of all the settlement paperwork. It was something that caused Mrs Calvert considerable stress in the lead-up to Isabella's marriage. 'We were in hopes the papers w[oul]d arrive in time for the wedding to be tomorrow, but they are not come yet,' she wrote in her journal, her agitation evident. Expecting another baby to add to her brood of seven and, by her estimate, already at her due date, all she could do was hope that the documents would arrive from Ireland before she had to lie in. Thankfully, her 'reckoning' proved to be inaccurate. The settlements arrived on 4 September, she was able to see Isabella married to Sir James Stronge on the fifth, and was not brought to bed of her new daughter until the eleventh.

Not only was the date a matter of practicality rather than preference, it simply mattered less, since genteel weddings were not celebrations that needed sunny weather or swathes of guests to be a success. While modern couples eagerly send out 'save the date' cards, their Regency counterparts were much less inclined to worry if the day they chose for their marriage meant close family or friends would be missing. Though she selected 24 December 1809 for her wedding day in the hope that it would allow her heavily pregnant sister Georgiana to be there, Lady 'Harryo' Cavendish doesn't seem to have considered for a moment delaying her marriage for a month or two to guarantee it – even though she had only been engaged for less than five weeks. In the end, Georgiana *was* absent, having given birth just the day before. It was much the same when the sisters' cousin Lord Althorp married in April 1814. He and his bride Esther sped out of town straight after the ceremony to pass the honeymoon in the country, despite the fact that it meant missing the union of his sister Gin and Lord George Quin, which took place the very next evening at Spencer House.

Strange as it seems to us to marry without all our loved ones gathered round, the wedding ceremony had not yet become sentimentalised in the way that it would in the Victorian era, when weddings consequently became larger, more choreo-graphed and more costly affairs. When Harryo's great-niece married over forty years later in 1852, the guests at church numbered 120, over ten times as many as witnessed the wedding of Harryo herself, as well as those of Ladies Sarah and Gin Spencer and all three Fane sisters, Ladies Sarah, Augusta and Maria (all six of whom, incidentally, were married by special licence).

The one part of the wedding preparations that did demand both effort and expense in the weeks beforehand was the bride's dress. The height of Regency bridal fashion was a gown of delicate, handmade Brussels lace, often laid over an under dress of white or silver and accompanied by a matching lace veil – an ensemble that, like a court outfit, did not come cheap. Heiress Lady Sarah Fane's lace robe was said to have cost upwards of 500 guineas (almost £50,000 today) when she married Lord Villiers (soon to be Lord Jersey) in 1804, while Harryo's lace veil alone was thought to be worth 100 guineas. In 1810, it was estimated that on her combined bridal attire, including feathered headdress and diamond ornaments, the new Marchioness of Ely had spent as much as 1,000 guineas. All astronomical sums when an everyday gown could be purchased for somewhere between one and eight guineas, and entirely out of reach of all but the most privileged of brides. With her parents feeling the pinch, and soon to have another mouth to feed, Isabella Calvert must have been delighted when her Aunt Knox made her a wedding gift of a splendid lace gown, veil and cap to be married in.

Since she was marrying in church, Isabella would have had an eye to the proprieties when deciding on her gown, factoring in long sleeves or adding a pelisse to cover up an otherwise fashionably low-cut dress. Those marrying in their own homes had more scope, and would probably pick a design that rivalled the most modish evening attire; perhaps something they might wear again, since white was not only the height of fashion for bridal wear, but on trend for women's clothing generally. Whatever style they opted for, there appears to have been no greater compliment for a bride than to be described as looking 'interesting' in her matrimonial ensemble, an epithet applied by the newspapers to a score of aristocratic young women married in the Regency.

While Isabella's dress was taken care of courtesy of her aunt, like all other genteel parents Mr and Mrs Calvert would have had to fund what later came to be known as a 'trousseau' – the cache of clothes that a young bride carried into her new life as a wife. In Isabella's case these took several weeks to procure, from both shops near her Hertfordshire home and smart West End establishments. The shopping list certainly included numerous muslin dresses, both silk and satin spencers,[9] a sealskin shawl, various caps and £100 worth of lace for trimming, the last a wedding gift from her grandmother. Normally, it would also have incorporated everything from hats and shoes to new undergarments and stockings, nightgowns and detachable pockets. How large exactly the hoard was depended on how deep the family's pockets were; it was entirely possible to find dressmakers proudly displaying in their warehouses trousseaus that ran to more than sixty dresses – a new morning and evening gown for every day of the honeymoon.

Naturally, the purchase of the trousseau could be an expensive endeavour. In 1801 the Duke of Devonshire laid out more than

---

9   The iconic cropped jackets with long sleeves.

£3,300 (over £250,000 today) on the wedding clothes of Harryo's older sister, sourced from the haberdashers who supplied the Princess of Wales. The £850 splashed out by the Earl Spencer on Sarah in 1813 was a comparatively moderate sum, but yet still colossal given that 98 per cent of the population had less money to live on in a year. Both brides would clearly be much-envied, though perhaps not so much as heiress Catherine Tylney Long, who was able to incorporate into her trousseau in 1812 – at a cost of over £20,000 – a selection of spectacular jewels, including matching sets of rubies, emeralds and pearls.

Jewels worn by a bride on the day of marriage – an essential part of her outfit – were usually either inherited or received as wedding gifts. Mrs Calvert scoffed at the sight of Lady Anna Maria Stanhope 'loaded with ornaments' at her wedding to the future Duke of Bedford in 1808, but the poor bride had no doubt felt duty-bound to wear not only the pearls that had belonged to her groom's grandmother, but also the 'superb diamond cross' and 'precious stones' given to her by Queen Charlotte and the Prince Regent. And all despite the fact that, as Mrs Calvert acknowledged, she looked far prettier in a simple muslin gown without any ornament whatsoever. She no doubt advised her own daughter to choose sparingly from a jewellery box overflowing thanks to the wedding gifts of her Knox cousins, who had supplied the bride with a selection of splendid necklaces, earrings, brooches and bracelets.

It was not uncommon for the bridegroom to bestow a gift upon his new wife, too. Catherine Tylney Long's scapegrace future spouse William Wellesley Pole made her a present of a stunning set of diamonds, comprising a necklace, drop earrings and tiara, to wear as she made her vows – though in a sign of things to come, the bill for 25,000 guineas (well over £1.5m today) had effectively been paid by plundering her own inheritance.

In addition to any more personal gift he might proffer, it was traditional for the groom to bestow at least one new carriage on his bride, too. Commissioning it was all part of the preparations for setting up home together – preparations that were far more important than those for the wedding itself. The weeks leading up to their marriage had found Lord Duncannon and Lady Maria Fane busy picking out soft furnishings and tableware, and engaging new servants. Lord Althorp gave up his bachelor pad in Albany[10] (promptly snapped up by Lord Byron) ahead of his wedding, taking on a lease of a house in Pall Mall for him and Esther; while Charles Arbuthnot oversaw the redecoration of a bedroom for his young bride, who felt pleasantly spoiled by the attentions. 'Let everything go on as it is,' Harriet had begged as to his other household arrangements, 'only take me & my maid in.'

When the wedding day dawned, a couple's smart new equipage would be on standby in the mews, four horses ready and waiting to whisk the bride and groom straight off to their honeymoon retreat, often as soon as the knot was tied. For if you married fashionably in the Regency, it seems the shorter your celebration, the more impromptu and informal the whole occasion felt, the better.

Even such an immoderately wealthy couple as Lady Frances Anne Vane-Tempest and Charles, Lord Stewart, whose penchant for opulence and pomp would be roundly condemned as vulgar in later years, kept most things about their wedding day relatively low-key. Their congregation of at least fifty 'intimate

---

10   The elegant apartment complex in Piccadilly, designed for bachelors of wealth and rank.

friends' was a pretty large one by Regency standards, but the
guests invited to Lady Antrim's house in Bruton Street on the
evening of 3 April 1819, ten days after the Chancery case was
resolved in the couple's favour, were simply invited to adjourn to
her drawing room soon after 9 p.m. to witness the brief marriage
ceremony, all over within the hour. With suitable nonchalance,
Charles's brother, Lord Castlereagh, arrived only after hosting a
dinner party at his own home.

Not only was the day not the long, meticulously planned and
minutely timetabled affair it is today, but the kind of mishaps
that might be deemed a major catastrophe if they occurred at a
modern wedding also seem to have been reported without any
angst whatsoever. Harryo and her affianced Lord Granville, the
*Morning Post* told its readers, were left kicking their heels for
nearly an hour after the Dean of Windsor failed to arrive at her
father's house in Chiswick by 9 p.m. as planned, leaving the
Duke of Devonshire to send for the local curate to come and
unite them instead. Worse happened at heiress Catherine Tylney
Long's wedding at St James's church, Piccadilly in 1812: halfway
through, the groom realised he had forgotten to purchase a
ring for his bride and the ceremony had to be paused while a
messenger was dispatched to a nearby jeweller.

Yet for all its informality, a contemporary British bride
stepping back in time would still find much about a Regency
wedding ceremony familiar. Frances Anne was one of many
women supported by two 'bride's maids' – friends in her case,
though often they were sisters. She was 'given away' like many
a modern bride too; the place of her father was filled by the
Duke of Wellington, who appears to have been a favourite
to perform the office, as was the Prince Regent, who happily

obliged the daughters of various noble friends. The conduct of the marriage ceremony and the content of the vows would likewise be recognisable to anyone who has wed in an Anglican church; albeit, of course, that the bride would promise 'to love, cherish, and to *obey*' her husband, and would be the only one of the pair to receive a wedding ring. There would not, however, have been any hymns during the service, nor a kiss between man and wife to seal the deal. Such a display in public would have been unthinkable.

The shedding of copious tears, though, has always been acceptable wedding behaviour. Lady Antrim proudly told Frances, Lady Shelley that her daughter had 'shed abundant tears' at her ceremony, much like Lady Anna Maria Stanhope, who 'cried all the time' on her wedding day in 1808, according to Mrs Calvert. And it wasn't only the ladies overwhelmed by what was, in Regency vernacular, an 'awful' (for which read awe-inspiring) occasion. As William Lyttelton's sister reported, their journey from Mayfair to Wimbledon for his wedding to Lady Sarah gave plenty of time for the bridegroom to grow nervous about his impending matrimonials. 'When she knows the carriage how her heart will beat!' she remembered he remarked as they entered the park, at which point his fond sister, surmising that his own heart 'was not at that moment very peaceably resting within him', was moved to take his hand. 'Do not make me shed tears before the time,' was the admonishment she received for her troubles. When it was time for the tiny congregation of eight to 'march in procession' to the estate's compact church, Mrs Pole-Carew thought her new sister-in-law looked overwrought by the event, too – 'as if she could hardly support herself,' she said.

Their walk back to the house after the service was rather more brisk. With daytime ceremonies, it was usual for the bride's parents to host a *dejeune* – a wedding breakfast, in the *ton's* parlance – and the Spencers had laid on a light collation by way of celebration, which included 'an enormous plumb cake' much enjoyed by Mrs Pole-Carew. In some cases, this post-ceremony party was a little more lavish. After the four o'clock marriage of Lady Anna Maria Stanhope and Lord Tavistock, for instance, the assembled company were also treated to the Regency equivalent of a wedding disco: music in her parents' garden from the band of the Life Guards, his Lordship's regiment.

Where the marriage was an at-home, evening affair, the bride and groom were more likely to have dined with their guests beforehand, since it was common with an 'owl light' wedding for the happy couple to hop into their carriage almost the minute they were officially man and wife. In 1804 Lady Sarah Fane and Lord Villiers were clattering over the cobbles on their way out of London as soon as the ceremony at her father's house was over. Her sister Lady Maria also departed post-haste after her 9 p.m. marriage the following year, leaving with Lord Duncannon within an hour of the parson beginning the service. Maria's new mother-in-law Lady Bessborough still had enough of her evening left to pay a call, dash off a letter to her lover and travel with her husband out to her sister's house at Chiswick.

Even those who married in daylight would not usually spend much more than a couple of hours celebrating with their loved ones. Mrs Pole-Carew, having set out from central London with her brother William at 2 p.m., was making her farewells to the Spencers at Wimbledon not long after 4 p.m., more than satisfied that all boded well. She left the newly married Lytteltons, 'one munching a hunch of dry bread, the other relishing a piece of hard biscuit, side by side on a sofa, looks beaming with love and joy.' In their case, there was no carriage waiting to carry them off. Instead, Lord and Lady Spencer were 'to leave the coast clear immediately after dinner' as the couple were to make the Wimbledon house 'their headquarters during the compleat honeymoon'.

Modern as it might seem, 'honeymoon' was a word in common usage by the Regency, though it then referred not so much to an indulgent post-nuptial holiday as to the period of time immediately after the wedding: 'the first month after marriage, when there is nothing but tenderness and pleasure', as Samuel Johnson's dictionary defined it. Yet the honeymoon as we know it was already well on its way to being established. In the previous century, travel in the honeymoon period had often been about visiting extended family to receive their congratulations, the happy couple commonly accompanied on their wedding tour by a sibling or bride's-maid. By the Regency, it was becoming conventional in upper-class circles for newly-weds to retreat from the eyes of society to pass the honeymoon (or at least part of it) alone, to consummate the marriage, of course, but also to get to know one another better.

The typical honeymoon retreat was a country house lent for the purpose by a family member. The new Lord and Lady Stewart followed the prevailing fashion, sweeping off in a handsome post-chaise and four to Lord Castlereagh's house at Cray in Kent on the night of their wedding, where they spent the first week of the honeymoon in company with his wife's collection of zoo animals. Clearly they relished their seclusion from the polite world, because when the Castlereaghs came down from London with a large party of guests, the newly-weds did not stay. Instead, they moved on to Wildernesse House, lent by Charles's uncle Lord Camden, for a further week of private pleasures.

For a young couple used to socialising primarily with members of their own sex, and hardly ever left alone before, a sudden period of absolute isolation can't have been easy, and their solitude was consequently rarely entirely uninterrupted. Before she left Wimbledon, for example, William and Lady Sarah extracted a firm promise from Mrs Pole-Carew that she would '*dine and sleep there, before it was long*'. Similarly, the new Lady Duncannon had been happy to receive visits from her stepmother and her sister Sarah, Lady Jersey, who was able to report to Lady Bessborough that Maria had sung and played for them in good spirits. Interestingly, though, the family were anxious to correct newspaper reports that the Duncannons had left their honeymoon retreat to dine with the Duke and Duchess of Devonshire less than a week after their wedding, which they clearly felt reflected badly on the fledgling marriage.

For debutantes fresh from the marriage market, the honeymoon period was their first taste of the freedoms that came with being a matron instead of a young miss. Harriet Fane was one of many who longed to spread her wings, begging Charles to take her to the Mediterranean, and more particularly to Spain, where her brothers had been fighting with the army. But with much of war-torn Europe still inhospitable to travellers at the time of her wedding in January 1814, she had settled for passing the honeymoon period with Charles in the Northamptonshire countryside instead, not abandoning but merely postponing her ambitions.

William Lyttelton and Lady Sarah, however, had been

determined to venture further afield for a little adventure before settling down to sensible married life, Sarah having heartily wished as a debutante that 'it was the fashion for young ladies to go and travel' and William being no less eager himself. Encountering the same issue as Harriet, they had picked out a safer destination off the typical European tourist route. They set sail for Sweden at the end of June 1813 and enjoyed (after a choppy journey lasting a fortnight) a few months of touring and sightseeing. The whole experience Sarah relished as much because of the 'incessant, undeservable, and, if possible, still increasing kindness and attention' of her 'Mr. L' as anything else. From Sweden, they made a spontaneous skip on to St Petersburg – a somewhat daring decision since Napoleon had only retreated from Moscow the previous year – and did not leave its icy-cold environs until the end of May 1814, by which time, thanks to Napoleon's abdication, they were able to travel safely home through Germany and France.

The Lytteltons might have been bold in refusing to let the long-running war shatter their dreams of a post-nuptial tour abroad, just the two of them – an adventure that lasted almost eighteen months. But their honeymoon was most certainly not the most unusual of the Regency period. That distinction must go to the De Lanceys, whose plans were not just curtailed by the war with France, but almost derailed completely. It was no more than ten days into the new Lady De Lancey's idyllic honeymoon in early April 1815 that duty had called for her new husband, forcing him to abandon their tranquil Scottish retreat and return to active service overseas.

Magdalene's had been a whirlwind romance. Colonel Sir William De Lancey, a distinguished army veteran, had strolled into her home city of Edinburgh just six months earlier, and into her heart soon after that. Tall, dark and handsome, the bright, American-born officer, with his fashionably windswept curls and shining military crosses, must have caused quite a stir among the ladies when he had arrived in the Scottish capital to take up his first ever peacetime posting, as Deputy Quartermaster General in North Britain. But it was Magdalene, the 21-year-old daughter of a Scottish baronet and prominent scientist, who had caught his eye, charming him with her girlish, gentle beauty and cultivated mind. By December, the 38-year-old De Lancey had become a fixture in the drawing room of her father's country house at Dunglass, thirty miles or so outside Edinburgh, and by March, the banns were being called for their wedding. Tied in holy matrimony in the city's historic Greyfriars Kirk on 4 April, they had travelled straight out to Dunglass for what they expected to be a quiet honeymoon period, with the estate's sweeping views of the wild Scottish sea and wooded Lammermuir hills providing a romantic backdrop for their first weeks of married life.

Or so it would have been, had not war clouds been gathering ominously on the continent again as their wedding day approached. On 26 February, Napoleon had sensationally escaped from the Mediterranean island of Elba, to which he had been exiled after his abdication the previous year, and headed back to France. Encountering little resistance from the forces he had so lately commanded, the former emperor had been able to re-establish his reign by the end of March and had begun putting the army on a war footing again. It was sudden and unexpected news, intensely unwelcome to a war-weary nation, let alone to the newly wedded De Lanceys. It possibly reached them ahead of their wedding, but like most military men Sir William had probably not felt unduly alarmed by what was, at first, considered to be simply an audacious attempt on the part of the deposed French leader, and likely to be swiftly quashed. It was only when a messenger came thundering up the drive at Dunglass with instructions for him to report to Horse Guards – immediately – that the true impact of Napoleon's flight became clear. The Duke of Wellington was already in Brussels preparing for a resumption of hostilities against the French, and one of his earliest actions had been to call for De Lancey, a trusted comrade of many years' standing, to return to his side as his quartermaster general. Powerless to refuse – even had he wanted to – William had been back in London a mere seventeen days after making his wedding vows. The honeymoon, he must have thought, was officially over.

But he had underestimated his new bride. Instead of meekly agreeing to wait in Scotland for news, Magdalene had urged William to let her follow him to Brussels, where she must have hoped to continue with a honeymoon of sorts. It was a brave move. While she could be fairly confident that as an officer's wife she would not be deprived of any home comforts, taking herself off to a theatre of war was not without risk. If the worst happened and the Allies were this time defeated by Napoleon, her husband killed in the fighting, she could be stranded abroad without friends and family, unable to make a safe passage home and vulnerable to potentially violent and vengeful French forces. Even if the Allies were successful in their mission, victory might not come quickly. Magdalene could endure weeks of uncertainty and anxiety, alone in a foreign country for the first time in her life. With a 22-year military career behind him, Sir William understood all this far better than his new wife. But the idea of keeping her with him seems to have been too tempting to resist. So in early June, Magdalene had left England behind. Quitting the country in 'violent spirits', she joined her husband at his lodging in the Count de Lannoy's townhouse, a few doors down from Wellington himself.

She had been greeted by a festive atmosphere that belied the very real preparations being made for war, and had observed with a touch of disapproval the gaiety and social round of British families like the Capels and the Lennoxes, still whirling on despite the ever-increasing number of troops and officers disembarking in Belgium. Neither Magdalene nor William had any appetite for the parties and picnics of the wealthy British set. They had time only for each other. 'Fortunately, my husband had scarcely any business to do, and he only went to the office for about an hour every day,' she recalled happily – if naively. The besotted colonel – renowned for being both conscientious and dutiful – must have sought help from his staff to ensure that he and his wife could enjoy some semblance of the honeymoon they had been forced to cut short. After all, as Quartermaster General he had overall responsibility for the movement and supply of an Anglo-Allied force numbering in the region of 70,000 soldiers. His painful struggles between head and heart had been evident for all to see. 'Poor De Lancey sighs for his Caledonia cottage in the middle of all his prospects of military reputation,' remarked one of his junior officers.

As she waited for him to return to her each day, Magdalene, still getting used to herself as Lady De Lancey, wife of an important military man, was content to sit at the window and watch her neighbours parading in the park. By her own admission she saw little of Brussels, and even less of its inhabitants. She and William generally walked out together at 3 p.m. when they knew most other people would be sitting down to dinner; and dined at 6 p.m., just as the rest of society was venturing out, occasionally inviting one or two of William's friends to join them. They accepted no invitations themselves. De Lancey had no interest in the race meetings and drunken dinners amusing other officers; and Magdalene wasted no time on morning calls or evening soirees. It was 'a scene of happiness, so perfect, so unalloyed,' she later said. 'I was entirely enjoying life.'

But of course, despite appearances, this was no conventional honeymoon. Close to the seemingly blissful surface, shadows lurked. Magdalene was horribly aware that a battle was coming and that she would be separated from her new husband much sooner, and in much more worrying circumstances, than she could ever have expected when, wreathed in smiles, she had walked out of church ten weeks earlier.

## Chapter Seven

# Fragile Lives

IT WAS ON the evening of 15 June 1815, as she watched her husband dress for the first dinner engagement he had been persuaded to attend since her arrival in Brussels, that Magdalene De Lancey began to grow uneasy. William was strangely reluctant to go, delaying for this reason and then that, lingering in their apartment, until at last she tenderly affixed his medals to his coat and ushered him out. It would be no more than an hour before she came to suspect what he knew already: that these were the last precious moments of their honeymoon.

She had begun to fear it when an aide-de-camp rode furiously up to the house and enquired as to Sir William's whereabouts. Unsettled by his demeanour, she had remained at the window after his departure, only to see her husband gallop past a few minutes later, dismount hastily at the Duke of Wellington's house and run inside. It looked ominous, but there was still a chance that it was a false alarm. William had been able to brush off all the rumours of an imminent battle that had been buzzing round Brussels in recent days; and, as she well knew, a swathe of officers – Wellington included – were confidently expecting to spend the coming hours in the Duchess of Richmond's ballroom, gaily whirling around the dance floor in their dress uniforms and sipping the best champagne the city had to offer. 'Duchess, you may give your ball with the greatest safety without fear of interruption,' the duke had assured their host just days previously.

The more time that passed, however, the more Magdalene had become convinced that this was the day she had been dreading ever since the messenger had arrived at Dunglass. Britain's interminable conflict with France, which had begun in 1793 and dragged on, near continuously, for the last twenty-one years, had then seemed to be over, for good. Yet now it appeared to be about to resume in earnest, and to wrench her husband from her side. When William arrived home at 9 p.m., he confirmed it. Napoleon's troops had stormed into the Netherlands and the Allied forces were readying themselves for a great battle the following day.

'Seeing my wretched face he bid me not be foolish, for it would soon be all over,' Magdalene remembered. As he flitted to and from the office that night, completely absorbed by the arduous task of mobilising the army; as the news filtered into the duchess's crowded ballroom, sending officers scattering, she had paced around their rooms in a sort of stupor. The carefree happiness of her wedding day, when they had promised to have and to hold, till death us do part, must suddenly have seemed a very long time ago. Marriage was always a vulnerable bond in Regency Britain: illness could strike suddenly and incurably;

childbirth snatch a woman years before her time. But Magdalene was about to find out what it was like to fear for the life of a husband, risked for the sake of King and country.

Though the appeal of a suitor in a smart uniform had waned somewhat as the war went on, it was still an experience familiar to plenty of her contemporaries. Not least because the ongoing fighting had provided opportunities for men of genteel birth without inherited money to obtain the riches and advancement in rank that made them look like good husband material. Captain Charles Paget of the navy, fifth of six sons of the Earl of Uxbridge, had married his wife Elizabeth after returning from the Mediterranean in 1805 with a '*whack* of Prize Money' that he estimated at about £50,000 – 'which for a younger brother is not a bad fortune to have made,' he boasted. Though the sum turned out to be about half as much in reality, it still meant he had sufficient wealth to settle on a bride, and to purchase a small country estate for their home. In a time of war, an ambitious and well-connected younger son like Charles looked like a pretty good catch to parents and chaperones alike: long stints in action meant long stints on full pay, guaranteeing his income, as well as a greater chance of promotion or honours and, of course, more prize money.

Balanced against that, though, had to be the risk of early widowhood. Even when a military man was not cast in the mould of former general, Charles, Lord Stewart – who was renowned for his gallantry and seemed at times during his career to have 'no other object in view than to go in quest of death' – losing him in service was still a very real prospect. Estimates suggest that between 1803 and 1815, about one army officer in every ten lost his life, many of them from aristocratic or landed gentry families.[11] Harriet Arbuthnot's favourite brother Charles was one of the 426 army officers – of a total force of around 10,500 – who died in 1813, killed at the battle of Vitoria in Spain, not long after she had announced her contentious engagement. As always, more men had died that year from disease or misadventure than were lost to enemy fire. In the navy especially, the risk was high: not only were the odds of survival shorter overall, but mishaps like ship fires and tropical illnesses were the cause of 80 per cent of all deaths. Harriet had lost another brother, Neville, to yellow fever six years earlier, when he was a naval lieutenant of nineteen, serving in Barbados.

If a husband did dodge both disease and enemy bullets and returned home alive, there was still a one-in-six or -seven chance that, if he was serving with the army, he would come home with a serious – possibly life-changing – injury, particularly in the latter years of the Napoleonic Wars. Lord Stewart's only lasting wound was to his face, his eyesight forever slightly impaired, but a fellow comrade of the action in the Iberian peninsula, Brigade-Major George Napier, returned to Britain in 1812 and began courting his future wife with only one arm, an amputation having been performed in the wake of the storming of Ciudad Rodrigo. Considering 'the service he was employed upon,' a mutual friend told his brother, 'one could hardly expect him to come off with whole bones.' That being so, another officer had learned from his sisters that as more and more men of his profession arrived back in Britain with 'Tanny, Emaciated'

---

11 Diaries and letters of the ladies of the *ton* make clear that there was scarcely an aristocratic family who did not have a close relative fighting, at some stage, in the Napoleonic Wars. Magdalene's brother Basil was in the navy, like two of the Spencers' sons, Bob and his younger brother Frederick. The Bessboroughs had a son, another Frederick, in the army, and so did both the Earl of Westmorland and Mrs Calvert, who also had a nephew in the navy. Harriet Arbuthnot had four brothers who donned military uniform in all.

faces, some of them 'wanting legs, others Arms & Eyes', the less inclined the ladies were to look favourably on a redcoat.

The likely periods of separation had also made marriage with a military man look a little less desirable. De Lancey was not, in fact, the only officer dragged away from his honeymoon by the call of duty: George Napier's brother William had left his wife a mere three weeks after their wedding in 1812 to return to Portugal, to assist an army depleted of officers after the siege of Badajoz. The new Mrs Caroline Napier had been left waiting at home for the Brigade-Major's woefully brief letters, unable to comfort him as he grieved over the death of his best friend, or to say a proper goodbye before he threw himself headlong into the bloody battle of Salamanca. Lord Stewart's first wife had faced similar trials. Charles was away for the better part of four years during the period he served alongside Wellington in Portugal, and was still abroad when she died, in his brother's arms, after an operation to remove a cyst from her head in 1812. 'The only, & God knows it is the only, reason I have for one instant to condemn myself for having married,' Captain Charles Paget once confessed, 'arises from the misery it is to both my poor dear Elizabeth and myself – these cruel intervals from each other.'

To 'follow the drum' as Magdalene had chosen to do was never much more satisfactory. It might appeal to a debutante who craved travel and adventure, but it still entailed an eventual separation from her spouse – unless, that is, she was prepared to suffer the worst hardships of life on campaign, which might include bedding down outside 'under the canopy of Heaven' as one colonel's wife did. In reality, most of the officers' wives who had come out to the peninsula in the previous phase of the war had remained in relative comfort in Lisbon instead of travelling with their husbands to the front.

None of it was what Magdalene had expected when she accepted William's proposals. 'I had no apprehension of the trials that awaited me,' she said of her whirlwind romance. When her future husband had marched into her life in the autumn of 1814, peace had seemed secure. Napoleon's armies had surrendered. The emperor himself had been safely exiled on Elba. Families had been flooding to the continent, for sightseeing trips and money-saving stays. Britain had only just finished its jubilant victory celebrations – the street parties and processions, fireworks, fêtes, grand balls and bell-ringing that had gone on right through the summer. William had no doubt assured his bride that, with his Edinburgh posting confirmed for the foreseeable future, he was at no risk of being sent off to the ongoing conflict in America like some of his fellow officers. In fact, the picture he sketched of their first few years of married life was probably free from all the worry and upheaval that had been known to women like Catherine Stewart and Caroline Napier. Perhaps he had even talked about selling out in the not-too-distant future.

But things had changed incredibly quickly – 'the return of Bonaparte broke upon the world like a hurricane,' one army officer put it. 'It seemed as if all was to begin again & that all our former toils & blood & triumphs had been in vain,' he had written with dismay. As Magdalene paced their Brussels apartment on the night of 15 June, she had almost as much reason to bitterly regret that the emperor had slipped his noose. It had put all her happiness at risk.

In the early hours of the morning when her husband's work was finally done, she had snatched some final moments alone with him, the two of them leaning out of the open window of their apartment, watching the infantry regiments march out of the city to the sound of the fifes and bugles. Then, at 6 a.m., they had parted, Magdalene making for Antwerp, where William, anxious that she not be exposed to any unnecessary danger, had arranged for her to wait for him in safety. Touched by his tender concern, she had gone without argument, his confident prediction that it would be a short and decisive battle ringing in her ears.

She had holed herself up inside the town's principal inn, shutting her windows to block out the distant rumbling of the artillery, and determining not to stir outside for fear of hearing either cannon fire or malicious rumours of an Allied defeat. Continuing to dispatch messages to her husband at the front, she had refused to be infected by the fear that engulfed the town when panicked families fleeing Brussels began to arrive, swiftly followed by the first casualties from the initial engagement at Quatre Bras. Restlessly, impatiently, she had just gone on waiting for word that all was over, struggling to believe that her confident, competent husband, who had survived so many campaigns, would really be hurt this time. 'The possibility of his being wounded never glanced into my mind,' she later wrote, 'till I was told that he was killed.'

In fact, in all the chaos that followed the final, decisive battle at Waterloo on 18 June, two days after the skirmish at Quatre Bras, poor Magdalene had to suffer the agony of several misreports: first, William had come through it all unscathed; then he had died on the battlefield from his wounds. From the heights of feverish happiness, she had been sent plunging into a state of 'violent agitation'. It was not until nearly two days after the British victory that she finally heard the truth: De Lancey was not dead, but he was critically injured.

Magdalene had convinced herself that as one of Wellington's right-hand men William would be 'less exposed than in the midst of the battle', but her husband had obviously shielded her from the reality of the situation, for, having served alongside him for the entirety of his five-year campaign in the peninsula, he knew the duke always liked to be right in the thick of the action, and consequently so were his loyal staff officers. A subaltern spotted their splendid cavalcade on the morning of that final overthrow of Napoleon at Waterloo, looking 'as gay and unconcerned as if they were riding to meet the hounds in some quiet English county.' This time, however, in one of the bloodiest battles most of them had ever experienced in their careers, the duke's inner circle had paid heavily. Two of his eight aides-de-camp had died. His military secretary Lord Fitzroy Somerset had been shot in the arm and knocked off his horse while riding close by his side. The cavalry commander Lord Uxbridge had been struck in the leg as they talked, and only kept in his saddle by the firm grasp of Wellington's outstretched hand. Sir William's luck had run out midway through the afternoon when, riding next to his old friend and comrade, he had been struck on the back by a ricocheting cannonball. He was thrown with great force over his horse's head, and eight of his ribs had been ripped from his spine, the splinters of one puncturing a lung.

As soon as the news of his survival was confirmed, Magdalene had become frantic in her determination to reach him. She embarked on a journey that proved to be a perilous one – the sort that might easily have overborne a young woman so sheltered from danger as she had always been. Military wagons heavily laden with wounded soldiers clogged the roads to Mont St Jean, where he had been taken, and she encountered more than one Prussian soldier inclined to violence, drawing up the blind of her carriage to plead with one who chased her vehicle with his sword drawn menacingly. Then, as she rattled through Waterloo, scene of the late battle, her horses screamed at the stench of blood and rotting bodies – all the horrors her husband had tried so hard to protect her from. Yet despite all that, she pushed on. Less than three months she had been William's wife, and she feared she might already be a widow. Finally, in what a fellow officer freely described as a hovel, she found her gentle husband, lying on a makeshift bed and holding out his hand to her. 'Come Magdalene,' was his greeting, 'this is a sad business, is it not?'

The scene that confronted her must have been unlike anything she had ever encountered before. The little cottage 'had been plundered and set on fire by the French,' she remembered, a broken teacup and sack of chaff for a pillow among its few remaining amenities. William himself was obviously in a bad way. Though his attendants hastened to assure her that the surgeons entertained hopes of a recovery, it was obvious that his newly-wed bride, bred in luxury and never yet touched by tragedy, would need to become his nurse. And with no one but her new maid Emma, engaged just before her departure from England, to offer her emotional support.

She handled it with incredible composure. Day after day, she tackled unfamiliar tasks without complaint: changing his soiled dressings, applying leeches and ripping up her petticoat to bathe his limbs. Night after night, she sat beside his bed, his hand tucked in hers, unwilling to leave him for even a moment. All the time, she was growing ever more aware that his situation was hopeless – though loving, noble William was valiantly maintaining the pretence of hope for her sake. 'Even if I recover completely,' she remembered him saying, 'I should never think of serving again, nobody would ask such a thing, and we should settle down quietly at home for the rest of our lives.'

It was a lovely thought. Twelve miles away in Brussels, Fitzroy Somerset, minus an amputated right arm, was already making plans with his wife Emily and five-week-old daughter; considerably thinner, weaker and in a great deal of pain, but thanking 'Providence for the preservation of [his] life, amid so many dangers.' Lord Uxbridge, too, was soon to be reunited with his wife. The loss of his leg was a life-changing injury, certainly, but she found him looking 'as lively or *more lively than ever*'. William, though, was steadily declining, as the doctors finally admitted to his young wife on 24 June.

On the night of the twenty-fifth, ten days after they had parted in Brussels, knowing they did not have long, Magdalene had climbed into his small, uncomfortably narrow bed and laid next to him again, both of them sleeping soundly for the first time since their ordeal began. The following afternoon, her husband of just twelve weeks succumbed to his injuries. As an eager young cornet in the Light Dragoons, he had been there right at the start of the French wars in 1793, and in their dying hours he had become one of their final victims.

Wellington, who had known and valued De Lancey for many years, shared some of his bride's engulfing sadness, declaring him an 'excellent officer' who 'would have risen to great distinction had he lived.' But for Magdalene, Sir William's prospects as a husband had been even better. 'I saw [him] loved and respected by everyone. My life gliding on, like a gay dream, in his care,' she later said in a unique account of her time in Brussels. Looking back on her three short months of marriage, she was filled with sadness – but also gratitude. 'I do not forget the perfection of my happiness – while it lasted – and I believe there are not many who after a long life can say that they have felt so much of it,' she wrote.

The bloody conclusion to the long-running conflict with France snatched from Magdalene a promising chance of happiness, but hers was not a sadness known only to military wives. For every couple who wed in the Regency, 'till death us do part' was a vow weighted with so much more resonance than in the modern world. Even on the home front, good health and long life was not to be taken for granted. Not even by the members of high society, who ate well, lived in clean, comfortable homes and were more than able to pay a physician's fees. In fact, life expectancy at birth for the generation of aristocrats who went looking for love in the first decades of the nineteenth century was just forty-six for a man and forty-nine for a woman. In reality, many lived to be at least seventy, if not older, but few newly-weds would be so bold as to enter the married state confidently expecting to reach their silver wedding anniversary.

Young couples would have been acutely aware that illness and death could haunt their marital home early on; many would have seen at least one sibling die in infancy or childhood, or lost a parent long before they reached adulthood. People might not die of 'little trifling colds' but a chill, or a fever, or an intermittent cough could not be considered trivial, however young the sufferer or however healthy they had previously seemed. They could be the signs of something both more serious and less treatable, as they were in the case of Catherine, Lady Aberdeen. After intermittent periods of illness, she was diagnosed in the spring of 1811, six years into her marriage, with 'an inflammation of the lungs' – almost certainly, as the family must have realised, the consumption, or tuberculosis, that had killed her mother, the first Lady Abercorn.

Catherine's condition had deteriorated quickly, and by December that year as many as four physicians had been attending the 28-year-old mother of three at the Aberdeens' house in London's Argyll Street, along with a specialist from Scotland. He was 'said to have performed wonders', according to her attentive husband, who swore to his brother that 'what medicine can do will be done'. Unfortunately, having no antibiotics in their armoury, there was very little that Regency physicians could do for a consumptive patient. They were not yet even firmly convinced that the disease was contagious, instead explaining away infections that rippled through families like Catherine's with talk of constitutional predispositions and inborn susceptibility. With no cure, their recommended treatments focused simply on slowing the progress of the illness, the favourite prescription being a prolonged stay in a warmer climate – preferably one reached by boat, since sailing on the sea was thought to be especially beneficial. Patients like Catherine, however, whose consumption was at a relatively advanced stage by late 1811, would probably simply be urged to rest, and given laudanum to ease the pain of the coughing that would have racked her body. She was certainly bled regularly, too, which, regrettably, left her considerably weaker. In spite of all her husband's determined efforts to save her, she died – as he had realised deep down that she would – at the end of February 1812, claimed by the same disease that had already killed her brother Claud and would also kill her sister Maria, and probably her eldest brother James as well.

Responsible for as many as one in three adult deaths in London, consumption was generally on the rise in the early nineteenth century. A disease that affected the rich just the same as the poor – a good diet and access to an expensive doctor conferring almost no advantage on the aristocracy – it robbed numerous members of the beau monde of loved ones, along with diseases like cancer, cholera and typhoid. Lady Gertrude Stuart lost her husband of seven years to the latter in August 1809 and tragically, it killed her too, a mere nineteen days later. She was obviously taken suddenly ill, as she died in a coaching inn on the road back to London; in the space of one fateful month her three sons and one daughter became orphans.

The most obvious threat to a young wife's health, however, was part and parcel of married life. Childbirth was a matter of course for most aristocratic wives; not just because motherhood was seen as their natural role, or because contraceptive options were limited, but because there remained considerable pressure on high-born women (particularly the wives of peers) to produce male heirs to inherit the family money and titles. Women could expect to 'lie in' multiple times during their marriage, bearing on average six or seven live children, the first often within a year of their wedding. Indeed, for some women, a failure to fall pregnant within weeks of the wedding day was a source of great stress and embarrassment. According to Harryo Cavendish, Sarah, Lady Jersey, 'burst into tears' when she heard about her younger sister's pregnancy and 'coloured like fire' when asked politely about it. Still not with child herself eighteen months after her marriage, Sarah had grown noticeably skeletal and pale, which her acquaintances attributed to her worry over her infertility and her attempts at 'quacking' herself.

Pregnancy itself was not usually a great trial for upper-class wives. Most were able to carry on their lives much as normal right up until their confinement, it being perfectly permissible to appear in public while heavily pregnant. Lady Jersey's sister, Maria, Lady Duncannon, was still out socialising – and staying out till gone midnight – little more than a fortnight before her first baby was born in 1807. Labour, on the other hand, was not an experience many Regency women relished. Maria's mother-in-law Lady Bessborough, herself a mother of six, called it 'a dreadful operation, however often it may come'.

It was also a potentially life-threatening one. Mortality rates were actually not as high as we might think: only 1 or 2 per cent of all women died in childbed, 10 or 20 in every 1,000. But that's still over a hundred times more than die during pregnancy, labour or from related complications in twenty-first-century Britain, and not reflective of the lifetime risk, which was higher, how much so depending on how many times a woman gave birth. Given that most wives knew a friend or close family member who had died, either in labour or not long afterwards, the odds must often have seemed much shorter than the statistics suggest, too. As Isabella Calvert prepared for her wedding in August 1810, she and her mother, then heavily pregnant herself, could name two friends lost that month alone to childbirth: Lady Deerhurst, married less than three years, and Lady Mildmay, barely a year. Both women were in their early twenties.

For both expectant mothers and their relatives, each birth seems to have felt almost like a game of Russian roulette, with unproblematic deliveries in the past considered no guarantee whatsoever of future safety. Having suffered a nail-biting wait for news of her younger sister Olivia's confinement in 1818, Sydney, Lady Morgan and her husband Charles together urged her to think better of risking another pregnancy, simply because she had 'fared so well' with her latest (though perhaps they would have done better to direct their pleas to her husband). What contributed to the sense of powerlessness was the fact that it was so difficult to predict which ladies would come safely through the ordeal and which would not. Only a year apart in age as they were, both in good health and both with access to the best medical advice money could buy, there was no apparent reason why Lady Sarah Lyttelton and her sister-in-law Esther, Lady Althorp, should not both have sailed through their labours when they found themselves in 'near expectation of lying in' at about the same time in June 1818; but, tragically, only one of them was to survive.

With thirty-year-old Esther awaiting the birth of her first child, Sarah had been the more experienced of the two women. Either by accident or design she had managed to avoid falling pregnant during her honeymoon tour in 1813 and 1814, but had come safely through labour twice in the past two and a half years. The baby she was carrying was set to be a sibling for pretty Caroline and her little brother George, the 'manly, stout, ugly son' his mother joked she had always wished for.

As their two due dates approached, Sarah had also been the more confident of the two, characteristically sanguine, and bantering with her brother Frederick about the possibility of an election taking both of the fathers-to-be out of town. Esther, on the other hand, was full of anxiety. Her four-year marriage with Althorp had been everything a wife could wish for. She had basked in his declarations that she was the only woman with whom he never felt shy; revelled in the trust he showed in her judgement by letting her open and sort his letters; and valued the effort and expense he poured into her beloved childhood home. The only thing wanting had been a child. Two miscarriages had made her doubt that they would ever be blessed with one. Althorp had been feeling positive this time, telling friends he had never seen his wife more well, but for months past she had been absolutely convinced that something would go wrong, seemingly unable to stop thinking about Princess Charlotte, the Prince Regent's daughter, who had died the previous November after an exhausting fifty-hour labour, at the end of which her baby boy had been stillborn. 'Poor Soul!' clucked a sympathetic Mrs Calvert, back on friendly terms with Esther now she was Lady Althorp, and much more supportive than Lady Spencer, who had no patience with her daughter-in-law's nerves. Mrs Calvert, however, had been similarly affected many times herself, most notably after the death of a childhood friend in 1805. 'I try not to think of it,' she had written then, 'for it is no rule because she has died in her lying-in, that the same thing is to happen to me, but I can't banish the idea, and I feel most terribly frightened this time – however, God's will be done.'

It was Esther who was the first of the two sisters-in-law to be brought to bed, on 8 June. Like Princess Charlotte's, hers was a long and difficult labour, at the end of which her son was also stillborn. She herself was said to be in 'great danger' – in 'high fever and delirious' according to a solicitous Mrs Calvert, who sent her servant for news. However, in a scenario eerily similar to that which had played out in the royal palace, by 11 June it looked like Esther had rallied. She had 'recovered her senses' and the doctors had left her eating a little bread and milk. Sarah, still waiting for her own labour to begin, must have breathed an enormous sigh of relief.

As with the late lamented princess, though, appearances proved deceptive. When the family physician looked in on her Ladyship he discovered that her pulse was dangerously weak. Brandy, immediately, he ordered. But as a horrified Lord Althorp attempted to get his wife to swallow a few drops, he realised she was struggling against him. As he looked on helplessly, she passed out. Not long afterwards, she was dead.

It was not until a full eight days later that Sarah's labour began – a wait that must have been excruciating for her. There but for the grace of God might she go, too. Thankfully, just a day after Esther and her baby were tenderly laid to rest in the family vault, she was safely delivered of her own son. Master Spencer Lyttelton came kicking and screaming into the world, totally oblivious to the mourning clothes and melancholy looks worn by his maternal relations.

For Althorp it was a particularly bleak time. Never was there 'deeper grief in any widowed heart,' thought Sarah, watching her adored brother wrestle with his sorrow. In the immediate aftermath of Esther's death the 36-year-old buried himself deep in the Nottinghamshire countryside at Wiseton, her family home, dressing in nothing but full mourning and shutting out the Spencers and their abundant attentions. When he wasn't listlessly wandering the garden his wife had carefully laid out, he was avidly reading – mainly the Bible. Not even the hunting he had always pursued with such a fervent passion had the power to interest him. 'I hear that Althorp is still quite wretched,' said their younger sister Gin in August. Indeed, when he eventually returned to town, the family were shocked at the change in him. An air of extreme dejection clung to his person, and it was clear he had no intention of joining in with any frivolous pursuits. 'If it were not for my duty, I should like to shut myself up for the rest of my life,' he told a friend.

Nobody expected a bereaved husband like Althorp to bounce back quickly from the loss of such a beloved partner, but few expected him to wear the willow for Esther for ever, either. Just as a loved one's death from consumption was a melancholy but all-too-frequent reality, death in childbirth was a fact of life – a tragic one, but a part of life nonetheless.[12] As the heir to an earldom, with a long life left to live and no heir of his own, Althorp's marrying again was something his contemporaries would find far more understandable than his staying true to Esther's memory. His fellow MP John Lambton was positively encouraged both to get back to work and to look about him for a new wife in the months after Henrietta – with whom he had eloped to Gretna Green – died of consumption in 1815, leaving him alone at twenty-three with three young daughters. In fact, much as we like to imagine handsome bachelor heroes, unburdened by children or past paramours, many Regency brides married a man who had been up the aisle before and then been bereaved once already, if not twice. There was even

---

12    In fact, the Spencers would be confronted by the grievous reality again just five years later. In 1823, Sarah's 'kind-hearted sisterkin' Gin, who had married Lord George Quin the very day after Althorp and Esther wed in 1814, lost her life eleven days after giving birth to her fourth child. She was just twenty-nine.

something quite attractive about a melancholy widower, if the letters of some young debutantes are to be believed.

While it was perfectly legitimate to move on, as with everything else there was etiquette around remarriage to be observed. Lord Worcester was considered to have swept aside with unseemly haste his grief after his wife Georgiana died unexpectedly in 1821, at the age of twenty-eight. Though he was reported to be 'in great despair' at the time of her death in May – attributed (surely mistakenly) to 'inflammation brought on by going into a cold bath' after a long night's dancing – by October that year, his engagement to Lady Jane Paget was an open secret. Rumour had it that he had (shockingly) 'proposed three weeks after Lady W's death' – although he had been sufficiently tactful not to go to her father so soon. Oddly, though, he opened himself up to criticism over a woman he never actually took to church. By January 1822, he had moved on again, and was 'very much in love' with Emily Smith, his late wife's 21-year-old half-sister, whom he eventually married in June that year. It was still a bare thirteen months after he had been widowed, but acceptable in the eyes of society, since convention demanded only a year's mourning for a spouse. In fact, period sources suggest he was not alone in remarrying shortly after his year was up. John Lambton did the same, while Lord Deerhurst did not even wait a year before wedding his second wife.

Hasty as it might still seem in our minds, families rarely wanted widowers, particularly those with children, to spend too long solemn and alone – and least of all their late wives, some of whom, like Lady Frederica Stanhope, bravely confronted their own mortality to tell them so. It was in the very last days of her pregnancy in January 1823 that she sat down to write the most difficult missive of her life. 'My dearest and best Husband my own beloved James,' it began, 'I write this to express my gratitude for the happiness you gave me happiness dearest James such as no mortal ever felt.'

Until then, the Stanhopes had lived out a fairytale romance. They had first met around 1815, when James was a lively, sociable army officer of twenty-seven, with a taste for poetry and a tendency towards piety, and 'Freddy' a thoughtful, serious schoolgirl of just fifteen; but according to family legend, James had known then that she was the woman he wanted to make his wife. They had eventually wed when Frederica turned twenty, and James, whose upbringing had been unconventional, his own family emotionally dysfunctional, had found genuine happiness as part of hers. Already the proud parents of a son, the couple were looking forward to giving her parents, Lord and Lady Mansfield, another grandchild when Frederica took up her pen to write what turned out to be her last ever letter to her husband.

She was far from the only woman who put a farewell down on paper in case childbirth claimed her life. Lady Jersey – who did eventually fall pregnant – wrote three such notes in three years, telling her husband in 1810, 'I have not my dearest Love, courage to bid you adieu, to speak such words would be impossible.' Frederica went further, though. The letter she wrote to James was not just a goodbye, nor just a mere declaration of her love for him. Her last words were a selfless attempt to encourage him to find happiness without her.

Above all, she wanted him to marry again; to preserve his virtue in the sacred bonds of matrimony, rather than to seek a sinful form of comfort in the arms of a mistress. 'Do not let the worldly idea of its being a want of affection to my memory deter you,' she wrote, before adding somewhat less selflessly, 'I do not expect anyone will make you as happy as I trust I have done, but I earnestly wish such a woman should be found.'

If there was another war, she hoped he would do his duty, but not chase it simply as an escape from his sorrow. She hoped he alone would undertake the religious education of their children, and that he would look to her mama for help with their care. Her only truly selfish request was that their unborn baby, if it was a girl, be given her name. 'Oh, if it is permitted to souls to look down to influence mortals, how I will watch over my James,' she assured him.

Sadly, her courageous note was written in vain. When Freddy's second experience of childbirth proved fatal, James was utterly devastated. Her labour had been mercifully short and uncomplicated but, like Esther, she had become worryingly feverish soon afterwards, and neither the drawing of thirty-six ounces of blood nor the application of thirty leeches to her stomach had stopped her from slipping away from him three days after the delivery of baby Frederick, who himself lived less than forty-eight hours. Sunk deep into mourning by the events of that fateful week, the once exuberant James's sorrowful story reached its ultimate conclusion two years later, when, burdened by grief, and in growing pain from the musket ball irreversibly lodged in his shoulder during his military service in Spain, his mental health broke down completely. As dusk fell on 5 March 1825, the 36-year-old left the mansion house at Kenwood, where he and his surviving son were living with Frederica's parents, and walked hurriedly past the gardeners to an outhouse in its wooded grounds. It was there that he was found by a search party of servants several hours later, suspended from one of the beams by his own braces.

At the ensuing inquest into his death, the jury concluded that he had put a period to his existence during 'a fit of temporary insanity' – the habitual verdict in cases of suicide, which prevented the deceased being punished for what was still a crime if committed when in a rational state of mind, and was still regarded by many as a deadly sin. Indeed, when barrister and politician Sir Samuel Romilly had taken his own life in November 1818, four days after the loss of his wife of twenty years, the manner of his death had been publicly lamented. One newspaper even mounted an attack against those willing to excuse his actions, arguing that his 'self-murder' betrayed if not an irreligious mindset then a lack of Christian fortitude or resolve.

James's 'insanity' the jury had readily attributed to the wound he had incurred at the siege of San Sebastian in 1813, the attending doctor having confirmed that resulting 'paroxysms of pain might produce temporary derangement'. In his testimony, however, the late colonel's valet, Wheeler, emphasised his master's grief at the loss of his wife, referring to it right before confirming that, of late, he had fallen into 'the habit of sitting a long time as if in a state of stupor' before starting up 'as if from sleep or upon an alarm'. He had also complained to his attendant of seventeen years that 'he could get no sleep in consequence of the pain he endured.' It was suffering that could easily be blamed on his old and chronically painful war wound, but Wheeler seems to have suspected another source. Certainly his master had been subject to worrying bouts of depression since his wife's death. And it was said that he was on the verge of remarriage, to a young lady actually on a visit to Kenwood at the time of his suicide. It's not hard to imagine that the burden of carrying out his beloved wife's plan for his future happiness had become more than James could bear.

Though thankfully not driven to such a desperate course, Lord Althorp also remained steeped in melancholy for years after his wife's death, giving up his marital townhouse in Pall Mall, returning to a set of bachelor rooms in Albany and becoming even more socially reclusive than in his younger days. He did make a half-hearted attempt at remarriage, perhaps for the sake of the succession: shortly before becoming Earl Spencer in 1834 – a full sixteen years after losing Esther – he offered his hand to a widowed cousin, Isabella, Lady Clinton, but she refused him, and there were to be no further proposals. Such lasting grief perhaps surprises us more than the swift remarriages of men like Lord Worcester, given the 'matchmaking and manoeuvre' that characterised so many Regency courtships. Yet however difficult it was to get to know one another in the social whirl of the season; however much passion had to be balanced with the practicalities; and however much marriage was about begetting heirs, it's clear that love matches were no rarity and that deep and conflicting emotions were often at play when it came to deciding whether to marry again.

That was certainly the case with Lord Aberdeen. It was said that 'the sunshine went out of his life for ever' after his wife Catherine's death from consumption in 1812. For a year, he recorded his almost daily visions of her in his diary. Yet scarcely had that first year of his widowhood passed before he was seriously contemplating marrying Miss Anne Cavendish, a niece of the 5th Duke of Devonshire. His conspicuously deep mourning troubled her friends, who thought him attempting 'a *mariage de convenance*', but his motives in his own mind do not appear to have been so straightforward. The practical – he was only twenty-nine, with no heir and three motherless daughters – jostled with the emotional – both the desire for affection and stability that came from being orphaned at an early age, and his attractiveness to the opposite sex, who tended to acknowledge that he was 'beautiful' to look at. There could be no forgetting Catherine. 'I have seen human nature under a form in which it never before existed. My heart must be more than metaphorically cold before this feeling can ever be changed or forgotten,' he assured her sister. But his heart was still beating, his mind, he said, still 'capable of entertaining sentiment for [Anne] more ardent and pure than I believe she is likely to meet with.'

If it was not mere convenience, however, it was not love either, as his tentative pursuit of another woman at the same time must have made clear to poor Miss Cavendish. In the end, neither courtship came to anything. Instead, in 1815, at the suggestion of his father-in-law, Lord Abercorn, the earl wed the widow of Catherine's eldest brother, Viscount Hamilton. Lady Hamilton – Harriet – had only been married herself for four and half years before a lingering illness (probably the consumption that killed so many of his siblings) ended her husband's life, and so could enter into all of Aberdeen's feelings on the subject of love and loss at a young age. The match seemed to make eminent sense, providing the widower with the domesticity he craved and the ailing Lord Abercorn's young grandson (and now heir) with a guardian already loved and trusted by the family; but despite what the practised matchmaker told his friends, it was not one of sensibility. Not on the groom's side, at least. Aberdeen's new wife was a woman he had not so long since described as 'rather well looking… but certainly one of the most stupid persons I ever met with.'

For her part, Harriet seems to have greeted her father-in-law's suggestion that she take his grieving son-in-law for a second husband with some enthusiasm. At only twenty-two, the prospect of being thrust back into singledom was perhaps not that appealing to her – nor the prospect of putting herself, a mother of three, in competition with the young and carefree debutantes on the marriage mart. Possibly she had even fallen for the handsome Aberdeen, whom she had known for some years as part of her husband's family circle.

In general, however, Regency women remarried far less often than men. Much depended on a widow's individual feelings, how fragile her financial circumstances were, and what hopes she had for the future. If she had a comfortable jointure, she might relish being 'her own mistress and very much at ease' for the first time in her life: in control of her finances, free to live where and how she pleased without reference to a man, and possibly even sole guardian of her children. But, equally, her jointure might be much less than the magnificent sum she was used to living on as a fashionable wife, or perhaps not paid as promptly as she would like, especially if her late husband had left his estates in debt. As for her future life, she might be extremely content to end a near-constant cycle of pregnancies; happy to sink into celibacy if it saved her from wearing out her body like poor Maria, Lady Duncannon, who spent much of her adult life pregnant and died at forty-six, just five years after her fifteenth childbirth. On the other hand, she might yearn for love and companionship, particularly if she was still young and childless like Magdalene De Lancey.

Not only was there much to weigh up about the lifestyle she wanted, but a widow also appears to have had to think far more carefully about her reputation than did her male counterparts. From their clothes to their conduct, mourning was supposed to be more conspicuous for the female sex. Certainly in the months after Sir William's death, Magdalene had to deal with snide insinuations from other women that she was not suitably anguished by his passing – something that never troubled the amorous Lord Worcester, whom the *ton* had generally agreed would soon console himself after his wife's death. 'She really must be composed of flint,' was the verdict of Lady 'Georgy' Lennox, daughter of the Duchess of Richmond, who had, presumably, wanted to see a properly feminine display of tears and female helplessness in the days and weeks after Waterloo, when instead the self-sufficient Magdalene had competently and confidently arranged for her husband's burial and her own passage home from Belgium. Georgy's words had been unconsciously echoed by an acquaintance of Magdalene's aunt, who described the short note she sent home to announce her husband's death as 'almost too composed to be comfortable to her friends.' The poignant account that Lady De Lancey penned of her time at Waterloo might well have been an attempt to rebut the rumours that were spreading and re-establish herself as the grief-stricken widow of a great man.

A swift remarriage could certainly leave women open to criticism that they were not sufficiently saddened by a husband's death, nor being sufficiently respectful to his memory. Despite the fact that Harriet saw out a full year of mourning before being united to Lord Aberdeen – just the same as Lord Worcester and many other men – her remarriage was described as 'an odd circumstance' by one lady, who remarked pointedly: 'she has not mourned her first husband long.'

There were her children's lives to think about, too. Her remarriage to a man of a lesser status might damage their prospects, especially those of her daughters. The widowed Countess of Lindsay's daughter Lady Charlotte would forever hold against her mama her decision to marry her cousin, the disreputable and drunken Reverend Peter Pegus. She retained a lifelong belief that her mother's 'unfortunate marriage' had closed doors that should have been open to the daughter of an earl and prevented her from marrying an aristocrat herself. It was obviously a legitimate belief. In 1818, Lady Charlotte Campbell had tried hard to keep secret her own engagement to her eldest son's tutor, the Reverend Edward Bury, who was some fifteen years her junior, precisely because she feared it might jeopardise the understanding that existed between her daughter and the son and heir of a marquis. In the event, all that was jeopardised when it became known was her own security: her son so violently disapproved of the clandestine romance that he threatened to cut off the allowance that he made her, which presumably had been topping up an inadequate jointure.

Second marriages could also be a struggle, as the new Lady Aberdeen found out. As the couple's son later wrote with crashing understatement, the earl's 'devotion to his first wife and all belonging to her naturally caused [her] some uneasiness, not always wholly concealed.'

Frederica Stanhope had envisaged just such difficulties when she wrote to her own hopelessly devoted husband about finding a second wife. In advice mature beyond her twenty-two years, she had encouraged him not to always be talking about what she would have done or felt, especially not if he and his new lady disagreed, but to think of her, and speak of her, like a sister. 'Let her hair be worn on the same chain as mine,' she told him generously. And 'if she should have children make no difference between them,' she counselled.

But if he ever received similar guidance from the women in his life, Lord Aberdeen failed to heed it. By all accounts affectionate towards his second wife and their children, in both deeds and words, he nevertheless continued to wear mourning for his first wife right up until the day of his own death almost fifty years later. Catherine's rings never left his fingers, and she seemed hardly ever to leave his thoughts. He was also zealously attentive to their three daughters, with whom he found intellectual companionship of the kind that had made his years with their mother so special, but was entirely lacking in his relationship with Harriet.

She had apparently entered their relationship with her eyes open, but his eternal and ever-obvious mourning pushed Harriet to the limit. She became consumed by jealousy and resentment, unable to bear the fact that she did not have first place in his heart. After just a few visits, she began refusing to make the week-long journey to her husband's Scottish seat, which Catherine had adored, instead taking herself off to Brighton every summer. To Catherine's daughters she was soon acting the part of the stereotypical wicked stepmother, treating them 'with indignation and disgust' and displaying a 'cruel and unnatural' hatred for them, or so her husband complained – and that despite the fact that all three were frequently unwell, having clearly inherited the family's fatal tendency to tuberculosis. She forced Lord Aberdeen into taking sides against his middle daughter Jane and, on one occasion, used intense emotional blackmail to compel him to leave 16-year-old Alice on the continent in declining health, with only her governess by her side. Blending their two families proved to be a spectacular failure, and Harriet's attempts to come between father and daughters ended only with their deaths. By 1829 all three had succumbed to consumption, with not one of them having reached the age of twenty. Harriet and Aberdeen had been living separate lives long before that.

Yet for all its risks, remarriage was an opportunity for some women. Lady Bessborough had once pondered how many wives there must be who would 'gladly separate' from a husband, 'and still more gladly chuse again, if they could do so without ruining their characters' – a scandalous elopement being their only real option for doing so, as she well knew. Widowhood, however, gifted them a chance to make a second choice in an entirely respectable fashion – and usually when they were older, wiser and, unlike debutantes, free to make a marriage of inclination, heedless of the practicalities. Louisa Hope, the wife of immensely wealthy art connoisseur Thomas Hope, was just one of many women who let her heart rule her head after she was widowed. According to rumour, her first marriage to the merchant banker had been forced on her by her parents. Meeting the couple at their vast London residence in 1810, the Persian envoy Mirza Abu'l Hasan had been shocked at the idea that simply for money, such a lovely woman had been tied to such a hideously ugly man – 'if you were to see him in a dream, you would never wake again!' he wrote emphatically in his journal, incensed on her behalf. He would surely have rejoiced at the news that a year after Hope died in 1831, Louisa married the man who family tradition said she had wanted to wed more than twenty-five years earlier, her illegitimate cousin, General William Carr Beresford.

Of course, it must have been far easier for those stuck in an unhappy or arranged marriage to see an upside to widowhood than for those like Magdalene, who had married for love and experienced happiness 'so perfect, so unalloyed!' Lady De Lancey did not, though, follow Lords Althorp and Aberdeen into lifelong mourning for her late husband. Despite all the pain that love had brought her, she was not afraid to open up her heart again. In a strange echo of her earlier romance, she not only fell once more for a military man, but married him after a swift courtship in Scotland that followed almost exactly the same timescale as her first. Captain Henry Harvey of the East India Company Army was befriended by her brother Basil, a captain in the navy, when they travelled back to Britain together on board the same ship, and introduced to her when he came on a visit to the family in Edinburgh. Having met in late 1818, they were engaged by December and married from Dunglass House the following March. If anything, Magdalene was more deeply in love with him than she had been with William – she was certainly more eager to meet her affianced at the altar, constantly hurrying on the already speedy preparations for her second nuptials. Out of her tragic and testing experience at Waterloo she had emerged more confident and more self-aware, but above all, more determined to seize happiness while she had the chance.

*Chapter Eight*

# Criminal Connections

O<small>N</small> 22 M<small>AY</small> 1808, a carriage and four horses swept into the yard at the Crown Inn in Lyndhurst, Hampshire. A gentleman, unquestionably a member of 'the quality', sprang out and handed his female companion down the steps. To anyone watching they must have looked like an ordinary, if strikingly attractive, married couple. But the man who followed Lady Boringdon inside to enquire about a room was not her husband but her lover; the man on whose arm her Ladyship had walked out of her marital home in London several days previously, in full view of the servants, and with absolutely no intention of coming back.

The two amorous fugitives were already the chief topic of conversation in the metropolis, the apparent break-up of the Boringdon marriage having created more of a sensation in fashionable circles than any split had done for some years. To the gratification of anyone not yet privy to all the juicy details of this latest elopement in high life, the *Morning Post* was well informed, able to confirm that 'about an hour before Lady B——'s departure, Sir A— P—— called' at her home in Cumberland Place, the use of initials doing nothing to obscure the identity of her partner in crime, handsome diplomat and third son of the Earl of Uxbridge, Sir Arthur Paget. 'They walked out of the house together, and have not since been heard of,' the report went on, noting that 'the absence of the Lady did not excite any surprise until the hour of dinner'. Then, it said, Lord Boringdon had become 'much agitated' and in an effort to trace his wife had dispatched couriers to all the postmasters and hackneymen in the neighbourhood. Not so long after that, the *ton* had begun to chatter.

'You will have read in the Paper that Lady Bo[r]ingdon has Left her Husband,' one matron told her daughter. 'She was Lady Augusta Fane, and is very pretty. Lord Bo[r]ingdon is a very handsome Man also, but had the indelible Stain of being her Husband.' It was a throwaway comment that did Augusta a disservice, as Lady Jerningham was soon to discover. 'Lord Bo[r]ingdon is now greatly Blamed,' she scribbled by way of an update three days later. 'He had kept up an intimacy, formed before his marriage… and the Knowledge of it had Caused a great deal of uneasiness to Lady Bo[r]ingdon.' Actually, or so those close to her said, four years into her marriage she had come to despise her husband.

When she had taken her marriage vows in June 1804, the eighteen-year-old Lady Augusta, daughter of the Earl of Westmorland and sister to Sarah, Lady Jersey, seems to have been entirely ignorant of the existence of a mistress in his life, let alone a mistress who had long since taken possession of his heart. If the rumours that circulated around town in the summer of 1808 were to be believed, it was in the earliest months of her marriage that she learned the truth when, entering Boringdon's study one morning, she had 'accidentally cast her eye upon a fond epistle from Lady ——, together with an unfinished note, written in reply, which was equally tender and explicit.'

The love rival who was to cast such a long shadow over her short marriage was 'flaming beauty' Lady Elizabeth Monck, eight years Boringdon's senior and married herself to an Irish gentleman, with whom she had two teenage daughters. When Augusta became his wife, Elizabeth had been in a relationship (of sorts) with his Lordship for ten years, during which time she had given him three illegitimate sons and had treated Saltram, his country seat overlooking Plymouth harbour, almost like her own home. It was no frivolous liaison. In fact, much to his sister's dismay, Jack – as he was known to the family – had wanted to marry his mistress, but Elizabeth had firmly rejected all his proposals, arguing that a divorce would be too hard on her daughters and her poor husband, Henry.

Nevertheless, she had taken it hard when her faithful lover had bounced back from her rejection and at the age of thirty-two found himself a teenage bride: an acclaimed beauty with captivatingly large, dark-blue eyes, an influential earl for a father, and a sizeable marriage portion courtesy of her grandfather, Robert Child. It did not appear to be a hugely passionate romance. Jack – not exactly famed for his powers of fascination, and nicknamed 'the Boring Don' by some of his contemporaries – had first encountered Augusta in 1803, when he lived next door to her father in Berkeley Square, and had proposed during what was probably her first season the following year. There had, though, been a fairly convincing display of newly wedded bliss – enough not only to gratify his female relations, but also to make Lady Elizabeth jealous. 'I think she sees all this wrong and encourages herself in wishes and aversions which are useless,' Lady Bessborough told her own lover Lord Granville Leveson-Gower – one of Boringdon's oldest friends – on Christmas Eve 1804. 'From my heart I pity her,' she added, 'for with the best resolutions and intentions her situation would still be dreadful.'

For despite the fondest hopes of his sister – who was 'decidedly of the opinion that it will not be [Augusta's] fault if she is not an excellent wife' – Jack had not parted with his mistress. And as rumours of discord in the Boringdon household had begun rustling as soon as the autumn after their wedding, it seems likely that Augusta had, indeed, become well aware of his ongoing affair in those first months of her marriage. The ever-informed Mrs Calvert had even heard that the couple were to part then, though only because 'she says he is so cross she can't live with him.'

The state of the newly-weds' relationship had still been the subject of tittle-tattle in the spring of 1805. 'I had the Pleasure of seeing Lord Boringdon look very well a few Days ago,' Lord Granville's mother, Lady Stafford, reported to him. 'I think Matrimony has improved his Hair dressing,' she added inconsequentially, before going on to say, 'he seems to be thoroughly happy, and, I am told, so is his little Wife, though Envy, Malevolence, and Disappointment have circulated very contrary reports' – perhaps a veiled reference to Lady Elizabeth, still stirring up trouble.

Yet while Lady Stafford was inclined to dismiss the reports that said all was not sunny in the Boringdon household, they may have been closer to the truth. By all accounts Augusta had a lot to put up with. For a start, Lady Elizabeth was not the only other woman in her husband's life. Around the same time that Augusta gave birth to their first child, a son, in May 1806, Boringdon became the father of a daughter, born to a ballet dancer in Bristol. And there had probably been other affairs, too. He had enjoyed a reputation as a ladies' man since long before his marriage and, in the wake of the elopement, the newspapers were full of gossip about his 'neglectful conduct' and 'notorious attachment to other females'.

Boringdon had also, it seems, been an overbearing and controlling husband. 'He directs not only her visits, but the hours she is to pay them,' the Duchess of Devonshire had observed in March 1805, adding laughingly, 'I imagine that he gives out his orders like a General, and that he points out her *route* and where her stations are to be. Attention! — turn to the Right; Halt at Ly. Bessboro's at 3, D. House 4, &c.' Augusta's own letters to her husband – addressed to her 'dearest love' – certainly betray an anxiety about displeasing him that is slightly uncomfortable to a twenty-first-century eye. 'I have myself been unwell, and induced to take laudanum (you must not scold me),' she wrote in 1806. Going on to say that it had prevented her going to church, she had added, 'do not believe that this was from neglect of your orders… it was from the violence of my cold.' Another time she had written to him, 'I hope, my dear Boringdon, you will like my going to the Play, as nothing could give me pleasure that was not agreeable to you.'

Most hypocritically of all, however, Boringdon expected his young wife to be the model of virtue and morality that he himself was not. When alerted by one of his servants to the growing frequency of Sir Arthur Paget's visits to his house, he had rained reproaches down on Augusta's head. She was to give up her lover for good (if lover he even was at that point) and return to the country. It was this peremptory command that had proved the last straw for Augusta. No doubt resentful of his blatant hypocrisy and total disregard for her feelings, she had determined to take charge of her own life. In what the newspapers described as 'preparatory steps' for her flight, she had pretended to dismiss her maid, by which means she had managed to have her clothes secretly conveyed out of the house, ready for her to follow at an opportune moment. And when that moment presented itself, she had seized it. It would probably be unfair to say that she did so with no regrets at all – only after 'a most tender and agonizing farewell' did she part from her little son Henry, the newspapers said – but as far as anyone could tell, she was not remotely sorry to have abandoned her errant husband.

Marital infidelity like Lord Boringdon's was still largely tolerated in aristocratic circles in the Regency period, provided, that is, that anyone indulging in an adulterous affair played by the rules. Above all, lovers were expected to be discreet, refraining from publicly displaying or avowing their affection for one another, and behaving with courtesy when out in company with their spouse. As long as they kept up appearances in public, unfaithful husbands usually avoided censure for their private conduct. Condemnation was primarily reserved for those who brought what should have been private transgressions, kept behind closed doors, out into the public sphere, humiliating their wife in the

*Right*: A fashion plate from 1816, displaying a bridal gown of gauze over a white satin under dress, with fashionable puffed sleeves, a low-cut bodice and a deep flounce of delicate Brussels lace.

*Below*: Plenty of aristocratic couples opted to marry at home, usually at a fashionably late hour and sometimes surrounded by only a handful of guests.

*Left*: Magdalene Hall, in her late teens.

*Right*: Colonel Sir William De Lancey, c. 1814.

*Above and below right*: The Battle of Waterloo by Jan Willem Pieneman, depicting Wellington and his staff. The wounded Sir William is seen in the bottom right-hand corner, and below in the artist's preparatory sketch.

*Below left*: The Army Gold Cross awarded to Sir William for his service in the Peninsular War. Each arm of the cross and each clasp on the ribbon was a reward for participation in a separate battle.

*Left*: John 'Jack' Parker, 2nd Baron Boringdon, in a portrait from 1804, the year of his marriage to Augusta.

*Right*: Lady Elizabeth Monck, painted by a female friend in Italy a couple of years before she and Lord Boringdon first became lovers.

With permission of the Carr-Ellison family and Northumberland Archives

*Left*: Sir Arthur Paget, c. 1804.

*The Elopement of Lady W— with Lord Paget.*

CRIM.CON.

*A Sketch taken from Life by Seignor Gabrielli. Valued by 12 Connoisseurs at Twenty thousand pounds!*

*Above*: A depiction of the elopement of Sir Arthur's eldest brother with Lady Charlotte Wellesley in 1809; produced for a book of tales of 'crim.con.' and divorce entitled The Annals of Gallantry.

*Below*: The scene conjured by artist Signor Gabrielli at the 1807 trial of Sir John Piers for criminal conversation with Lady Cloncurry was a gift for satirical cartoonists.

*Above*: Frances Anne, Lady Londonderry, in 1859, laying the foundation stone of the new blast furnaces she built at Seaham. She gave a speech to the assembled crowds on the occasion.

*Left*: The rumour that Harriet Arbuthnot was the Duke of Wellington's mistress persists even to this day. This sketch of them walking arm in arm in the park was published days before her death in 1834.

*Right*: Sydney, Lady Morgan, in a portrait which appeared in the Illustrated London News in 1856.

*Left*: Sarah, Lady Lyttelton, photographed in her 70s, c. 1860.

process. The Marquis of Abercorn, for instance, was denounced for allowing a double portrait of his long-time mistress and their illegitimate son to be exhibited at the Royal Academy; while Sir Arthur's younger brother, the Hon. Berkeley Paget, was unceremoniously 'cut' by the Duke of York (among others) after first abandoning his wife and children to live with courtesan Amy Wilson, and then parading about in public with her, 'thus insulting the town… and the feelings of his unfortunate wife.'

Such was the tolerance for infidelity, in fact, that plenty of aristocratic women appear to have entered the married state expecting that their husbands would feel *tempted*, at the very least, to stray, and were fairly sanguine about it. Frances, Lady Shelley anticipated it, but as a new bride, she was determined to be proactive. Knowing that not only were acknowledged beauties (including Augusta) flirting hard with her husband Sir John, but that his mistress of twelve years Lady Haggerston had no wish to lose him, she determined on her marriage in 1807 to make him so happy at home that he would not look elsewhere. 'I exerted every power with which nature and study had endowed me, to fascinate him as a mistress, and to enchain his affections as a wife,' she remembered. 'I firmly believe that I was completely successful,' she added; although she did admit that since she had begged him not to tell her if he was unfaithful, she could not be completely sure.

Similarly, by no means did adultery prompt all women to take action as Augusta had done – even in cases of more extreme provocation. Sophia, Mrs Berkeley Paget, a mother of five, took her wandering husband back into the family home in 1819 after he was cast off by his courtesan. 'I am sorry for it,' wrote Lady Williams Wynn, 'as I fear she can have no prospect of any permanent comfort in him, & will therefore only be subjecting herself to fresh pangs.' To those on the outside, the unfortunate reconciliation appeared to be a complete one, with Berkeley accepted not just into the marital home but also the marital bed, as the couple went on to have two more children.

Unthinkable as it may seem to us, Sophia's was generally the course of action recommended by the conduct books targeted at young female readers – and not just those by men like James Fordyce (whose famous sermons bluntly declared that women usually had themselves to blame for their husbands' neglect), but even the ones penned by the likes of Elizabeth Lanfear, once part of the literary circle of feminist icon and passionate campaigner for female equality, Mary Wollstonecraft. In her 1824 manual for young ladies, Elizabeth advised that a wife simply adopt a 'dignified reserve' in the face of infidelity, and maintain a 'forbearing silence on the subject of her wrongs'. Where a husband confessed to his failings and asked for his wife's forgiveness, 'let not the hour of reconciliation be delayed, nor marred by nugatory stipulations or useless and offensive recrimination,' she counselled. Indeed, 'the woman who is a mother,' she thought, 'should make many sacrifices before she either exposes or drives from her the father of her children.' No doubt there were many women who knew Augusta's pain, but were silently enduring it like Sophia, or steadfastly looking the other way like Lady Shelley.

Of course, it wasn't only adultery that turned Regency marriages sour. Unhappy unions were made of many things. Viscount Lismore and his wife Eleanor clashed over their lifestyle; feeling suffocated in the Irish countryside, she was desperate for a London home, while he maintained that they could not afford it. The first Lady Worcester, meanwhile, must have wished her husband was so prudent; her marriage had been made exceptionally uncomfortable by his enormous and ever-increasing debts. Not long before her untimely death in 1821, the bailiffs had descended on their home in Upper Brook Street; and if her uncle, the Duke of Wellington, 'had not given her rooms in his house, she w$^d$ not have had a hole to put her head into,' according to Harriet Arbuthnot. More serious than either, Lady Abercorn's young half-sister, Lady Julia Lockwood, suffered for over ten years at the hands of a physically abusive husband, army captain Robert Lockwood, whom she had begged to be able to marry in the face of family opposition. Since a now horrifying degree of marital abuse was unrecognised as such by the law, she would certainly not have been alone.

However, whether they were neglected, humiliated and trapped in a loveless marriage like Augusta, or pushed to breaking point by a husband's abusive or reckless behaviour, Regency wives had very little scope to change their situation. Parliamentary divorces – the only kind that permitted remarriage – were both rare and socially taboo. Trifling by modern standards, the numbers averaged just over three a year between 1800 and 1852 – nowhere near as high as the frowning moralists of the period made out. And while, technically, a woman could sue for one, actually obtaining it was near-impossible. The sole ground was adultery, but, unlike a husband, a wife could not sue for divorce in England on the basis of adultery alone. She had to prove an aggravating offence, such as bigamy or incest.

When Augusta left her marriage in 1808, only one woman had ever been granted an English divorce: a Mrs Addison in 1801, whose husband had, luckily, chosen to take her sister for his mistress, a relationship deemed by law to be incestuous. Never yet had a husband's infidelity been sufficient on its own, no matter how cruel or humiliating his behaviour had been. A Mrs Teush had tried and failed in 1805 to secure her divorce in London, even though her spouse was acknowledged to have 'exhibited the grossest infidelity' by living openly with his lover and allowing her to take his surname, actions far more brazen and insulting than anything Augusta could attribute to Lord Boringdon. Likewise, though Jack's domineering personality must have been maddening to her at times, no Regency judge would have been persuaded that a man telling his wife what to do was cruelty.

The other legal options for a wronged wife, while marginally less taboo than divorce, were far from satisfactory, especially for a young woman not ready to commit to a life of celibacy. The ecclesiastical court required only proof of a husband's adultery (or life-threatening cruelty) to grant a separation from bed and board – a remedy somewhat confusingly known as a divorce *a mensa et thoro*. However, while it was akin to a parliamentary divorce in that a female petitioner could – assuming there was no evidence of her own adultery – come away with a generous annuity and the possibility of living an independent life, it was unlike it in one crucial sense: neither party was permitted to remarry. That might not bother the erring husband so much, particularly if he already had a legitimate heir and a spare. He could find companionship – and more – in the arms of a lover. But his wife could not do the same. Separated from him, she was akin to an unmarried woman in the eyes of the polite world, and her reputation – like her maintenance allowance – depended on her remaining chaste. There could certainly be no more children for her if she wanted to maintain her place in polite society. It was an uneasy situation for her socially, too – neither spinster nor widow, her status was unclear. Many separated women found they could live more comfortable lives abroad, far removed from the fashionable world and its inflexible rules.

It was the same with a private separation effected by deed. A quasi-legal form of divorce, this involved the couple themselves, their lawyers or their trusted relatives thrashing out the financial and practical arrangements for a parting of ways. The only option available where a woman had no evidence of adultery or cruelty (or none that would stand up in court), it also had the advantage of keeping a couple's marital troubles out of the public eye, stopping them providing fodder for the gossip-loving ladies of the *ton* – for which reason, it tended to be the most palatable of all for a woman's family, too.

It was a private, out-of-court separation that Lady Caroline Parnell opted to broker with her husband in 1816, when she decided that, much like Augusta, she was no longer prepared to go on in a relationship that afforded her little pleasure. Born Lady Caroline Dawson, she, too, had drifted indifferently into her marriage with MP Henry Parnell at the age of eighteen. Her mother, the Countess of Portarlington, who had no great expectations for her impecunious daughters, had been delighted when, after meeting her girls again on a visit to a mutual friend in 1800, Henry, a former playmate of theirs, had written and unexpectedly offered for Caroline. It was, the countess told her sister, singleton Lady Louisa Stuart, 'the match of all others I would have wished'; she had 'known him from a child' and had 'a great regard for all his family and connections'. Caroline, though extremely surprised, she said, had no objection 'but the very natural one of feeling not sufficiently acquainted with him' – a circumstance the family eagerly remedied by taking her straight to town to see a little more of him. But it was only a little more; the couple were married not twelve weeks after the proposal.

Unbeknown to any of them, however, it had all been a terrible mistake. It was never Caroline Henry had wanted to marry, but her younger sister, Lady Louisa. Somehow, he had managed to bungle his letter to Lady Portarlington, couching it in such a way that she had understood him to be proposing for Caroline, the only one of her daughters then out of the schoolroom. Either too cowardly or too honourable to undeceive her, Henry had said nothing, but his new bride had felt his coldness and lack of affection. For twelve years she surged on with him in a kind of mutual apathy, until she lost, in quick succession, both her youngest daughter and her mother. On doctor's orders there followed a trip to the continent, which seemingly prompted a period of soul-searching. Caroline, happily settled in France with her three surviving daughters and two younger sons, delayed again and again their return to England until, in 1815, an increasingly impatient Henry insisted that the children come home. His wife agreed, but declined to accompany them, and Henry admitted defeat. In July 1816 a separation agreement formalising their split was signed, the terms of which granted Caroline £560 a year for her maintenance: an allowance of £360 from Henry, plus the £200-a-year pension inherited from her mother, to which he relinquished all his claims.[13]

In fact, had he so desired it, Henry would have been well

---

13  The sum does not seem particularly generous, but that probably had more to do with Henry's income than anything else. When the Duchess of Gordon's separation from her philandering husband was made official in 1805, she came away with an allowance of £4,000 a year.

within his rights to insist on Caroline's return. He could even lawfully have seized her by force and brought her back to their marital home in England, such were the privileges conferred on men by marriage. But Henry must also have realised that their relationship, such as it was, had run its course. As for insisting on the return of the five children she had taken with her, again, he had the perfect right to do so. Though attitudes were softening, common law still said he alone was legally entitled to custody of them, no matter what sort of father he was; and it was his right alone to direct their upbringing, their education, their employment and their marriages. He could be drunken, violent or in jail and would usually still be deemed the more proper of the two parents to have care of his children. A private separation deed such as the Parnells signed could *in theory* give their mother custody of them, either permanently or for a specified period, and some husbands did willingly agree to such an arrangement, particularly in the case of daughters or young children. But these agreements were effectively toothless because they did not hold up if challenged in court. If her offspring were subsequently snatched away by their father because he changed his mind on a whim, or in pursuance of a vendetta, a woman separated from her husband would find herself powerless to stop him. The same was often true if he decided to prevent his separated wife visiting her children or writing to them. Her right to a relationship with them was, again, entirely at her husband's discretion.

In the Parnells' case, Lady Caroline was able to keep up a very regular correspondence with all her children from her French home, but most of them never saw her in person again after 1816. That was, however, her choice rather than their father's command – perhaps her guilt at putting her own needs ahead of theirs was simply too much.

Given that leaving a marriage had significant downsides for a Regency wife, it's not surprising that some women resorted to other means of dealing with a husband's infidelity, neglect or oppression. Sydney Owenson's patron Lady Abercorn tackled her problems head-on. Like Mrs Berkeley Paget, she stayed with her philandering spouse, perhaps feeling unable to complain too vociferously about his conduct without provoking accusations of hypocrisy. When her sister Lady Elizabeth Monck had first met Lord Boringdon in Italy in 1794, Lady Anne Hatton (as Lady Abercorn was then) had been there too, a merry widow hopping between the beds of handsome young peers doing the Grand Tour, 'very pretty, very foolish, and very debauched'. Somehow, though, she succeeded in separating her second husband from his favourite mistress. Frances Hawkins – she of the vulgar Royal Academy portrait – was dislodged from the comfortable house she had long inhabited just across the park from Lord Abercorn's home at Stanmore, and shipped off to Ireland, initially becoming a housekeeper at Baronscourt. Perhaps in setting up the flirtatious Sydney with Charles Morgan – who looked unlikely to be a complaisant husband – Lady Abercorn had been making a similarly tactical strike.

For those women who preferred just to keep an objectionable husband at arm's length, cultivating an air of delicacy or discovering a recurrent illness – one, perhaps, that required frequent visits to friends to soak up the country air, or the warmth of the continent – was an alternative strategy. Playing him at his own game and taking a lover of their own was another.

While a double standard inevitably existed that meant that

adultery was considered less sinful when indulged in by husbands than wives, female infidelity was tolerated by the upper classes. Women were, of course, expected to have provided their husbands with a couple of legitimate sons before they indulged in any extramarital pleasures, but as long as they then followed the unwritten rules – keeping their affairs as private as possible and maintaining a united front with their husband in public – they usually avoided any social penalties. Some of the lady patronesses of Almack's are a good case in point. Emily, Lady Cowper (née Lamb) and Sarah, Lady Jersey both strayed from their husbands, both of them being at some point mistresses of the notoriously promiscuous Lord Palmerston, who was rumoured to be the father of more than one of Emily's children. Countess Lieven's long-running affair with the Austrian Chancellor Metternich was an open secret, too. Yet any respectable woman was gratified to have these ladies attend one of her parties, and all were greeted unblinkingly by the pious Queen Charlotte, who adamantly refused to receive at court any woman whose adultery had caused a scandal that publicly tarnished her reputation.

Any woman who indulged in an adulterous relationship, however, was putting more than just her reputation or access to court at risk. Socially acceptable as adultery might be, it was always a much more dangerous pursuit for a wife. She could not be sure how her husband would react on discovering an affair – or worse, an illicit pregnancy. Some couples, Lord and Lady Cowper included, went on for years in almost open marriages, each aware of the other's extramarital relationships; but not every spouse was as willing to turn a blind eye to a wife's affairs as Lord Cowper or the firmly cuckolded Mr Monck – however discreetly (or not, in the latter case) they had been conducted. When he was thrown into a 'violent fit of jealousy' in February 1811, Lord Cahir, for one, made absolutely clear to his wife that he was no complaisant husband. 'Lady Cahir has not been allowed to come out for these five days, and he is taking her back to Ireland,' her friend Lady Bessborough reported. 'Not by force,' she added, 'she has consented. The struggle was long, she withstood scolds, threats, and entreaties, but yielded to a service of plate, fresh from Rundell and Bridge's, which goes with them.'

Submitting to a period of rustication, armed with a shiny new dinner service straight from the royal goldsmiths (starting price in 1818, £30,000), sounds like no serious hardship – unless Lady Cahir's heart was engaged in her affair, of course. Some of those caught out in adultery faced a far worse fate: being divorced, whether they liked it or not. That, at least, was what happened to Lady Cloncurry, sent home to her father in disgrace in 1806 after her husband discovered her brief and much-regretted dalliance with his old school friend, Sir John Piers.

When the pitiful affair eventually hit the press, the story was one that set the *ton* giggling. On one occasion, so preoccupied had her Ladyship been with her lover that she had failed to remember the Italian mural-painter at work up a scaffold, who observed the couple locking themselves into the drawing room together only to emerge with flushed faces some ten minutes later. The scene conjured by Signor Gabrielli was a gift for the satirical cartoonists. But embarrassing as that was for her Ladyship, what emerged was worse. Sir John Piers had seduced the 19-year-old mother of two purely to win a lucrative wager.

She had confessed everything to her husband of three years and, in tears, begged him to forgive her. But though he had pardoned her – instantly, according to his obsequious Victorian biographer – he had still set in motion a permanent separation, which led, in the end, to a divorce. As Cloncurry's legal counsel put it, 'he refused to take back to his arms the tainted and faithless woman who had betrayed him. He refused to expose himself to the scorn of the world and his own contempt; he submitted to misery; he could not brook dishonour.' While this was overexaggerated courtroom eloquence, Cloncurry would have known that there was a stigma attached to the cuckolded husband, whose wife's adultery was a symbol of his inability to control her as a proper man should, making him fair game for mockery. His thinking in pursuing the separation (and no doubt that of other men in a similar position) seems to have been that to take his erring lady back, to forgive and forget her youthful indiscretion, would be a sign of weakness on his part – a notion reportedly rooted in his mind by his closest male friend.

Whatever the exact reason for his reaction to the affair, it hit his wife hardest of anybody. While her shameless scoundrel of a lover fled with his long-term mistress to live on the Isle of Man, she lost her comfortable home, the husband she loved, her formerly unblemished reputation, and, most distressingly, the chance to watch her two toddlers grow up. She was escorted home under a cloud to live in quiet retirement near her family, and reverted to her maiden name.[14] Her situation embodied all

---

14  Gratifyingly, Lady Cloncurry's story did not end there. She received a considerable inheritance from a childless (and obviously sympathetic) uncle in 1812 and seven years later married for the second time, a respectable clergyman and art lover named John Sanford, with whom she had another daughter.

the real risks of a casual love affair for a married woman; the harsh consequences that might well follow effectively acted as the Regency patriarchy's most efficient curb on female adultery and family break-up.

The hazards for women of indulging in adultery aside, the hypocrisy of a marriage where neither partner was faithful to the other didn't suit everyone. Attitudes were changing in the early nineteenth century. As society began to consider affection an ever more essential ingredient of a successful marriage, adultery was increasingly seen not just as an economic matter – relevant only as it affected inheritance of property and family honour – but as an emotional one. American tourist Louis Simond was one of those inclined to applaud women who were brave enough to expose themselves to all the adverse publicity that accompanied an elopement or divorce for the sake of honesty. 'The woman who leaves her husband to follow her lover, shews at least that she could not bear the indelicacy of a double connection,' he decided.

Whether it was a similar sensibility that motivated Augusta, the knowledge that Boringdon intended to make her do severe penance for her relationship with Arthur by shutting her up in the country, or simply the desire for a happy, mutually loving marriage, she had obviously been intent on leaving her husband, rather than conducting a parallel life as Lady Elizabeth Monck had done. Indeed, if Lady Shelley is to be believed, she had been looking around for the right man with whom to start afresh for some time. 'The lovely Lady [Boringdon]' was, she remembered, 'desperately in love with my husband. She tried, by every artifice, to induce him to go off with her.'

Augusta was by no means the first wife who thought that allying herself with another man was a better option than calling in the lawyers. But what concerned her well-wishers in the summer of 1808 was that she had, as Lady Jerningham put it, 'flung herself for Protection on the man Least Likely to behave decently towards Her, Sir Arthur Paget being notoriously ill tempered and having made a Practice of Playing with the feelings of the miserable women He Could engage to notice Him.' So numerous were the voices expressing that view that one newspaper, helpfully summarising for its readers all the latest *on dits* about the elopement, regaled them with talk of the 'inconstancy imputed to her gallant, who, it is confidently predicted, will be satiated in a short time'.

His track record was certainly not promising. This was not Arthur's first love affair. It was not even his first elopement. Only the previous year he had seduced and carried off the Duke of Bedford's cook. And he was the father of at least one illegitimate child, born to an Italian mistress in 1801 and being raised by his sister as her own. All his previous attempts at matrimony betrayed not only a regrettable tendency to chase after women with money, but a woeful distaste for commitment. In 1799 he had put himself in the running for the hand of heiress Joan Scott, whose dowry was said to be as much as £100,000. Around 1800, with his close friend the Prince Regent as his willing go-between, he had ardently courted the Dowager Duchess of Rutland, a wealthy widow some fourteen years his senior – only to then shy off before making an offer of marriage, to her intense disappointment. Then, in 1804, a much-publicised engagement with Lady Catherine Harris, the daughter of an influential diplomat, had been broken off when the settlements fell short of expectations, her father – *most* unreasonably – declining to pay half of the £10,000 debt (over £900,000 today) that he had run up during his time as Ambassador at Vienna. That breach was, in any event, fortuitous, since Arthur had already fallen hard for one of his Viennese acquaintances, Princess Leopoldine Esterházy. Her parents, however, soon stepped in to depress his pretensions there, clearly all too aware of his notorious inconstancy. 'The utmost pains have been taken to make her believe that my only object was to gain her Person, because it is beautiful, and that at the end of a year or two, I should abandon her for the first woman whose external appearance pleased me,' the disappointed swain had complained bitterly to his mother.

Fifteen years her senior, Augusta's lover was a handsome devil by all accounts – droll apparently, too, and with friends in high places – but he was not a man in any doubt of his manifold charms. 'I know your excellency likes to show your shapes to advantage,' a friend had once joked on recommending a breeches-maker for him in Naples. The very matter of his diplomatic career should perhaps have rung alarm bells in Augusta's mind, too. Only the month before their elopement, even as he and Lady Boringdon were spotted flirting at the season's assemblies, Arthur and his brother had been talking about the prospect of his returning to Vienna. A recall abroad might so easily have served as an excuse to leave his married lover to her fate – as presumably he had done with the Duke of Bedford's former cook.

All things considered, it seems hardly surprising that even the ladies of the *ton* sympathetic to Augusta's plight thought eloping with Paget was a bad bet. For women, married or single, elopement was always a gamble, and there was every chance that Augusta would find herself abandoned twice over: first by a bored lover, then by a hostile husband, loath to take her back, just as Lady Cloncurry had been.

While a husband might forgive an affair, a wife's elopement was typically only a prelude to a permanent separation or divorce. Not only a very public breach of the code that governed polite society, it was a well-publicised pique to her husband's pride, a dereliction of her duty towards him and their children and, potentially, a threat to his family property, since she might well be carrying her lover's child. Often, of course, it must have been exactly what the runaway herself wanted: to break free of her marriage and to unite herself with a new partner. Divorce and remarriage must certainly have been Augusta's goal when she walked away from Jack on Arthur's arm. According to courtesan Harriette Wilson, whose infamous memoirs have her condoling with the cuckolded Boringdon when he came to take tea with her, he had been prepared to take her back for the sake of their son, but she had refused.

As Augusta found out, though, fleeing a marriage was not an experience for the faint-hearted. After an elopement a cuckolded husband held all the cards. If he chose, he might easily hold his wife in a form of marital purgatory, just as the Earl of Derby had done in a similar situation in 1779. When his wife of just four years had embarked on an affair with her first love, the Duke of Dorset, the earl had resolutely refused either to reconcile or to divorce, condemning Lady Derby to a long and lonely life in social exile. Withholding a divorce could then be a means of exacting revenge on an unfaithful wife, depriving her of the opportunity to wed her lover and through remarriage recover her reputation. It could be punishment, pure and simple.

Even if it wasn't about revenge, going so far as a parliamentary divorce might not be to a husband's advantage. There was the expense to consider, the very public scrutiny it entailed of his private affairs, and the knock-on impact of that on both his career and the prospects of his children. If he had a perfectly satisfactory mistress and plenty of legitimate heirs, a separation from bed and board might serve the purpose just as well – for him, at least. Of course, his wife wouldn't be able to marry her lover, or anyone else, until he died. And she might find it very hard to make ends meet. Maintenance was only rarely granted to an adulterous wife in the ecclesiastical court, meaning that until her jointure kicked in she might have only the pin money she was entitled to under her marriage settlement. Any fortune she had brought to the union was also forfeited in such a case. A privately agreed separation might be more generous, but only if she had some kind of leverage to bring him to the negotiating table to discuss terms: perhaps embarrassing evidence of his own adultery that she could threaten to bring forth in court, or proof of his tacit acceptance of hers.

The statistics are certainly testament to the lack of appetite for parliamentary divorce in the upper echelons of society. Between 1800 and 1829, only sixteen titled couples were divorced by Act of Parliament – a number that in no way reflected the number of aristocratic spouses, male and female, seeking solace outside the marital bedroom. Not if diarists like Countess Lieven are to be believed, anyway. At one fête in 1820, she reported, so many couples strolled off into the garden – where the 'paths were well screened with thick laurel bushes' – that by the end of the evening almost the only guests left in the ballroom with her were the debutantes and a few old women.

Augusta, however, must have felt reasonably confident that her husband would want a divorce as much as she did. 'The Don' – as his closest friends called him – was only thirty-six, a year younger than Arthur, and had only one legitimate child. He was also socially ambitious: hopeful of taking a leap or two up the peerage ladder from his barony, to which end a respectable wife and willing hostess by his side would be an advantage. Tall, with handsome features and a calm demeanour, according to an acquaintance, his romantic career to date suggested that he would have no real struggle filling the vacant position, either. The press certainly seemed in little doubt that divorce was on the cards. Before the amorous fugitives from Cumberland Place had even been located, the papers ventured that 'as soon as the forms of law shall permit', Augusta would be Sir Arthur's wife.

For a man who did want to marry again, divorce was a three-step process. First, he had to sue his wife's lover for 'criminal conversation' – the euphemistic term for adultery, commonly referred to as 'crim.con.'. Then, he had to successfully obtain a separation from bed and board in the ecclesiastical court, and finally, he had to present a private bill in Parliament for divorce. The first step, the crim.con. trial, was traditionally his chance to exact financial retribution from his love rival for the loss of the comforts of his married life, for which damages could be eye-wateringly large. £5,000 was relatively commonplace where the parties were aristocrats and £20,000 not unknown – the first equivalent to more than £400,000 in today's money and the second a sum in excess of £1.5 million. Since Arthur, an indebted younger son whose parents claimed to be 'as poor as Poverty', was largely reliant on the income from his diplomatic work, Augusta was not the only one taking a risk when they eloped. An order to advance such a significant sum to Lord Boringdon had the potential to put his future financial security in serious jeopardy.

And if the reports doing the rounds in Mayfair were correct, it was not only his wealth but his health that the diplomat had put on the line when he carried her Ladyship off. 'We fear that, ere this, a duel has taken place between a Noble Lord (not Lord B——N) and Sir A.P,' one newspaper reported at the end of May 1808, adding, rather unnecessarily, that 'the most extreme agitation pervades every branch of the W——ND family; they are deeply interested in the event of this hostile meeting.' Since the journalist supposed that 'the Earl has taken every step possible, to prevent this much dreaded encounter', it appears to have been Augusta's older brother Lord Burghersh, a proud soldier, who was rumoured to have called her lover to account. However, if they did meet, Arthur came through it unscathed, ready to face his crim.con. trial.

The erstwhile ambassador decided not to contest the allegation that he had been 'criminally connected with the Plaintiff's wife' and by this admission of guilt contrived to keep the kind of salacious tittle-tattle so relished by the reading public out of the courtroom. Instead of combing over the usual evidence of rumpled sofa cushions and crumpled gowns to decide whether or not he and Augusta had actually committed adultery, the jury settled onto the benches at the sheriff's court on 19 July were concerned only with assessing the amount of damages.

Knowing that his opponent's lawyers would be doing their level best to demonstrate that their client had enjoyed a happy, harmonious married life with a chaste woman before the arrival on the scene of her practised seducer, a defendant like Sir Arthur usually resorted to publicly abusing his stolen lady. If she was imprudent, immodest and debauched, no comfort at all to a respectable man, her husband could need no large sum in compensation for his loss. Lawyers for Sir John Piers, for example, made sure to emphasise that Lady Cloncurry was alleged to have succumbed to his charms the very first time they happened to be alone together. It was, agreed the chief justice, 'a conquest of no great difficulty' and consequently 'her value could not be highly estimated.'

Sure enough, Lord Boringdon's counsel talked of 'uninterrupted harmony and matrimonial felicity' until the 'constant and unremitting visits' of the defendant began. Sir Arthur, however, had clearly instructed his barrister not to slander Augusta, who, like all women, was neither party to the case nor permitted to testify, and was therefore unable to defend herself. So, instead of treading the usual traitorous path, Mr Garrow confined himself to attacking the 'fashionable state of morals and manners' that had carried a young lady into an alliance at the age of eighteen, 'before her notions of happiness' could be fixed, or 'her inclinations known'. What was his client to do, he asked the jury, when she flew to him? 'His visits had brought a beautiful and accomplished woman into trouble and disgrace. He could do no otherwise than become her protector,' he concluded. Unfortunately, it proved an unsuccessful argument. Taking no more than twenty minutes, the jury set damages at £10,000, to which was added £111 for costs – half of which Sir Arthur must have struggled to raise.

In reality, he probably never had to; or if he did, it was only temporarily. He, Augusta and Lord Boringdon were almost certainly among the many who cooperated in the divorce process for their mutual benefit. According to Lord Eldon, the future Lord Chancellor, by 1800 as many as nine out of ten crim.con. trials were 'founded in the most infamous collusion'. The majority of cases, he said, were 'previously settled in some room in the City' and then, by agreement between the parties, damages were 'never paid to, nor expected by, the injured husband.' Such a bargain – effectively divorce by mutual consent – was repugnant to those who viewed adultery as a crime, but it was obviously in the interests of the three parties in a love triangle if they were united in their desire to move on and remarry. The cuckolded husband would commit to the parliamentary divorce that would allow them to achieve it, while his wife and her lover would agree not to contest any stage of the process, and specifically not to bring forward evidence of his own adultery, which – aside from being damaging to his career and reputation – would cause the whole case to collapse. If a husband was found to be guilty of infidelity himself, the law prevented him from obtaining either a full divorce or a separation from bed and board – something Georgiana, Lady Astley and her financially harassed lover Captain Tommy Garth turned to their advantage in the late 1820s, when her husband Sir Jacob Astley sued him for criminal conversation and attempted to sue her for a divorce. By convincing the courts that not only had her husband consorted with 'women of abandoned character' right in front of her face, but that he had also spent time 'with a common prostitute' in a house of ill repute, the lovers were able to reduce the crim.con. damages to just one shilling, and to scupper the divorce suit entirely, meaning that Georgiana retained all the protection of her husband's name and wealth.

Telling the courts all about Boringdon's *chères-amies* was obviously not in Augusta's interests, however. If she contested the suit he duly commenced in the ecclesiastical court, there would be no separation from bed and board, without which there could be no parliamentary divorce. Her best hope of marrying Arthur was to stay silent, to allow her own name to be blackened, her own character besmirched, while her philandering husband presented himself as a model spouse, 'scrupulously attentive to his moral habits and religious duties'. The thought of such public denigration must have been enough to put many gently bred ladies off any serious adulterous affairs, let alone an elopement. It must, surely, have been the reason that Lady Elizabeth refused Boringdon's proposals; the fallout of a divorce would be incredibly damaging for her unmarried daughters, just emerging into the world and seeking husbands of their own.

In fact, Augusta got off relatively lightly. It was much worse for those women like Lady Cloncurry, whose lovers had no intention of marrying them and might well stoop to promulgating lies about their promiscuity in an attempt to minimise damages; or those whose husbands had trumped up charges of adultery with the assistance of servants bribed to give false evidence. Though, like them, she could not defend her position, at least Arthur was taking steps to protect her reputation.

Thanks to the decision not to contest the adultery at any stage, no particularly salacious details made their way into the papers, either. All that Augusta was publicly accused of doing prior to her elopement was taking a few walks with her lover in Kensington Gardens, and regularly receiving him in Cumberland Place. Admittedly, her husband was conspicuously absent when these visits occurred, but her handsome visitor was – or so his barrister said – 'exposed to the intrusion of all the male and female acquaintance of the family'. Even the evidence of improper relations after she left her husband's house was couched in the most delicate terms, with the maid at the Crown Inn at Lyndhurst, where the fugitives were discovered, confirming little more than that it looked like two persons had slept in the bed made up in the room the couple had taken, and that 'the Gentleman's Clothes lay in the Bed Room the whole Time he was there.' There was certainly nothing to unduly amuse or titillate as there had been with painter Signor Gabrielli's recollections in Lord Cloncurry's action – possibly intentionally. In cases of collusion, the story the parties chose to reveal in court sometimes bore little resemblance to reality.

The lack of juicy details didn't stop pamphlets containing transcripts of the crim.con. trial being produced for the delectation of the scandal-hungry public – purchasable for as little as a shilling and still available on the shelves of Hookham's circulating library in Bond Street two decades later – but given the evidence, they were also a comparatively bland affair. Granted, they did, like some of the newspapers, repeat (and seemingly embellish) some of Augusta's private correspondence, which must have been extremely unpleasant; but the testimony of the various servants involved no suspicious noises, sofas in disarray or dresses discomposed. There was not even the mention of a locked drawing-room door. Nor did Augusta have to suffer, as other women had, the indignity of a degrading 'likeness' of her adorning the frontispiece, one naked breast exposed to signify her lost virtue.

As for Boringdon's shameless portrayal of himself as an affectionate husband with not the smallest stain on his character or morals, the press had helped Augusta out there, insinuating that his Lordship was no paragon of virtue, but rather a neglectful, unfaithful husband. And, while some (male) journalists pontificated that 'the faults of a husband cannot extenuate those of a wife' and (male) nobles talked about it never being a tie of 'interest or affection' on the part of the lady, many women, like Lady Jerningham, while they could not approve Augusta's actions, made up their minds to direct all their sympathies towards her.

Indeed, in the Hampshire neighbourhood where she and Arthur had set up home, effectively as man and mistress, so many people were making friendly overtures to her that the local clergyman delivered a sermon 'evidently meant... against the countenancing those who had openly infringed the laws of virtue & decency,' according to the Dowager Lady Spencer, then on a visit in the area. She commended him for it, having felt herself that Augusta ought to be living a little more quietly and repentantly. 'She has been & I believe still is at Portsmouth,' she had written to her daughter a few weeks earlier, 'walking about with S$^r$ A.P. with an effronterie that has certainly never been assumed by anybody in her situation.'

The couple had been waiting patiently away from London for the lawyers to clear each hurdle but, as Christmas approached, the stakes were rising for Augusta. By the time the usual separation from 'Bed, Board and mutual Cohabitation' was granted to Lord Boringdon in the ecclesiastical court on 16 December 1808, his wife was more than six months pregnant with another man's child. If her unborn baby was not to suffer all the disadvantages of illegitimacy, she had just a month or two to marry its father, an event on which her own social rehabilitation entirely depended, too – something that concerned the Dowager Lady Spencer. 'If it is true that she declares she never was so happy, I should greatly fear... that [Sir Arthur] might take her at her word, &

not alter her situation, when it is in his power to do it,' she wrote ominously. There was also the matter of money yet to be resolved. The ecclesiastical court had decided (as was their customary practice) that, adultery being proved, her Ladyship was not to be granted a maintenance allowance. But Augusta had brought a fortune of over £30,000 into her marriage, and was understandably anxious – especially given Arthur's less-than-plump pockets – to be compensated for its loss.

Armed with the necessary prerequisites, Boringdon at last brought his divorce bill before the House of Lords on 20 January 1809. If there was a deal between the three of them, he had stuck to it. Yet Augusta still teetered on the brink of ruin. The Lords would not hesitate to reject the divorce if they scented even a whiff of collusion. Just months later they would throw out the bill of Colonel Thomas Powlett, whose wife Letitia and her lover, Viscount Sackville, had been sensationally exposed when staff at the White Hart Inn in Winchester, where they had met for a furtive mid-afternoon tryst, sold the story to the papers. Even though the colonel had been granted the necessary separation and awarded damages of £3,000 at a crim. con. trial, Parliament was uneasy about the introduction of new and damning testimony. They suspected that Mrs Powlett had tipped off her husband about evidence her maid could supply about a soiled gown. If she had, it was an own goal, as without a divorce act from Parliament there was no way she could ever marry again and reinvent herself as a respectable wife.

For Augusta, it must have been an enormous relief when Boringdon's divorce act was passed, somewhat ironically on Valentine's Day 1809. With his public commitment to pay her an annuity and also settle £10,000 on her acting as an unintended but most welcome wedding present, she and Arthur hastened straight to church. They were married in Hampshire two days after she was officially divorced. Four weeks after that, they became the proud parents of a daughter, whom they named Leopoldine, presumably (if oddly) after her father's Viennese sweetheart. Arthur retired from the diplomatic profession, swapping his salary for a pension of £2,000, and they began to look about them for a permanent country home to rent near to his brothers. All boded well for a happy life together. But it was by no means guaranteed. Lady 'Harryo' Cavendish had it right when she lamented that an elopement would 'bring its own punishment' for a woman. As Lady Cloncurry had discovered, there were all too many reasons for a wife to bitterly regret a divorce.

The greatest of all was undoubtedly her separation from the children of her first marriage. With no hope of gaining custody and very little chance that her ex-husband would be generous enough to permit regular contact – adulterous women being considered morally unfit to care for children – most divorcees had to reconcile themselves to a virtual banishment from their sons' and daughters' lives. The situation appears to have been no different for Augusta. Her son Henry, heir to Boringdon's title and substantial property, remained permanently with his father. The three-year-old had so little memory of his mother that, rather tragically, he was able to mistake his new stepmother for her in the autumn of 1809. It was Frances, the second Lady Boringdon, to whom his care was from then on solely entrusted. She raised him alongside her own children, as well as his father's illegitimate sons with Lady Elizabeth, who remained ignorant of their true parentage but often spent their summer holidays at Saltram. For Augusta, as for most divorced women, the best that could be hoped for was to build a relationship with her son once he reached adulthood; but sadly, the opportunity never materialised. Henry died in November 1817 after swallowing an ear of rye, which the physicians believed had travelled down his windpipe and lodged in his lungs, causing an abscess. Whether she was actually prohibited from visiting him on his sickbed or not, Augusta did not travel to Paris where the eleven-year-old was then staying – though her sister Lady Jersey was said to have been with her nephew often during the last weeks of his life, carrying with her, one assumes, the blessings of his absent mother.

It wasn't only relationships with children that were impacted by divorce, however. Precious relationships with parents, siblings and cousins could suffer almost as much, since a Regency woman's honour was closely entwined with that of her family. A 'false step' by a member of the female sex, one contemporary writer explained, 'does not confine its ignominy to the guilty, but it is extended to those, who are connected to [her] by the dearest ties.' No matter if her near relations were 'free from the imputation of neglect, ill advice or bad example,' he said, they nevertheless 'seem to share in the disgrace.' Indeed, Caroline, Lady Paget, the wife of Arthur's oldest brother, was 'much blamed' for her encouragement of her brother-in-law and his married lover, with her visit to Augusta in the wake of the elopement described as 'injudicious'. That being the case, adulterous women might well find themselves given the cold shoulder for the sake of preserving the rest of the family's reputation – though, pleasingly, Augusta seems to have remained on very good terms with hers, or at the very least with her father and her sister Sarah. The family narrative seems to have been that she had detested Lord Boringdon for his behaviour and was deserving of kindness; it was certainly what her cousin Harriet Arbuthnot, still in the schoolroom at the time of the elopement, was told. 'It was very unfortunate, for she is a very amiable person, with a thousand good qualities, & ever since… her conduct has been irreproachable,' she wrote after a visit to Lady Augusta and her second husband many years after the event.

Augusta was also welcomed with open arms into the Paget family – again, something not guaranteed. When Lady Sarah Spencer's Uncle Richard had eloped with Lady Elizabeth Howard in 1793 – four years after she had been pressured by her parents to give him up and marry the Duke of Norfolk's heir – his youngest sibling, her aunt, Lady Anne Bingham, had positively refused to receive either the adulteress or her child. Augusta, however, was routinely given the Pagets' 'kindest love' in their letters to Arthur, which often contained messages for his lady – even when she was living with him unmarried. Her new sisters-in-law were happy to invite her to their homes, and her brothers-in-law to send back presents from their travels. Like her own relations, the Pagets seem to have felt that she had been badly used by Lord Boringdon and was deserving of their support. In truth, the morally dubious Lady Elizabeth Monck was no great favourite of theirs – though, awkwardly, she was the mother-in-law of Arthur's younger (and favourite) brother, Captain Charles Paget. Perhaps they were simply relieved that Arthur was settling down at last, and with a suitably well-born and likeable woman. Even so, the warmth of their reception appears somewhat surprising – not least because Augusta was not the only adulterous wife to join the family, and the other,

Lady Charlotte Wellesley, was greeted not just frostily but angrily after her elopement with Arthur's eldest brother Henry, Lord Paget, the following year.

Henry (later Lord Uxbridge who lost a leg at Waterloo) was, unlike Arthur, married with eight children at the time of his flight, and his wife 'Car' a much-liked member of the family. Whether that was the reason for the difference in treatment, in Charlotte's case there was no question of the Paget clan sending her their love. Arthur's father threatened to cut off his heir without a penny, while letters between the Paget brothers and their brothers-in-law variously described Charlotte as a '*maudite sorcière*' (damn witch) and 'the most wicked and profligate whore and liar that ever hell itself could or ever will produce.' Similarly, the Paget ladies always disliked meeting Charlotte: 'going… to *Swallow my Pill*' was how Lady Caroline Capel (née Paget) described a courtesy visit a full six years after the notorious elopement. At the same time, she expressed her pleasure that her brother being made Marquis of Anglesey meant that his second wife (whom he married after they had both obtained divorces) would 'no longer bear the same name' as her 'pure, virtuous, precious' mother.

Just as difficult to repair as family relationships was a divorcee's public reputation, though a swift remarriage to her lover helped enormously. A repentant retreat from town for a period and then re-emergence with a new name appear to have been sufficient to see a lady readmitted into the polite world, to some extent at least, as the *New Bon Ton Magazine* confirmed sardonically in 1819. 'Adultery,' it said, 'does not exclude females now from society; on the contrary, it gives eclat to their name, especially when they wing the bird, and fix him in their snare.'

But that's not to say that social rehabilitation was ever entire, nor easy. Even decades after her elopement and divorce, some doors still remained closed to the formidable Whig hostess Lady Holland. Similarly, Lady Charlotte Wellesley's scandalous flight with Lord Paget still tainted her reputation nearly twenty years later. 'The strict moralist perhaps may not approve of my taking my daughter to visit [her],' conceded one of her second husband's near neighbours. Her conduct could not be justified, he firmly agreed, but he was satisfied that a visit was unexceptionable since other respectable women were known to have stayed at her house.

Even if a divorced woman did manage to reclaim her reputation sufficiently to enjoy some sort of social life, there was still plenty of scope for disappointment and disenchantment in her new relationship. A man who made an exciting or considerate lover was not necessarily a good bet financially – at least not for an aristocratic woman who had probably never even had to think about regulating her spending, let alone running a household on a small budget. Lady Astley, for one, traded a life of great ease and comfort for something entirely different when she eloped with Captain Garth in 1826. Despite almost certainly being the illegitimate son of King George III's daughter, Princess Sophia, the unacknowledged Garth subsisted on his half-pay from the army alone, and was perennially indebted. Though they had successfully staved off a dangerously large damages payout by exposing Sir Jacob's fondness for the company of 'fallen' women, the couple – who were unable to marry precisely because they had scuppered the divorce – were obliged to live between lodgings and inns until Georgiana, sister of a marchioness, eventually followed her lover into the King's Bench debtor's prison. They were still residing there when their daughter was born in 1835. Sadly, Georgiana lived for only a few days after the birth, the scarlet fever putting 'an end to her sufferings', as one obituary described it.

While the Garths might be an extreme case, it was true that for aristocratic women, walking away from a husband could well mean leaving the lap of luxury, and perhaps taking a step down the social ladder, too. Money was certainly a greater concern for Augusta and Arthur than it was for Lord Boringdon, especially in their early years together. Arthur wasn't able to carry his bride over the threshold of a magnificent Palladian country seat, like the one her former husband had inherited, nor anything so imposing as the Jacobean Apethorpe Hall, her father's property in Northamptonshire. The couple's choice of residence was limited to the one they could afford to rent, Arthur having previously admitted to his brother that his 'means did not admit of [his] taking Houses at £300 and £400 a year'. They had no permanent base in town like Boringdon or her father, either; and if one diarist was to be believed, in the first year of married life they were keeping 'one man servant only' – 'such is Her change of situation in life,' he said of Augusta with a touch of disdain.

All in all, it isn't too difficult to understand why women like Lady Elizabeth Monck simply decided that a marital split had too many disadvantages to be contemplated. Happily for Augusta, though, her second marriage seems to have been worth every moment of heartache over little Henry, every smear on her character, every snide remark by her contemporaries and every bit of penny-pinching. She and Arthur settled in supreme contentment in the Hampshire countryside, enjoying visits from a steady succession of family and friends (including the fastidious Beau Brummell), and producing an ever-growing number of siblings for Leopoldine. Depending on the source, the dust kicked up by their elopement had either proved a convenient excuse for Arthur to abandon the diplomatic career that he had never liked, on account of it keeping him so far from home and his close-knit family; or it had forced him to retire, since he would not be able to present the divorced Augusta at any foreign court. Either way, living on his government pension and his younger son's portion, he immersed himself fully in countryside pursuits and family concerns – no doubt much to the previously neglected Augusta's delight.

Boringdon, too, seemed more content and settled with his second wife Frances, the daughter of a Norfolk surgeon, who had no fortune to speak of and was pleasing rather than pretty. The one-time rake – apt to talk of 'his present wife and her *predecessor* just as one would of a new butler' – did not entirely reform his womanising ways in the wake of their marriage, six months after the divorce, but his Saltram estate became the scene of comfortable fireside evenings à deux, and somewhere his genteel country neighbours were, for the first time, happy to visit. The second Lady Boringdon, while not born to their world, also won the universal approval of his inner circle. 'She seems to suit him exactly and to like him extremely,' observed Harryo Cavendish, soon to marry Boringdon's best friend, Lord Granville Leveson-Gower. 'How they all do surprise me by accepting him,' she did, though, admit to her brother. 'His success, just as to that, is wonderful. I do not envy his wife and happy in my mind was she who ran.'

*Chapter Nine*

# The Tomb of Love?

As the Regency proper drew to a close at the end of the 1810s, a satirical glossary poking fun at the members of the *haut ton* raised smiles. Along with their sense of morality – a word, it said, to be interpreted in 'modern polite conversation' as 'a troublesome interrupter of pleasure' – it took aim at their approach to matrimony, defined as 'a blind bargain, wherein a fashionable man and wife revolve like the sun and moon, shunning and eclipsing each other.' Certainly to those looking in on high society – seeing princes and their well-born friends parading mistresses around Mayfair, news of separations and elopements filling society columns, and Almack's branded a 'matrimonial bazaar'– real love and happy marriage must have seemed like concepts that belonged only in the world of novels.

But not so, said Sydney, Lady Morgan. 'I intend to write a book to explode the vulgar idea of matrimony being the tomb of love,' the authoress laughed to a friend. 'Matrimony,' she declared, 'is the real thing.' Admittedly, the words were those of a bride, wed for just a matter of weeks and still basking in the attention of a man she (somewhat cockily) described as 'desperately in love with his own wife.' Yet in thirty years of marriage she never came to feel differently. Sir Charles was ever to be her 'beloved' husband, her 'most dear and true friend' in the world. The once-reluctant wife was even known to declare that the best thing a woman could do was marry.

It helped that the devoted, besotted Charles proved to be an ideal husband for a woman hostile to the shackles that were part and parcel of the married state. He had been quite happy to allow Sydney to have charge of her own earnings. In their marriage settlement, they took a strikingly modern approach to their finances, agreeing that Sydney would have 'sole and independent control' over all her income, past and future. His money would be settled entirely upon his young daughter from his first marriage, who continued to be cared for by her grandparents in England. And just as he had assured her during their tumultuous courtship, he showed no 'tyrannical pretensions to *man's* superiority' either – indeed, Sydney had much success 'in getting him to do whatever she wished, or to go wherever she liked', according to her memoirs. The good-natured Charles had envisaged *equality*, but it seems to have been Sydney who wore the breeches most of the time.

It similarly helped that one-time local physician Charles came to be seen as quite a catch in his wife's literary circles. 'I see no such husband anywhere: the women all think him handsome, and the men very clever, and I am very proud,' Sydney was able to boast to her sister Olivia from London, where the couple were mingling in the fashionable world; she eagerly, he a little less so.

It was a mere visit, because Charles had never insisted on the much-dreaded move to England. Instead the bride and groom had settled themselves in a house right near Olivia in Dublin, her children – to whom Sydney and Charles were 'little mamma and big papa' – more than compensating (if compensation were needed) for the lack of any offspring of their own. The Morgans moved to London only when Sydney desired it, taking up residence in the sleek streets of Belgravia in 1837.

In fact, none of Sydney's worries were ever realised, and especially not those about her work. 'It is quite clear, that like all heroines, I no longer interest when I gain a husband,' she might, shortly after the wedding, have mock-indignantly chastised an old friend, but there was no real fear of it. With Charles's full support and encouragement, within three months of the wedding she was working on her next book – *O'Donnel* would be the first British novel to feature a governess as its romantic heroine. Not only would she continue to earn a respectable living through writing and to publish proudly under her real name, but she carried on negotiating the terms of all her book deals herself. Consistently she bettered the original bargain – commanding £550 (more than twice what some naval captains on full pay earned in a year) for the copyright of her first novel as a married woman – and managed to secure even more lucrative commissions for travelogues, which enabled her and 'dear Morgan' to jaunt about the continent together. With Charles soon picking up the pen himself, they became mutual editors and collaborators, on everything from the travel books to magazine articles. A visitor stepping into their drawing room in January 1843, seven months before Charles died, stumbled upon a typical scene: husband and wife 'sitting over the fire and laughing… at some nonsense' soon to be transformed into a paid commission.

It's not the sort of lifestyle that springs to mind when we think of married women in the early nineteenth century. The Victorian ideal of the 'angel in the house' has done much to shape our view of their lives, almost convincing us that they require our sympathy: marriage providing their financial security but the price being submission to a husband, and suppression of any ambitions or intelligence. Yet the childless, sociable Sydney, busy with work that exercised her mind and with a firm hand on the purse strings, was not actually that unusual – not in upper-class circles, anyway. Not only did the women who moved in Regency high society enjoy extraordinary rights over their own property, but there was very little expectation that their lives would be solely confined to the cosy domestic sphere, limited to the tender care of children and creation of a comfortable home, while their spouse made his mark in the big wide world. In fact, aided by stewards, housekeepers, nannies and nursemaids, to whom they could delegate numerous household concerns, many aristocratic wives looked forward to a married life spent serving – at the very least – as a companion and collaborator of their husband: inhabiting his world, travelling alongside him and sharing the burden of his responsibilities. Marriage opened up outlets for their intellect and industry outside the home and, often, opportunities to find a deeply fulfilling sense of purpose.

Harriet Fane was, as she gleefully acknowledged, propelled right into 'the vortex of politics' by her marriage to Charles Arbuthnot in 1814. As Treasury Secretary, responsible for ensuring government support in the House of Commons, as well as chief confidant to the Tory Prime Minister Lord Liverpool, her new husband enjoyed the 'intimacy and unreserved confidence' of an extraordinarily large number of statesmen and cabinet ministers. Not to mention he was, by necessity, privy to almost everything that went on in government. With her voracious appetite for politics, enquiring mind and allegiance to the Tory cause, his world was a thrilling one for the twenty-year-old Harriet. As his sounding board, and an enthusiastic hostess to the stream of prominent politicians who beat a path to the door of their Downing Street home, she was, almost from the very moment of her union, given an extraordinary insight into the political landscape. Finding her 'so perfectly discreet', Charles and his colleagues 'talked openly in her presence' and she was to be witness to all kinds of off-the-record conversations – in fact, to a great deal of history in the making. She had no need to read the gossip printed in the papers about King George IV's attempted divorce in 1820; all of it and more came to her direct. And when there was a plot to murder the whole of the cabinet the same year, she was able to visit the loft in Cato Street where the conspirators had been arrested.

Being a ringside spectator was one thing, but Harriet was able to go much further, stepping almost into the political realm herself. Having become a frequent visitor to 'the ventilator' – the loft space above the House of Commons, which, for those women who could secure admission, afforded through its ventilation shaft an opportunity to listen to debates[15] – her well-informed

---

15  Lady Shelley must have been among the first women to visit the new space after its creation in 1818. She described it as 'a room about eight feet square, resembling the cabin of a ship', with a window, a couple of chairs and 'a thing like a chimney in the centre', which opened into the Commons chamber below. 'Sound ascends so perfectly,' she marvelled, stirred by the debates she was able to hear. The shaft also offered its visitors – who included Lady Bessborough and Sarah, Lady Jersey, too – a view of proceedings, albeit a limited one.

views were soon proving of value to her husband's colleagues, many of whom became firm friends of Mrs Arbuthnot in her own right. So highly did they come to rate her frank, unvarnished opinions, sensible advice and sense of discretion that she would go on to serve, with the encouragement of her husband, almost as a special adviser to some high-profile statesmen. Before his death in 1822, Foreign Secretary Lord Castlereagh would visit the couple at breakfast time nearly every day to talk over the debates of the previous night – and 'to take his orders' from Harriet, he joked. To the Duke of Wellington she became a tried and trusted counsellor, held in high regard, said a mutual friend, because she 'gave him her clear and honest opinion on matters of which others were afraid to speak'. Harriet was the 'fireside friend… quite without nerves' that he needed.

That Harriet was no mere conduit for her husband's opinions, nor acting only within the bounds of his permission, is clear from Charles's occasional bursts of alarm when it seemed her actions might be jeopardising his own position. In 1822, he was 'made ill by the idea of Lord Liverpool imagining that he was opposing him' when his wife began canvassing for the man standing for election against the Prime Minister's favoured candidate. On that occasion, Harriet was quite happy to explain the matter to the premier herself, seizing the opportunity to remind him of the toll her husband's long hours and heavy workload were taking on his health, and entreating him to hasten the arrangements for his move to a new role.

In his fifties and struggling with a bad case of burnout as his wife hit her stride in the early 1820s, whether Charles appreciated her vicarious sense of ambition and determination to see him continue in a government post seems doubtful. 'Were I to consult my own inclinations I would retire upon my pension,' he wrote that same year. 'I am sick of everything political and so worn out that no post horse ever more wanted repose.' Yet Charles was bound to admit that his second wife, despite being inconveniently fond of the cut and thrust of politics, was his 'guardian angel' – 'I got into agitations & anxieties which made me unfit for everything; but she relieved me from all troubles,' he said touchingly.

For in what feels like as modern an arrangement as that of the Morgans, Harriet managed all of their finances. It was into her account that all of her husband's income was paid: 'I even went to her for mere Pocket Money,' Charles later recalled, without a shadow of irritation or embarrassment. Again, it was not so unusual a state of affairs as we might think. The death of the Duchess of Rutland Harriet described as a 'most dismal loss to her husband' since 'she managed all his affairs for him; he did nothing himself, and his estates, his houses, his family, everything was under her rule.'

Modestly, she drew no comparisons with herself, but Harriet certainly had no need to sit stitching chair covers or reading sentimental novels to pass her time. Like the duchess, who masterminded the Regency-era transformation of Belvoir Castle, her husband's ancestral seat, it was Harriet who oversaw improvements to what she described as Charles's 'perfectly hideous' property at Woodford in Northamptonshire. She began with work in the garden, and then turned her hand to the farmhouse itself, extending it and moving the old farm buildings to create a French parterre.

Unlike the duchess, a mother of ten, Harriet had no children of her own – something she seems not to have regretted; she confessed that she was not fond of infants. She was, however, an affectionate and involved stepmother, especially to Charles's two daughters – 'my two girls', as she referred to them. At the age of just twenty-six she took over from their governess, happily joining the chaperones at Almack's and a succession of other assemblies; the names of 'Mrs and Misses Arbuthnot' regularly seen in the society sections of the London newspapers.

That she was a young and beautiful chaperone, whirling round Regency London in political circles, and not always in the company of her much-older husband, was, inevitably, the thing that cast a shadow over what was a very successful marriage. One rumour then raged more fiercely than any other, and still does even to this day. 'Mr Arbuthnot & I have been greatly annoyed by another anonymous letter accusing me of being in love with the Duke of Wellington, of being always in *holes and corners* with him, & of being so jealous of him that I never can bear him to speak to any other woman!' Harriet scribbled angrily in her diary in 1824. It was the 'holes and corners' jibe that most rankled. She hardly ever, she wrote defensively, sat down by the duke at assemblies, was always one of a large party with him at the opera, and if she received him in Downing Street, it was only ever when her door was 'open to the whole town unless Mr A. is at home & chooses we sh$^d$ be a trio.'

And choose he very often did. The affinity between Harriet and Wellington might have been strongest, but all three of them had been tied in a triangular bond of friendship since 1815, a trio who seethed together privately over the 'base insinuations' in the letters, which all of them knew to be untrue. Harriet certainly had opportunity to be unfaithful during her married life, if not with Wellington then with any number of other admirers who talked appreciatively of her charm, which, 'when intellectual women can boast of it,' according to one, 'renders them mistresses of all hearts.' She was perhaps unwise in taking no pains to conceal her intimacy with the duke, readily taking his arm as they walked in the park and seeking him out at parties, but to those who knew her the idea that she ever indulged in an adulterous relationship was almost ridiculous. Harriet the arch-Tory was a straitlaced Victorian matron before such a thing ever existed. 'I do not see how it is possible to accuse a lady of more gross indecency,' she spat when *The Times* reported – incorrectly, of course – that she had attended a fancy dress ball in men's clothes. Besides that, it was clear to many of their acquaintances not only that Wellington was 'equally attached to husband and wife' but that Harriet lived with Charles 'in the most affectionate union in conscious innocence'. There was certainly no doubt whatsoever in the mind of Lady Shelley, close friend and confidante of both Harriet and the duke. 'He admired her very much – for she had a manlike sense,' she said, unconsciously betraying that however wealthy and liberated she was, she was still a product of her time. 'But,' she went on, 'Mrs Arbuthnot was devoid of womanly passions, and was, above all, a loyal and truthful woman.'

The temptation to stray was far greater for Frances Anne Vane-Tempest, the new Lady Stewart. Like Harriet, she found herself catapulted into a new sphere after her marriage to Charles, then Ambassador at Vienna, in 1819, and one in which she would have a part to play. Unlike Harriet, she was far from enchanted with her new life. Chief among her responsibilities was dispensing hospitality to foreign dignitaries and statesmen, but as an ambassadress she was a public figure in her own right, tasked with supporting embassy work, maintaining useful contacts and, importantly, avoiding either showing favouritism or giving offence. Harryo – by then Lady Granville – stepped into the same role when her husband was made Ambassador at the Hague in 1824, and reported wryly to her sister, '[I] do not let myself go to any likes and dislikes, but, like the sun, rather a dim one by the way, I shine on all alike.' The intensive socialising required of her she found the harder part of her new job – all the 'going out' was, she said, her 'favourite aversion'.

Frances Anne embarked on her own passage to the continent with pleasure – finally freed from the shackles of a governess, the purse strings firmly slackened, and her new husband, who had dutifully swapped his surname for hers, seemingly inclined to gratify her every whim. 'They dote on each other,' observed one of the embassy staff not long after the newly-weds arrived in Vienna. Her new position, however, the nineteen-year-old had quickly discovered she liked less. She found no friends of her own age in the city; was bored 'to death' by the diplomatic dinners at which she had to play hostess; and discovered, by the time she had given three glittering receptions for European royalty, hampered by the stifling court etiquette, that any vestige of excitement had well and truly worn off. Not to mention that acquaintances of her husband would keep telling 'uncomfortable' stories of 'former times and other attachments' that dented her confidence. Languishing in 'discontent and idleness' during her time in post, she engaged in a brief emotional affair with Alexander, the charismatic Russian Emperor, who combined, she said, 'every thing that could please the eye, fascinate the ear, flatter the vanity and captivate the heart.'

But that early wobble aside, she and her husband would

prove to be a strong partnership. Each found in the other a kindred spirit: both shared a well-developed sense of their own consequence, and both revelled in their combined spending power and considerable estates, which stretched to more than £80,000 a year and somewhere close to 50,000 acres after Charles became the 3rd Marquis of Londonderry in the wake of his brother's suicide in 1822. They certainly shared a penchant for extravagance, and a tendency towards exhibitionism. 'I should lose my taste for luxury in that house: it is displayed in such a vulgar way,' declared Countess Lieven after a visit to their rented home in London, while an acquaintance in Vienna sniped that 'when they give an entertainment... 'tis an ostentatious display of *their* Superiour riches and grandeur. She... receives you with *freezing* pomp,' she went on. 'He is *her* most humble slave.'

Indeed, for all Mrs Taylor's pre-wedding worries, Charles was much more affectionate and attentive towards his young wife than any mere fortune-hunter might be. In private letters to his brother written in the earliest years of their marriage 'Fanny' (as he always knew her) was his 'incomparable little companion, who has behaved like an angel'. Twenty years on, he would pay tribute to her as the one to whom 'I owe more than I can repay, although not more than I feel... the partner of my joys, my sorrows, and my fate.'

The management of the Vane-Tempest collieries, in which Charles had been granted a life interest under their marriage settlement, Frances Anne left chiefly in his hands. Ceding day-to-day oversight of her inherited empire may have been what was expected of her, as a woman and a wife, but it was by no means an inevitability. When she came of age in 1806, Sarah, Lady Jersey declined to make her new husband a partner in Child & Co, the bank that formed part of her sizeable inheritance from her grandfather. Even in her childbearing years, during which she became the mother of eight children, Lady Jersey remained its senior partner, involving herself in everything from the accounts to staff salaries during her tenure, and keeping a desk in their Fleet Street offices for the purpose. All of which she did alongside being heavily involved in the day-to-day running of Almack's. Frances Anne, however, trod a slightly more conventional path, her husband effectively becoming her agent – and a hard-working one. Within months of their wedding, Charles had assumed control of the collieries on her behalf and, having conducted a detailed enquiry into their operation, promptly replaced the failing management team. He would go on to take informed but speculative risks that later paid significant dividends, most notably building a harbour at Seaham to facilitate the shipping of their coal, and a railway to move it between the colliery and port.

But if she was not quite so hands-on as her husband, Frances Anne clearly considered the administration of her inheritance as a joint enterprise. 'We forgave [my mother] 2000£ balance... which she owed us for furniture, books, plate etc. sold and carried off,' she wrote of the period immediately after her marriage, in which Lady Antrim's plunder of her daughter's birthright had come fully to light. There is certainly no doubt that Frances Anne was well aware of everything that was happening in her inherited empire in the north-east, matched her husband's enthusiasm for his large-scale projects and was in many respects actively involved. Far from being cloistered away, concentrating on domestic matters, she played a central role in electioneering in County Durham, oversaw the building of schools for her employees' children, and even petitioned the government for a peerage that could be passed on to her own eldest son. So, too, was she instrumental in the remodelling of her own ancestral home, Wynyard Park; with the planning and building of a holiday home for herself on the Irish estates she inherited from her mother; and with the eye-wateringly expensive refit of the couple's new London property, Holdernesse House, which they combined with the mansion next door. Here she positioned herself as a Tory hostess, the thrower of particularly sumptuous parties (at which she habitually appeared dripping in jewels) and the patron of aspiring young politicians, among them Benjamin Disraeli. And all of this she combined with nine pregnancies in the space of seventeen years; suffering two miscarriages but giving birth to three sons and four daughters.[16]

It was, however, after Charles died of influenza in 1854 that Frances Anne was able to prove definitively to the world that she was more than the 'mere fine lady' she had so often seemed – something her husband had made it easy for her to do. After she came of age in 1821, he had arranged for all of her Durham and Irish estates, including her collieries, to be left at her 'absolute disposal' after his death – wanting to make her 'more powerful and a free agent in every future contingency,' he told his brother. When the time came, Frances Anne had stepped into his shoes without hesitation. Under her sole direction came everything

---

16  Frances Anne was not an especially hands-on mother during their early childhood – nurses plural accompanied her and the children on social visits in Vienna – but in time, she would have much to concern herself with when it came to her children, because the young Vanes proved every bit as defiant as their parents. Their youngest daughter Adelaide eloped with her brother's tutor, a recently ordained clergyman; their youngest son Ernest enlisted as a mere private in the army at seventeen and had to be bought a commission; while their second son Adolphus made a hasty marriage to the Duke of Newcastle's daughter, much frowned upon because of his struggles with his mental health in the wake of his return from the Crimean War.

from 'Estates to Docks, from draining to Railways, quarries to timber' – a sizeable industrial empire that included the largest, most profitable coalfield in the north of England, as well as 12,000 acres of land. Frances Anne was to be no mere figurehead either, but every inch the equivalent of a contemporary CEO. She proved herself unafraid to show the door to agents who attempted to take advantage of a woman in business; undaunted by extensive expansion; and unflinching at the prospect of making public speeches to several thousand of the pitmen on her payroll.

'I wish I had your energy and activity,' said her stepson Frederick. Somewhat surprised at the turn of events, he added, in a backhanded compliment, 'I wonder at your work for you never seemed as if you would rouse yourself to great exertion.' Frances Anne's former protégé Disraeli did not wonder so much. 'One must find excitement if one has brains,' he wrote after visiting her in 1861 at her 'regular office' in Seaham. Queen Victoria might have been uncomfortable about the power she held in her hands – 'we women are not *made* for governing,' she famously said, 'and if we are good women we must *dislike* these masculine occupations' – but not all of her female subjects agreed. Frances Anne could easily have delegated her commercial responsibilities to an agent, or to one of her three sons. Yet she chose not to, considering them, she said, 'a charge confided to me'.

Like Frances Anne, it was only after her husband's death that Sarah, by then Lady Lyttelton, made her mark on history. For the previous twenty-five years, her focus had been almost entirely on their family. It was a life that would not have suited Lady Morgan or Mrs Arbuthnot, but one which she had relished. 'They are said to be the happiest couple in the world,' a new acquaintance had been able to remark about her and William in 1833, a full two decades after their Wimbledon wedding. By that time the couple were, at last, settled at Hagley Hall, William's ancestral home, having spent much of their married life on the move between short-term rented homes and relatives' houses, managing a limited budget.

With her warm heart, caring disposition and plentiful experience with her younger brothers, motherhood had always been Sarah's most natural vocation – although she had hoped to avoid too large a family. She did not, she said, '*mean* or *wish* to have as many by about half' as her sister-in-law Mrs Pole-Carew, who had five children of her own and at least six stepchildren. To the upbringing of the three sons and two daughters who did arrive between 1816 and 1821, she had, however, dedicated herself, becoming a devoted and hands-on mother. 'Sal is up to her ears in alphabets, copy books, and gamuts,'[17] Lady Spencer clucked in 1823. 'Her babies are really uncommon fine ones, and very clever and sensible ones. And they will be admirably brought up, for she thinks and does nothing else.'

It was a slight exaggeration. Sarah was not so occupied outside the family as Frances Anne or Harriet, but, ever interested in current affairs, she remained a valued confidante for William, still active in politics. She was renowned as a friendly, accomplished hostess and continued to be a diligent correspondent to all her nearest and dearest. But home would always be her favourite place; family always her driving force. When Mr Pole-Carew died in 1835, she and William were quick to offer a home to their four orphaned nieces, who joined the Lyttelton clan at

---

17  Scales of musical notes.

Hagley – though minus their canaries. 'Ld. L has *no preference* (to speak mildly) for their music,' Sarah told them. 'We have already one, who undergoes many risks and banishments, and much abuse into the bargain, poor fellow.'

It seems to have been a tacit acknowledgement that William, plagued by health problems, was not the easiest of husbands to live with, illness making him increasingly impatient and short-tempered. He was certainly not unloving – 'how can I be thankful enough to Heaven for the Gift, and the long continuance of it to me,' he wrote of his wife on her forty-sixth birthday – but he was quite obviously the dominant partner in their relationship. Still lacking in confidence almost as much as in her debutante days, Sarah admitted to having been 'guided and prompted' by him throughout their many 'bright years' together.

His death in 1837, however, had ushered in an entirely new era. For Sarah, at the age of forty-nine, began a widowhood that would last three decades; for the nation began the long, stable reign of Queen Victoria. And it was the teenage monarch who gave Sarah a whole new sense of purpose. Persuaded by her brother Althorp (by then Earl Spencer), in the early months of 1838 she took up a post as lady of the bedchamber, which allowed a degree of both distance and independence from her eldest son, newly installed as master of Hagley Hall and eager to marry.

Her ready sympathy, good sense and amiable nature quickly made her a favourite at court, and when the Queen and Prince Albert began looking around for a governess for the royal children, she was their first choice for the post. Thus from 1842, Sarah went from month-long stints 'in-waiting' to something very much like a full-time job, taking total charge of the education of the Princess Royal and the Prince of Wales (and in due course a number of their siblings). As with Frances Anne, it was no mere ceremonial role. Sarah's duties included everything from managing the nursery staff, keeping accounts and sending bulletins to the Queen to giving the children their first lessons. And at her own insistence, she had considerable authority, including the almost-treasonous right 'to maintain her own opinions by argument, without reserve'.

Despite being as diffident as ever, she enjoyed the complete confidence of her royal employers during her eight years in post – along with the sincere affection of her royal charges, to whom she was known as 'Laddle'. And while doing her duty to the monarch had many downsides, there was satisfaction to be found in it for her, too. 'I sometimes feel glad, as well as thankful, that I am doing what I used to fancy I wished to do,' she wrote, 'really *working* for my bread.'

For all that, though, family still came first. It was without hesitation that Sarah resigned her post after her daughter Lavinia died in 1850. There were four young children who would stand in need of their grandmother and her 'far-reaching power of intensely loving'.

Delving into the diaries and letters of the real women who lived and loved in the Regency brings an incredibly satisfying reward: a glimpse of a reality that's both comfortingly familiar to us from our favourite fiction, and yet surprising at the same time.

The heroines of true tales of Regency romance, their voices reveal, were gratifyingly every bit as independently minded and determined as their invented counterparts. They could, and did, fight for love. They had agency, and the ability to make choices about how and with whom they spent their lives, whether that was as a contented singleton or a spouse. They chose men who valued them as friends and partners. They resisted attempts to surrender their rightful property. They sought adventure, proved courageous and capable in the face of adversity and, despite considerable penalties, dared to leave unhappy marriages. In a male-dominated world, they stepped into roles of trust and responsibility with confidence, and proved themselves more than up to the task. In so many ways, from their attitudes to their actions, they seem startlingly modern, strikingly relatable.

And while many of their opinions and experiences give us a thrill of recognition as readers of Regency romance, arguably more interestingly they also push us to challenge some of the stereotypes that we have a tendency to swallow without question: that all single women of the era were doomed to penury and a depressing state of dependence; that debutantes married in their first season or two or got left on the shelf; that women's property ownership was just a fanciful dream before Victorian reform; and that wives had to bury any intelligence and enterprise in domestic oblivion.

What we get by following women like Sarah and Sydney, Frances Anne and Harriet, Magdalene and Augusta behind drawing room doors, into ballrooms and courtrooms, to country house parties and off on campaign with the army, is a new perspective on a period of history that's exercised a powerful hold on our imaginations for so long. We see what Regency romance was *really* like, for the aristocracy, at least – from the marriage market, with its constant scrutiny and its seemingly enviable rules of engagement, which actually turned tying the knot into more of a gamble than we'd be prepared to accept today; to the months and years of matrimony that followed, in which, despite the burden of childbirth and a system skewed against their sex, plenty of women found happiness and fulfilment. We see how little human emotion has changed in two centuries, too, from the power of love to the pain of grief; and we satisfy ourselves that while classic tales of Regency romance might sometimes read like fantasy, they absolutely have their parallels in reality.

Lady Augusta Paget was amply rewarded for her courageous decision to break free from her miserable marriage to Lord Boringdon. She and Arthur went on to have nine children together, raising them in a country house that they had built, overlooking the sea at Southampton. His notorious inconstancy seemingly never troubled her, and this loving second union ended only with his death in 1840. The remaining thirty years of her life Augusta spent living in a grace-and-favour apartment at Hampton Court Palace, where, in a twist worthy of a novel, her old adversary Lady Elizabeth Monck was a near neighbour.

Magdalene De Lancey lived out the happy ending that had been cruelly snatched from her at Waterloo with her second husband – albeit just heartbreakingly briefly. She and Captain Harvey had a honeymoon tour around Europe; with their first daughter born in Rome just over nine months after their wedding day and followed, in quick succession, by a brother and sister. Magdalene celebrated her third wedding anniversary, but died just a few months later, probably from the consumption that had killed her sister. She was just twenty-nine.

Harriet Arbuthnot also died young, passing away suddenly at the age of forty after being struck down with cholera. Money worries had plagued her and Charles throughout their twenty-year marriage, just as her older brothers had foreseen, but she never repented her choice. The journal she left behind, scribbled down in secret, fizzes with her love for the life that he gave her, while her letters are full of affection for the man himself. 'God bless you, my dearest love, I hope at the end of another ten years you will love me as much as now,' she wrote to him a decade into their marriage in 1824, adding fatefully, '& if I am alive I am certain I shall love you more.'

Frances Anne, Lady Londonderry, who had fought equally hard to wed her own Charles, never regretted her marriage either. 'It seems as if there was only ½ myself left,' she said after his death, bereft of her 'friend and partner of 35 years'. Testament to her pride in him is the statue of the marquis as a dashing Hussar in the city of Durham, along with the church she had erected in his memory in Seaham, a town that owed its very existence to his endeavours. After her own death at the age of sixty-five, she was buried next to him, in *her* family vault in County Durham, resplendent to the last in two large turquoise rings. She had gone to the grave happy in the knowledge that her estates were in excellent shape, free from debt thanks to her late stewardship, and safe in the hands of her eldest son, the Earl Vane. He would, in a twist of fate, inherit, and thus unite, both the Vane-Tempest property of his mother and the Londonderry acres of his father – a fitting conclusion to the conjugal partnership that had so nearly never happened.

Sydney, Lady Morgan, too, died content with her legacy. 'The world has been a good world to me,' she was often heard to say. She published no fewer than seventy works in all – not just novels and travelogues, but poetry and pamphlets, a women's history and an autobiography. She also became the first woman to be awarded a literary pension – worth £300 a year – by the British government. Firmly in control of her own story right to the end, her exact age was never revealed, not even on her death certificate, which stated only 'about 80 years' – a circumstance which made her male critics fume. Of her finances, too, she remained fully in control her whole life long, and, after succumbing to a short illness in 1859, left an estate worth almost £16,000. The bulk of her accumulated fortune she left to her two nieces, but there was also a £200 gift to the Governesses' Benevolent Institution, a nod to the life that might have been hers.

Sarah, Lady Lyttelton, at one point the most high-profile governess in the whole land, remained on good terms with Queen Victoria until the end of her days. Her Majesty 'laughed immoderately' the last time the two widows met in 1869; even as an 'old codger' (as she put it) of eighty-one Sarah approached life with just the same humour and sunny cheerfulness as she had in her youth. When she died the following year, it was surrounded by her loving children, at Hagley, where the memories were strongest of William and their family life. So ended, as her son wrote, 'a life full of blessings given and received.'

# Selected Bibliography

All quoted matter in each chapter is taken from the
sources itemised in this section.

## Introduction

A.M.W. Stirling (ed.) *The Letter Bag of Lady Elizabeth Spencer-
Stanhope*, 2 Vols (London: John Lane, 1913), Vol I.

Harriette Wilson, *Memoirs of Harriette Wilson*, Written by Herself,
4 vols (J.J. Stockdale, 1825), Vols I and IV.

## Chapter One: Spring Campaigning

*The Morning Post*, February 1803.

*The Morning Post*, 23 March 1804.

*The St. James's Chronicle*, 30 May 1805.

[Privately Printed] *Letters from Sarah, Lady Lyttelton 1797–1873*
(London: Spottiswoode & Co., 1873).

Anon., *The Mirror of the Graces; or, The English Lady's Costume*, 2nd edn. (London: B. Crosby & Co., 1811).

A.M.W. Stirling (ed.) *The Letter Bag of Lady Elizabeth Spencer-Stanhope*, 2 Vols (London: John Lane, 1913), Vol I.

Castalia Countess Granville (ed.), *Lord Granville Leveson Gower (First Earl Granville) Private Correspondence 1781–1821*, 2 Vols (London: John Murray, 1916), Vol I.

Charles Spencer, *The Spencer Family* (London: Viking, 1999).

Countess of Ilchester and Lord Stavordale (eds.) *The Life and Letters of Lady Sarah Lennox 1745–1826*, 2 Vols (London: John Murray, 1901), Vol II.

Francis Paget Hett (ed.) *The Memoirs of Susan Sibbald, 1783–1812* (London: John Lane, 1926).

Hermann Pückler-Muskau, *Tour in England, Ireland and France in the Years 1826, 1827, 1828 and 1829* (Philadelphia: Carey, Lea & Blanchard, 1833).

Hon. F. Leveson Gower, *Letters of Harriet Countess Granville, 1810–1845*, 2 Vols, 3rd edn. (London: Longmans, Green, and Co., 1894), Vol I.

Hon. Mrs H. Wyndham (ed.), *Correspondence of Sarah Spencer, Lady Lyttelton 1787–1870* (London: John Murray, 1912).

Louis Simond, *Journal of a Tour and Residence in Great Britain During the Years 1810 and 1811*, 2 Vols, 2nd edn. (Edinburgh: Constable, 1817), Vol I.

Lord Hylton (ed.), *The Paget Brothers, 1790–1840* (London: John Murray, 1918).

John Feltham, *The Picture of London for 1809* (London: Richard Phillips, 1809).

Margaret Morris Cloake (trans. and ed.) *A Persian at the Court of King George 1809–10, The Journal of Mirza Abul Hassan Khan* (London: Barrie & Jenkins, 1988).

Mrs Warenne Blake (ed.) *An Irish Beauty of the Regency* – Compiled from *'Mes Souvenirs'* – *The Unpublished Journals of the Hon. Mrs Calvert 1789–1822* (London: John Lane, 1911).

Rachel Leighton (ed.) *Correspondence of Charlotte Grenville, Lady Williams Wynn and her three sons* (London: John Murray, 1920).

Richard Edgcumbe (ed.) *The Diary of Frances Lady Shelley 1787–1817* (London: John Murray, 1912).

Richard Rush, *A Residence at the Court of London* (London: Richard Bentley, 1833).

Sir George Leveson Gower and Iris Palmer (eds.), *Hary-O: The Letters of Lady Harriet Cavendish, 1796–1809* (London: John Murray, 1940).

Sir Jonah Barrington, *Personal Sketches of His Own Times*, 2 Vols. (London: Henry Colburn, 1827), Vol I.

Theophilus Christian, Esq. (pseud. John Owen), *The Fashionable World Displayed* (London: J. Hatchard, 1804).

**Chapter Two: Conquests and Admirers**

British Library: Add. MS 75922 (Letters to George, 2nd Earl Spencer from his mother, the Dowager Lady Spencer, 1809–1813) and Add. MS 75934 (Letters to George, 2nd Earl Spencer from his wife, Lavinia, Countess Spencer, December 1810–1812).

A.M.W. Stirling (ed.) *The Letter Bag of Lady Elizabeth Spencer-Stanhope*, 2 Vols (London: John Lane, 1913), Vol I.

Betty Askwith, *The Lytteltons: A Family Chronicle of the Nineteenth Century* (London: Chatto & Windus, 1975).

Castalia Countess Granville (ed.), *Lord Granville Leveson Gower (First Earl Granville) Private Correspondence 1781–1821*, 2 Vols (London: John Murray, 1916), Vols I & II.

Earl of Bessborough and A. Aspinall (eds.), *Lady Bessborough and Her Family Circle* (London: John Murray, 1940).

E.S. Turner, *A History of Courting* (London: Michael Joseph, 1954).

Joseph Friedman, *Spencer House: Chronicle of a Great London Mansion* (London: Zwemmer, 1993).

Lord William Pitt Lennox, *Fashion Then and Now*, 2 Vols (Chapman and Hall, 1878), Vol I.

Hon. Mrs H. Wyndham (ed.), *Correspondence of Sarah Spencer, Lady Lyttelton 1787–1870* (London: John Murray, 1912).

*Mabell, Countess of Airlie, In Whig Society 1775–1818*, compiled from the hitherto unpublished correspondence of Elizabeth, Viscountess Melbourne, and Emily Lamb, Countess Cowper, afterwards Viscountess Palmerston (London: Hodder and Stoughton, 1921).

Mrs Warenne Blake (ed.), *An Irish Beauty of the Regency* – Compiled from *'Mes Souvenirs'* – *The Unpublished Journals of the Hon. Mrs Calvert 1789–1822* (London: John Lane, 1911).

Richard Edgcumbe (ed.), *The Diary of Frances Lady Shelley 1787–1817* (London: John Murray, 1912).

Sir George Leveson Gower and Iris Palmer (eds.), *Hary-O: The Letters of Lady Harriet Cavendish, 1796–1809* (London: John Murray, 1940).

*The London Magazine,* 4 (January to April, 1826) (London: Hunt and Clarke, 1826).

Tim Clarke, *The Countess: The Scandalous Life of Frances Villiers, Countess of Jersey, 1753–1821* (Stroud: Amberley, 2016).

**Chapter Three: The Power of Refusal**

A. Francis Steuart (ed.), *The Diary of a Lady-in-Waiting by Lady Charlotte Bury*, 2 Vols (London: John Lane, 1908), Vol I.

Alice Marie Crossland, *Wellington's Dearest Georgy: The Life and Loves of Lady Georgiana Lennox* (London: Universe Press, 2016).

Amanda Vickery, *Behind Closed Doors: At Home in Georgian England* (London: Yale University Press, 2009).

A.P.W. Malcomson, *The Pursuit of the Heiress: Aristocratic Marriage in Ireland 1740–1840* (Ulster Historical Foundation, 2006).

Cindy McCreery, *The Satirical Gaze: Prints of Women in Late Eighteenth Century England* (Oxford: Oxford University Press, 2004).

*Confessions of Julia Johnstone, written by herself, in contradiction to the fables of Harriette Wilson* (London: Benbow, 1825).

Dorothy Howell-Thomas, *Lord Melbourne's Susan* (Gresham Books, 1978).

Edith, Marchioness of Londonderry, *Frances Anne: The Life and Times of Frances Anne Marchioness of Londonderry and her husband Charles Third Marquess of Londonderry* (London: Macmillan & Co., 1958).

Elizabeth Lanfear, *Letters to Young Ladies on their Entrance into the World* (London: J Robins and Co., 1824).

Emma Sophia, Countess Brownlow, *Slight Reminiscences of a Septuagenarian from 1802 to 1815* (London: John Murray, 1867).

Francis Bamford and the Duke of Wellington (ed.) *The Journal of Mrs Arbuthnot 1820–1832*, 2 Vols (London: Macmillan & Co., 1950), Vol I.

*Fraser's Magazine* for *Town and Country* Vol LXVII, January to June, 1863 (London: Parker, Son, and Bourn).

Henry Reeve (ed.), *The Greville Memoirs, A Journal of the Reigns of King George IV, King William IV and Queen Victoria* (Cambridge University Press, 2011), Vol VI.

Hon. F. Leveson Gower, *Letters of Harriet Countess Granville, 1810–1845*, 2 Vols, 3rd edn. (London: Longmans, Green, and Co., 1894), Vol I.

Hon. James A. Home (ed.), *Letters of Lady Louisa Stuart to Miss Louisa Clinton* (Edinburgh: David Douglas, 1901).

Jane West, *Letters to a Young Lady*, 3 Vols (Longman, Hurst, Rees, and Orme,1806), Vol III.

John Gregory, *A Father's Legacy to his Daughters* (London: W. Strahan and T. Cadell, 1775).

Kenneth Bourne (ed.), *The Letters of the Third Viscount Palmerston to Laurence and Elizabeth Sulivan, 1804–1863* (London: Royal Historical Society, 1979).

*La Belle Assemblée*, or *Bell's Court and Fashionable Magazine*, Vol XV, (London: J. Bell, 1817).

Lord William Pitt Lennox, *Fifty Years' Biographical Reminiscences*, 2 Vols (London: Hurst and Blackett, 1863), Vol I.

Mabell, Countess of Airlie, *In Whig Society 1775–1818*, compiled from the hitherto unpublished correspondence of Elizabeth, Viscountess Melbourne, and Emily Lamb, Countess Cowper, afterwards Viscountess Palmerston (London: Hodder and Stoughton, 1921).

Mary Campbell, *Lady Morgan: The Life and Times of Sydney Owenson* (London: Pandora Press, 1988).

Mrs Warenne Blake (ed.), *An Irish Beauty of the Regency* – Compiled from *'Mes Souvenirs'* – *The Unpublished Journals of the Hon. Mrs Calvert 1789–1822* (London: John Lane, 1911).

Pamela Hunter, *Through the Years: Tales from the Hoare's Bank Archive*, Vol 2 (London: C. Hoare & Co., 2018).

Priscilla Wakefield, *Reflections on the Present Condition of the Female Sex; with Suggestions for its Improvement* (London: J. Johnson, 1798).

*The Athenaeum, Journal of Literature, Science, and the Fine Arts, For the Year 1843* (London: J. Francis, 1843).

The Marquess of Anglesey (ed.), *The Capel Letters, Being the Correspondence of Lady Caroline Capel and her daughters with the Dowager Countess of Uxbridge from Brussels and Switzerland 1814–1817* (London: Jonathan Cape, 1955).

W.H. Dixon (ed.), *Lady Morgan's Memoirs: Autobiography, Diaries and Correspondence*, 2 Vols (London: W.H. Allen & Co., 1862), Vol I.

## Chapter Four: Objections

*The Morning Chronicle*, 2 March 1805.

*The Sailsbury and Winchester Journal*, 27 May 1811.

*The St James's Chronicle*, 28 January 1812.

*The Times*, 22 April 1818, 24 April 1818, 24 June 1818, 14 July 1818, 31 May 1830.

Volume 9; Frances Pery Calvert Diaries, C0621, Manuscripts Division, Department of Special Collections, Princeton University Library [Online].

A. Francis Steuart (ed.), *The Diary of a Lady-in-Waiting by Lady Charlotte Bury*, 2 Vols (London: John Lane, 1908), Vol I.

Adam Nicolson, *The Gentry: Stories of the English* (London: Harper Press, 2011).

A.M.W. Stirling (ed.), *The Letter Bag of Lady Elizabeth Spencer-Stanhope*, 2 Vols (London: John Lane, 1913), Vol I.

A.P.W. Malcomson, *The Pursuit of the Heiress: Aristocratic Marriage in Ireland 1740–1840* (Ulster Historical Foundation, 2006).

Diane Urquhart, *The Ladies of Londonderry: Women and Political Patronage* (London: I.B. Tauris, 2007).

Edith, Marchioness of Londonderry, *Frances Anne: The Life and Times of Frances Anne Marchioness of Londonderry and her husband Charles Third Marquess of Londonderry* (London: Macmillan & Co., 1958).

Egerton Castle (ed.), *The Jerningham Letters (1780–1843)* 2 Vols. (London: Richard Bentley, 1896), Vol I.

Geraldine Roberts, *The Angel and the Cad: Love, Loss and Scandal in Regency England* (London: Macmillan, 2015).

Hon. F. Leveson Gower, *Letters of Harriet Countess Granville, 1810–1845*, 2 Vols, 3rd edn. (London: Longmans, Green, and Co., 1894), Vol I.

Hon. Mrs H. Wyndham (ed.), *Correspondence of Sarah Spencer, Lady Lyttelton 1787–1870* (John Murray, 1912).

John Dodson, *A Report of the Judgment in the cause of Dalrymple the Wife against Dalrymple the Husband* (London: J. Butterworth, Fleet Street).

Leonard Cooper, *Radical Jack: The Life of John George Lambton* (London: The Cresset Press, 1959).

Leslie A. Marchand (ed.), *Byron's Letters and Journals*, 13 Vols (Harvard University Press, 1973), Vol II.

Lionel G. Robinson (ed.), *Letters of Dorothea, Princess Lieven, during her Residence in London, 1812–1834* (London: Longmans, Green, & Co., 1902).

Lucille Iremonger, *Lord Aberdeen: A biography of the fourth Earl of Aberdeen, K.G, K.T, Prime Minister 1852–1855* (London: Collins, 1978).

Mrs Godfrey Clark (ed.), *Gleanings from an Old Portfolio containing some Correspondence between Lady Louisa Stuart and her sister Caroline Countess of Portarlington*, 3 Vols (David Douglass, 1898), Vol III.

Mrs Warenne Blake (ed.), *An Irish Beauty of the Regency* – Compiled from *'Mes Souvenirs'* – *The Unpublished Journals of the Hon. Mrs Calvert 1789–1822* (London: John Lane, 1911).

Peter Orlando Hutchinson, *Chronicles of Gretna Green*, 2 Vols (London: Richard Bentley, 1844), Vol II.

Rachel Leighton (ed.), *Correspondence of Charlotte Grenville, Lady Williams Wynn and her three sons* (John Murray, 1920).

Reider Payne, *War and Diplomacy in the Napoleonic Era: Sir Charles Stewart, Castlereagh and the Balance of Power in Europe* (London: Bloomsbury, 2019).

Robert Elliott and Rev. Caleb Brown, *The Gretna Green Memoirs* (London, 1842).

T.C. Smout, 'Scottish Marriage, Regular and Irregular, 1500–1940' in R.B. Outhwaite (ed.), *Marriage and Society: Studies in the Social History of Marriage* (New York: St Martin's Press, 1981).

The Right Hon. Sir Herbert Maxwell (ed.), *The Life and Letters of George William Frederick, Fourth Earl of Clarendon*, 2 Vols (London: Edward Arnold, 1913).

The Marquess of Anglesey (ed.), *The Capel Letters, Being the Correspondence of Lady Caroline Capel and her daughters with the Dowager Countess of Uxbridge from Brussels and Switzerland 1814–1817* (London: Jonathan Cape, 1955).

Thomas Moore, *The Poetical Works of Thomas Moore* (London: Longman, Brown, Green, and Longmans, 1845).

W.H. Dixon (ed.), *Lady Morgan's Memoirs: Autobiography, Diaries and Correspondence*, 2 Vols (London: W.H. Allen & Co., 1862), Vol I.

## Chapter Five: The Price of Love

Lincolnshire Archives: Records of the Fane Family, specifically 1 FANE 6/4.

Volume 9, *Frances Pery Calvert Diaries*, C0621, Manuscripts Division, Department of Special Collections, Princeton University Library [Online].

Volume 10, *Frances Pery Calvert Diaries*, C0621, Manuscripts Division, Department of Special Collections, Princeton University Library [Online].

A. Aspinall (ed.), *The Correspondence of Charles Arbuthnot*, Camden Third Series, Vol 65 (Royal Historical Society, 1941).

A. Francis Steuart (ed.), *The Diary of a Lady-in-Waiting by Lady Charlotte Bury*, 2 Vols (London: John Lane, 1908), Vol I.

A.P.W. Malcomson, *The Pursuit of the Heiress: Aristocratic Marriage in Ireland 1740–1840* (Ulster Historical Foundation, 2006).

E.A. Smith, *Wellington and the Arbuthnots: A Triangular Friendship* (Stroud: Alan Sutton, 1994).

Henry Reeve (ed.), *The Greville Memoirs, A Journal of the Reigns of King George IV, King William IV and Queen Victoria* (Cambridge University Press, 2011), Vol VI.

Jane West, *Letters to a Young Lady*, 3 Vols (London: Longman, Hurst, Rees, and Orme,1806), Vol III.

Richard Edgcumbe (ed.), *The Diary of Frances Lady Shelley 1787–1817* (London: John Murray, 1912).

William Blackstone, *Commentaries on the Laws of England, 13th edn. with notes and additions by E. Christian* (A. Strahan, 1800).

### Chapter Six: Marriage à la Mode

*The British Press*, 5 April 1819.

Volume 9, *Frances Pery Calvert Diaries*, C0621, Manuscripts Division, Department of Special Collections, Princeton University Library [Online].

David Miller (ed.), *Lady De Lancey at Waterloo: A Story of Duty and Devotion* (Stroud: Spellmount, 2008).

E.A. Smith, *Wellington and the Arbuthnots: A Triangular Friendship* (Stroud: Alan Sutton, 1994).

Gareth Glover (ed.), *Eyewitness to the Peninsular War and the Battle of Waterloo* (Barnsley: Pen & Sword, 2010).

Hon. Mrs H. Wyndham (ed.), *Correspondence of Sarah Spencer, Lady Lyttelton 1787–1870* (London: John Murray, 1912).

Jack Lynch (ed.), *Samuel's Johnson's Dictionary, Selections from the 1755 Work that Defined the English Language* (Walker, 2003).

Mrs Warenne Blake (ed.), *An Irish Beauty of the Regency –* Compiled from *'Mes Souvenirs' – The Unpublished Journals of the Hon. Mrs Calvert 1789–1822* (London: John Lane, 1911).

Richard Edgcumbe (ed.), *The Diary of Frances Lady Shelley 1818–1873* (London: John Murray, 1913).

Violent Dickinson (ed.), *Miss Eden's Letters* (London: Macmillan and Co., 1919).


**Chapter Seven: Fragile Lives**

*The Times*, 8 March 1825.

A. Francis Steuart (ed.), *The Diary of a Lady-in-Waiting by Lady Charlotte Bury*, 2 Vols (London: John Lane, 1908), Vol I.

Adeline Hartcup, *Love and Marriage in the Great Country Houses* (London: Sidgwick & Jackson, 1984).

A.J. Heesom and E.M. Lloyd, Charles William, Third Marquess of Londonderry, *Oxford Dictionary of National Biography* entry.

Alice Marie Crossland, *Wellington's Dearest Georgy: The Life and Loves of Lady Georgiana Lennox* (London: Universe Press, 2016).

B.R. Ward (ed.) *A Week at Waterloo in 1815: Lady De Lancey's Narrative* (London: John Murray, 1906).

Betty Askwith, *The Lytteltons: A Family Chronicle of the Nineteenth Century* (London: Chatto & Windus, 1975).

Castalia Countess Granville (ed.), *Lord Granville Leveson Gower*

*(First Earl Granville) Private Correspondence 1781–1821*, 2 Vols (John Murray, 1916), Vol II.

David Miller (ed.), *Lady De Lancey at Waterloo: A Story of Duty and Devotion* (Stroud: Spellmount, 2008).

Edward Clarence Paget, *Memoir of the Hon^ble Sir Charles Paget G.C.H, 1778–1839* (London: Longmans, Green and Co., 1913).

Francis Bamford and the Duke of Wellington (ed.), *The Journal of Mrs Arbuthnot 1820–1832*, 2 Vols (London: Macmillan & Co., 1950), Vol I.

Gareth Glover (ed.), *Eyewitness to the Peninsular War and the Battle of Waterloo, The Letters and Journals of Lieutenant Colonel The Honourable James Hamilton Stanhope, 1803 to 1825* (Pen & Sword, 2010).

Georgina Battiscombe, *The Spencers of Althorp* (London: Constable, 1984).

H.A. Bruce (ed.), *Life of General Sir William Napier, K.C.B*, 2 Vols (London: John Murray, 1864), Vol I.

Hon. F. Leveson Gower, *Letters of Harriet Countess Granville, 1810–1845*, 2 Vols, 3rd edn. (London: Longmans, Green, and Co., 1894), Vol I.

Hon. Mrs H. Wyndham (ed.), *Correspondence of Sarah Spencer, Lady Lyttelton 1787–1870* (John Murray, 1912).

Jane Austen, *Pride and Prejudice*, ed. Vivien Jones (London: Penguin, 2003).

Joseph Friedman, *Spencer House: Chronicle of a Great London Mansion* (London: Zwemmer, 1993).

## Selected Bibliography

Judith Schneid Lewis, *In the Family Way: Child-bearing in the British Aristocracy, 1760–1860* (New Brunswick: Rutgers University Press, 1986).

Lord Hylton (ed.), *The Paget Brothers, 1790–1840* (John Murray, 1918).

Lord Stanmore, *The Earl of Aberdeen*, 2nd edn. (London: Sampson, Low, Marston & Company, 1894).

Lucille Iremonger, *Lord Aberdeen: A biography of the fourth Earl of Aberdeen, K.G, K.T, Prime Minister 1852–1855* (London: Collins, 1978).

Margaret Morris Cloake (trans. and ed.), *A Persian at the Court of King George 1809–10, The Journal of Mirza Abul Hassan Khan* (Barrie & Jenkins, 1988).

Mark Guscin, *The Life of James Hamilton Stanhope (1788–1825): Love, War and Tragedy* (Cambridge Scholars Publishing, 2021).

Muriel Chamberlain, *Lord Aberdeen: a political biography* (London: Longman, 1983).

Mrs Warenne Blake (ed.), *An Irish Beauty of the Regency –* Compiled from *'Mes Souvenirs' – The Unpublished Journals of the Hon. Mrs Calvert 1789–1822* (London: John Lane, 1911).

Nick Foulkes, *Dancing into Battle: A Social History of Waterloo* (London: Phoenix, 2007).

Philip Henry, 5th Earl Stanhope, *Notes of Conversations with the Duke of Wellington, 1831–1851* (London: John Murray, 1888).

Rory Muir, *Gentlemen of Uncertain Fortune: How Younger Sons Made Their Way in Jane Austen's England* (London: Yale University Press).

Sheila Simonson, *Following the Drum: British Women in the Peninsular War* (1981) [Thesis available online].

Sir George Leveson Gower and Iris Palmer (eds.), *Hary-O: The Letters of Lady Harriet Cavendish, 1796–1809* (London: John Murray, 1940).

Sydney, Lady Morgan, *Passages from my Autobiography* (London: Richard Bentley, 1859).

The Earl of Bessborough (ed.), *Lady Charlotte Guest: Extracts from her Journal, 1833–1852* (London: John Murray, 1950).

The Earl of Ilchester (ed.), *The Journal of the Hon. Henry Edward Fox, 1818–1830* (London: Thornton Butterworth, 1923).

Trevor Lummis and Jan Marsh, *The Woman's Domain: Women and the English Country House* (London: Viking, 1990).

Violent Dickinson (ed.), *Miss Eden's Letters* (London: Macmillan and Co., 1919).

**Chapter Eight: Criminal Connections**

*Bell's Weekly Messenger*, 29 May 1808.

*The Examiner*, 22 May 1808.

*The Morning Chronicle*, 21 May 1808.

*The Morning Post*, 20 May 1808, 21 May 1808, 24 May 1808.

*The National Register*, 23 May 1808.

*The St. James's Chronicle*, 26 May 1808.

*The Times*, 20 July 1808.

A. Aspinall (ed.), *The Later Correspondence of George III*, 5 Vols (Cambridge University Press, 1970), Vol V.

Augustus B. Paget (ed.), *The Paget Papers, Diplomatic and Other Correspondence of the Right Hon. Sir Arthur Paget G.C.B., 1794–1807*, 2 Vols (London: William Heinemann, 1896), Vols I & II.

Castalia Countess Granville (ed.), *Lord Granville Leveson Gower (First Earl Granville) Private Correspondence 1781–1821*, 2 Vols (John Murray, 1916), Vols I & II.

Earl of Bessborough and A. Aspinall (ed.), *Lady Bessborough and Her Family Circle* (London: John Murray, 1940).

Earl of Ilchester (ed.), *The Journal of Elizabeth Lady Holland (1791–1811)*, 2 Vols (London: Longmans, Green, and Co., 1908), Vol I.

Edward D. Ingraham (ed.), *Reports of Cases Argued and Determined in the English Ecclesiastical Courts*, Vol III (Philadelphia: P.H. Nicklin and T. Johnson, 1832).

Egerton Castle (ed.), *The Jerningham Letters (1780–1843)*, 2 Vols (London: Richard Bentley, 1896), Vol I.

Elizabeth Lanfear, *Letters to Young Ladies on their Entrance into the World* (London: J. Robins and Co., 1824).

Francis Bamford and the Duke of Wellington (ed.), *The Journal of Mrs Arbuthnot 1820–1832*, 2 Vols (London: Macmillan & Co., 1950), Vol I.

Francis Bickley (ed.), *The Diaries of Sylvester Douglas (Lord Glenbervie)* 2 Vols. (London Constable and Co., 1928), Vol II.

James Greig (ed.), *The Farington Diary by Joseph Farington, R.A.*, (London: Hutchinson & Co., 1925), Vol V.

John Burton, *Lectures on Female Education and Manners*, 4th Edn. (Dublin: John Milliken, 1796).

John Macqueen, *A Practical Treatise on the Appellate Jurisdiction of the House of Lords & Privy Council, Together with the Practice on Parliamentary Divorce* (London: A. Maxwell & Son, 1842).

Journals of the House of Lords, Vol XLVII (1809).

Lawrence Stone, *Road to Divorce, England 1530–1987* (Oxford: Oxford University Press, 1990).

Lord Hylton (ed.), *The Paget Brothers, 1790–1840* (London: John Murray, 1918).

Louis Simond, *Journal of a Tour and Residence in Great Britain during the Years 1810 and 1811*, 2nd edn., 2 Vols (Edinburgh: Constable, 1817), Vol II.

Mrs Godfrey Clark (ed.), *Gleanings from an Old Portfolio containing some Correspondence between Lady Louisa Stuart and her sister Caroline Countess of Portarlington*, 3 Vols (Edinburgh: David Douglass, 1898), Vol III.

Mrs Warenne Blake (ed.), *An Irish Beauty of the Regency –* Compiled from *'Mes Souvenirs' – The Unpublished Journals of the Hon. Mrs Calvert 1789–1822* (London: John Lane, 1911).

Niamh Howlin, *Adultery in the Courts: Criminal Conversation in Ireland* (2016) [University College Dublin Working Paper].

Peter Quennell and Dilys Powell (ed.), *The Private Letters of Princess Lieven to Prince Metternich, 1820–1826*, (London: John Murray, 1937).

Rachel Leighton (ed.), *Correspondence of Charlotte Grenville, Lady Williams Wynn and her three sons* (London: John Murray, 1920).

Richard Edgcumbe (ed.), *The Diary of Frances Lady Shelley 1787–1817* (London: John Murray, 1912).

Sir George Leveson Gower and Iris Palmer (eds.), *Hary-O: The Letters of Lady Harriet Cavendish, 1796–1809* (London: John Murray, 1940).

Susan C. Law, *Through the Keyhole: Sex, Scandal and the Secret Life of the Country House* (Stroud: The History Press, 2015).

Sybil Wolfram, *Divorce in England 1700–1857 in Oxford Journal of Legal Studies*, Summer 1985, Vol 5. pp 155–186.

*The Gentleman's Magazine*, Vol IV (London: William Pickering, 1835).

*The New Bon Ton Magazine*, Vol II (London: J. Johnston, 1819).

The Marquess of Anglesey, *One-Leg, The Life and Letters of Henry William Paget, First Marquess of Anglesey K.G. (1768–1854)*, (London: Jonathan Cape, 1962).

The Marquess of Anglesey (ed.), *The Capel Letters, Being the Correspondence of Lady Caroline Capel and her daughters with the Dowager Countess of Uxbridge from Brussels and Switzerland 1814–1817* (London: Jonathan Cape, 1955).

*The Trial of Sir Arthur Paget, K.B Late Ambassador to the Courts of Vienna and Constantinople, for Criminal Conversation with Countess Borringdon, Wife of Earl Borringdon, and Daughter to the late Earl of Westmorland* (London: J. Day, 1808).

William John Fitzpatrick, *The Life, Times and Contemporaries of Lord Cloncurry* (Dublin: James Duffy, 1855).

## Chapter Nine: The Tomb of Love?

A. Aspinall (ed.), *The Correspondence of Charles Arbuthnot*, Camden Third Series Vol 65 (Royal Historical Society, 1941).

A.C. Benson and Viscount Esher (eds.), *The Letters of Queen Victoria: A Selection from her Majesty's Correspondence between the Years 1837 and 1861*, 3 Vols (London: John Murray, 1907), Vol II.

Betty Askwith, *The Lytteltons: A Family Chronicle of the Nineteenth Century* (London: Chatto & Windus, 1975).

Diane Urquhart, *The Ladies of Londonderry: Women and Political Patronage* (London: I.B.Tauris, 2007).

Dorothy Howell-Thomas, *Lord Melbourne's Susan* (Gresham Books, 1978).

Edith, Marchioness of Londonderry, *Frances Anne: The Life and Times of Frances Anne Marchioness of Londonderry and her husband Charles Third Marquess of Londonderry*, (London: Macmillan & Co., 1958).

Elizabeth Longford, *Wellington: Pillar of State* (St Albans: Panther Books, 1975).

E.A. Smith, *Wellington and the Arbuthnots: A Triangular Friendship*, (Stroud: Alan Sutton, 1994).

Francis Bamford and the Duke of Wellington (ed.), *The Journal of Mrs Arbuthnot 1820–1832*, 2 Vols (London: Macmillan & Co., 1950), Vol I.

Hon. F. Leveson Gower, *Letters of Harriet Countess Granville, 1810–1845*, 2 Vols, 3rd edn. (London: Longmans, Green, and Co., 1894), Vol I.

Hon. Mrs H. Wyndham (ed.), *Correspondence of Sarah Spencer, Lady Lyttelton 1787–1870* (John Murray, 1912).

Lewis Melville (ed.), *The Huskisson Papers* (London: Constable, 1931).

Lord William Pitt Lennox, *Fifty Years' Biographical Reminiscences*, 2 Vols (London: Hurst and Blackett, 1863), Vol II.

Peter Quennell and Dilys Powell (ed.), *The Private Letters of Princess Lieven to Prince Metternich, 1820–1826* (London: John Murray, 1937).

Richard Edgcumbe (ed.), *The Diary of Frances Lady Shelley 1818–1873* (John Murray, 1913).

Sydney, Lady Morgan, *Passages from my Autobiography* (London: Richard Bentley, 1859).

W.H. Dixon (ed.), *Lady Morgan's Memoirs: Autobiography, Diaries and Correspondence*, 2 Vols (London: W.H. Allen & Co., 1862), Vol I.

W.H. Dixon (ed.), *Lady Morgan's Memoirs: Autobiography, Diaries and Correspondence*, 2 Vols (London: W.H. Allen & Co., 1862), Vol II.

## Selected Additional Sources

### ARCHIVES

Parliamentary Archives: 1809 Act to dissolve the marriage of Lord and Lady Boringdon.
University of Southampton Library: Deed of separation of Sir Henry Brooke Parnell and Lady Caroline Parnell, 1816.
The Bedford Estates: Letters relating to the engagement of 7th Duke and Duchess of Bedford.

British Library: Add. MS 76183 (Accounts of receipts and expenditure of 2nd Earl Spencer, August 1812–June 1813); Add. MS 48406 (Letters to Sir Arthur Paget from his sisters and Lady Jersey).

### BOOKS

Amanda Vickery, *The Gentleman's Daughter: Women's Lives in Georgian England* (London: Yale University Press, 1998).

Brian Southam, *Jane Austen and the Navy*, 2nd. Edn. (London: National Maritime Museum Publishing, 2005).

Carolyn A. Day, *Consumptive Chic: A History of Beauty, Fashion, and Disease* (London: Bloomsbury, 2017).

Colin Gibson, *Dissolving Wedlock* (London: Routledge, 1994).

Donna T. Andrews, *Aristocratic Vice: The Attack on Duelling, Suicide, Adultery, and Gambling in Eighteenth-Century England* (London: Yale University Press, 2013).

F.M.L. Thompson, *English Landed Society in the Nineteenth Century* (London: Routledge, 1963).

K.D. Reynolds, *Aristocratic Women and Political Society in Victorian Britain* (Oxford: Clarendon Press, 1998).

Hannah Greig, *The Beau Monde: Fashionable Society in Georgian London* (Oxford: Oxford University Press, 2013).

Hilary Davidson, *Dress in the Age of Jane Austen: Regency Fashion* (London: Yale University Press, 2019).

Ian Mortimer, *The Time Traveller's Guide to Regency Britain* (London: The Bodley Head, 2020).

Judith M. Bennett and Amy M. Froide (eds.), *Singlewomen in the European Past, 1250–1800* (Philadelphia: University of Pennsylvania Press, 1999).

Lawrence Stone, *The Family, Sex and Marriage in England 1500–1800*, abridged edition (New York: Harper & Row, 1979).

Robert D. Hume, *Money in Jane Austen, The Review of English Studies*, April 2013, New Series, Vol 64, No. 264 (April 2013), pp. 289–310.

Samuel and Sarah Adams, *The Complete Servant* (London: Knight and Lacey, 1825).

Susan Staves, *Married Women's Separate Property in England, 1660–1833* (London: Harvard University Press, 1990).

Venetia Murray, *High Society in the Regency Period, 1788–1830* (London: Penguin, 1999).

## WEBSITES

The History of Parliament Online (https://www.historyofparliamentonline.org/).

# Acknowledgements

IT'S A TRUTH universally acknowledged that writing a book is never entirely a solo effort and there are two people who deserve special thanks for helping to bring *The Game of Hearts* into the world. Firstly, my agent, Ella Kahn, who spotted its potential, encouraged me to be more ambitious, and has done a sterling job of supporting me at every step on its path to publication. Secondly, my editor Ellie Carr, who understood and shared my vision from the beginning, and whose insightful comments and suggestions have helped enormously in its creation. Thank you both for your endless enthusiasm for the subject of Regency romance.

My thanks are also due to the rest of the team at Bonnier, too, and especially Clare Kelly and Eleanor Stammeijer for all their hard work on publicity.

I am also indebted to a number of people who helped me at the research stage. Particular thanks to Pamela Hunter at Hoare's Bank, who very generously shared her research on Lady Caroline

Bruce; the team at the University of Southampton Archives, who saved me having to decipher the separation deed of the Parnells; Sian Thomas and Anida Rayfield at the National Trust for offering information about Saltram's one-time chatelaine, Augusta; and Rebecca Probert, who very kindly gave her time to offer some brief thoughts on the complicated subjects of marriage settlements and maintenance, and in particular to direct me towards some useful sources.

Last, but not least, I'm grateful to family and friends for their patience and moral support, especially Sarah (cheerleader-in-chief) but also Julie, Gareth, Emily, Lucy and Dan. And, of course, Mum and Dad, my first readers and occasional research assistants, without whose love, support and encouragement this book would never have been started, let alone finished. Thank you both, for everything.

# Index